ISBN 978-1-331-51526-5
PIBN 10200467

Similar Books Are Available from
www.forgottenbooks.com

This book is **DUE** on the last date stamped below

FACTS, THOUGHT, AND IMAGINATION

THE MACMILLAN COMPANY
NEW YORK · BOSTON · CHICAGO · DALLAS
ATLANTA · SAN FRANCISCO

MACMILLAN & CO., LIMITED
LONDON · BOMBAY · CALCUTTA
MELBOURNE

THE MACMILLAN CO. OF CANADA, LTD.
TORONTO

FACTS, THOUGHT, AND IMAGINATION

A BOOK ON WRITING

BY

HENRY SEIDEL CANBY, Ph.D.
FREDERICK ERASTUS PIERCE, Ph.D.
WILLARD HIGLEY DURHAM, Ph.D.

OF THE

DEPARTMENT OF ENGLISH, SHEFFIELD SCIENTIFIC
SCHOOL, YALE UNIVERSITY

New York
THE MACMILLAN COMPANY
1917

Norwood Press
J. S. Cushing Co. — Berwick & Smith Co.
Norwood, Mass., U.S.A.

PREFACE

THE authors of this volume have long felt the need of a book on writing which should view the subject as it presents itself to the writer, that is, as the problem of how to prepare the raw material of thought, knowledge, or experience for expression in words. They have wished to put into the hands of their students a book that should take up the study of English composition where formal rhetorics of an elementary character leave it, a book upon handling facts and developing thought. The three theoretical chapters of this volume represent an attempt to supply this need. They are to be regarded as three essays upon writing, to be read by students who have subjects ready, and need advice. This departure from the usual textbook method will commend itself to teachers who wish to break free from the conventional ruts of composition work. These essays not only give instructions for writing, but also, directly or by implication, suggest an abundance of subjects; they will be found, the authors hope, to be comprehensive in plan and thorough in detail. But their chief aim is to teach principles, not rules, to discuss the practical requirements for handling facts and thought. It is as a second-year or second-term book that this volume is presented, to be used by men or women who have been taught all they can absorb of Unity, Coherence, and Emphasis, and need most of all to write.

This experiment in a new method is based upon a successful course, now three years old. The course itself begins

42080

with a careful drill in the difference between fact and no fact or part fact. The use of important and interesting documents from contemporary writing makes the student feel the significance of this training for his intellectual self-respect. At the same time he is given practice, both oral and written, in *précis* making, as a means of guaranteeing accuracy and thoroughness in his reading, and precision in the planning of his own work. Next comes the study of the means and methods of thought development, freely illustrated as before from good writing, and driven home by practice in composing articles, essays, editorials, and arguments. Next and last is the indirect method of handling ideas, too little considered in textbooks, the method of the story with a moral, the play with an idea, the satiric sketch, and all those forms of writing where the imagination serves as a bridge over which thought may progress to its desired end.

For such a course this book has been planned; and therefore, throughout the three following chapters, subject matter has been given precedence over form. Facts, thought, imagination in the service of thought, have taken the place of the usual rhetorical categories.

The selections included in this book have been tested by classroom experience. They are not to be regarded merely as illustrations of rhetorical theory, but also as material for laboratory practice in the technique of composition. It will be noted, however, that in conformity with the plan of the volume they have been selected for the interest of their subject matter as much as, if not more than, for technical excellence. The grouped reports of historical events will provide an exercise in the testing of fact more instructive than a hundred pages of comment. The essays, the stories, and the plays have been chosen because the ideas they present are fresh, definite, often debatable, and always interesting to the college undergraduate. A nucleus of excellent material for *précis* writing, for the analysis of fact, and the pursuit of thought, is thus made part of this book. The value of such an accessible body of tested material is known to every teacher; but the book is not limited by its contents. It is designed to be used in closest connection with good reading of every kind, whether drawn from other courses the student may be pursuing, or from such periodicals as "The Atlantic Monthly," "The New Republic," or "The Yale Review." With such additions of material from without, the theory presented can be made the basis of a full and satisfying year's work. Indeed, the scope of this volume is as wide as the intellectual needs of the undergraduate writer.

CONTENTS

		PAGE
PREFACE		v
ACKNOWLEDGMENTS		xi

PART I

THEORY

CHAPTER I. FACTS . . .	*Frederick Erastus Pierce*	1
CHAPTER II. THOUGHT	*Henry Seidel Canby* .	24
CHAPTER III. IMAGINATION IN THE SERVICE OF THOUGHT	*Willard Higley Durham*	45

PART II

ILLUSTRATIONS

GROUP ONE

(To accompany Chapter I)

HABIT FORMATION AND REFORMATION	*Eliott Park Frost*	65
THE ODYSSEY OF THE SOCKEYE SALMON	*William Charles Scully*	84
THE CORONATION OF CHARLES THE GREAT	*From various sources* .	100
ACCOUNTS OF THE NAVAL BATTLE OF JUTLAND	*From various sources*	111

Group Two

(To accompany Chapter II)

PAGE

A Defence of Penny Dreadfuls . . . . . G. K. Chesterton 155

The Case of the Forgotten Man . . . . . William Graham Sumner 161

Life, Art, and America Theodore Dreiser 173

The Moral Equivalent of War William James 195

The Prolongation of Peace Simeon Strunsky 210

Group Three

(To accompany Chapter III)

The Speech of Ellis (from "A Modern Symposium") . . G. Lowes Dickinson 225

The Passing of the Third Floor Back . . . . . Jerome K. Jerome 236

The Story of the Last Trump H. G. Wells . 261

Two Plays . . . . . Alfred Sutro

    The Man on the Kerb 279

    The Bracelet 292

APPENDIX

Directions for Making a Précis . . . 317

ACKNOWLEDGMENTS

Acknowledgment is here made of the kindness shown by the following publishers in allowing material to be reprinted from works copyrighted by them: "The Atlantic Monthly"; Dodd, Mead, & Co.; The George H. Doran Co.; Doubleday, Page & Co.; Harper & Brothers; "The New York Times"; "The Seven Arts"; "The Yale Review"; The Yale University Press. Detailed acknowledgments will be found in connection with the separate articles.

PART I

CHAPTER I

FACTS

I

ANCIENT writers usually bracketed war and pestilence together as the two great evils of mankind. War remains with us; but the most terrible forms of pestilence during the last eighty years have been almost driven from the earth by the advances of medical science. Yellow fever no longer ravages Havana; the Black Plague is being hunted even from its lair in dirty, primitive Asia. Throughout once deadly Panama — over the bones of uncounted Chinese coolies whom the mosquitoes and climate killed — delicate women now make their homes and grow strong. In the Crimean war seven-eighths of the deaths were due to sickness, about twelve per cent. to wounds received in battle. During the far greater conflict that began in August, 1914, these proportions have been nearly reversed. The comparison of such figures from different periods shows a mighty revolution in the living conditions of the race; and that far-reaching revolution was made possible by the patient accumulation and the wise interpretation of facts. Millions of apparently petty details had to be observed and recorded by thousands of men before the causes and cures of bubonic plague, smallpox, typhus, and yellow fever were discovered. Could all the note-books, memoranda of experiments, and painfully gathered tables of statistics, that through decades prepared the way for these great discoveries, be piled together, they would form a pyramid perhaps not incomparable to Cheops in size, and certainly far more useful to mankind.

The history of this hygienic revolution well illustrates how completely our modern system of thought is based upon a wide and accurate knowledge of facts. This is hardly more true of hygiene than of other sciences. War is no longer decided either by the physical might of Achilles or by the sudden inspirations of Joan of Arc. Before the first cannon booms, millions of facts, military, geographical, historical, and economic, have been accumulated in the war offices of the prospective belligerents; and these facts would enable their possessors to outgeneral an unprepared Napoleon. "Now I can take a holiday," said Von Moltke, the German chief of staff, when he learned that his country in 1870 had declared war on France. Soon after, being informed of some unexpected development in French strategy, he pointed to his card catalogue, the accumulated data of half a lifetime, and answered, "It is all in drawer number so-and-so." In the same way a painstaking knowledge of detail often lies at the bottom of industrial success. According to the newspapers, when the battleship *Oregon* was on her trial trip, a reporter said to the head of the firm that built her: "Are you not worried? The breaking of a ten-cent bolt may cost you a hundred thousand dollars in premiums for extra speed." "No bolt will break," he is reported to have answered, "I know them all personally."

"But," exclaim readers who are more literary than scientific, "is not this glorification of facts rank sordidness and commercialism? Does it not substitute the card catalogue and microscope for the altar and art gallery?" By no means. The greatest poets, painters,

and architects have been supreme partly through their
mastery of facts. The details which they observed were
æsthetic, not utilitarian, but none the less facts. The poet
who first saw the beauty of

> "The yellow wall-flower stained with iron-brown,"

or of the sunset sky,

> "With its peculiar tint of yellow green,"

just as definitely added a new fact to our mental store-
house as the scientist who first observed the hookworm.
It was partly by their greater wealth of observed facts —
glorified by the imagination, if you will, but none the less
facts — that Wordsworth, Burns, and Keats excelled in
their nature poetry the vague, generalizing rhymers of
Queen Anne. When Tennyson describes a young lady's
nose as

> "Tip-tilted like the petal of a flower,"

he shows himself a keen observer of details in regard to
both flowers and faces. Wherein lies the success of Sir
Joshua Reynolds as a portrait painter if not in his minute
scrutiny of a thousand details concerning the rounding of
a cheek or the precise curve in a lock of hair? Whether
men are following business for money and position or are
artists and visionaries in quest of beauty, they need ability
to see and use the uncounted facts in their particular field
of existence. "The great heart, *the clear deep-seeing eye*,"
says Carlyle, "there it lies; no man whatever, in what
province soever, can prosper at all without these."

  In one sense of the word, everything which truly exists
is a fact. According to one definition, the relation of God
to his universe could be considered a fact, incomprehensible
to mortal mind, but actually there. Such an all-embrac-

ing conception, however, would defeat the purpose of this volume. The word "fact," as used in the following pages, stands in the first place for separate details ascertained by the five senses: the odor of a shrub, the contour of a mountain, the peculiar tint of overheated metal, the fatal dagger thrust that some one saw. It would include also similar facts of experience drawn from a wide field and tabulated as statistics. It stands in the second place for isolated details that must be determined by reason because nobody was present to see or hear them. The height of a prehistoric animal whose thigh bones only are found, the exact nature of a crime that nobody witnessed, these would be facts as far as they could be determined. Under the word are also included truths demonstrated by experiment, such as the fact that oxygen and hydrogen mixed in due proportions form water. For the sake of clearness the present book draws a fairly sharp distinction — sharper than that found in actual life — between this realm of facts and the realm of ideas. To the latter belong studies of far-reaching general principles, brilliant suggestions that come spontaneously and can be tested by facts later, problems of the relationship between man and man or between man and his environment.

Facts, as we have said, may be employed for either utilitarian and scientific or for æsthetic and literary ends. The latter use will be considered in a later chapter; the former concerns us at present.

II

This is a book on writing, and discusses facts only as a means to that end. Whatever his material, it is every writer's duty toward his reader to see that his data are in some respects new and in all important respects true. If he fails in the first requirement he is usually a bore; if in the second, he is — intentionally or unintentionally — a liar. Hence the problem for the would-be author is always a double one: to amass a wealth of material, and to handle it discerningly and honestly.

It is when he is writing on facts gathered by firsthand personal observation that this problem confronts him in its simplest phase. The traveler preparing a lecture on scenery and manners in countries he has visited; the spy transmitting his report of fortresses examined; the geologist giving an account of regions surveyed by him; the inspector reporting on factories under his charge; the polar explorer writing a book on his hardships and discoveries — all of these men face certain similar problems. These same considerations confront also the undergraduate who writes of some locality, building, or exciting situation.

Before all things else, before the planning of paragraphs or the polishing of phrases, must come the power to see much and clearly. Details which an ordinary man would overlook may be precisely the factors that give beauty to a description or significance to a spy's report. But, beyond this consideration, the author must realize the significance of facts and distinguish the essential from the unessential. Every man daily sees a thousand things not worth remembering; he may notice a few, the recording and interpretation of which are a service to the community. The haggard face that shows disease and unsanitary conditions in the workshop is something more than a mere face, it is a revelation. When the first explorer among the Niam-niam savages saw quarters of human bodies hanging like pork in the market place, he beheld a sight the significance of which was not to be forgotten. In a hundred similar ways the trained eye can derive from its surroundings a truth worth uttering.

When a man has observed life until he has a mass of new

and valuable data to present, then, and not till then, should he attempt to reduce it to written form. The problems of actual composition are many; and any elementary text-book will give rules for expressing the gathered material in clear, orderly, and condensed form. What concerns us here is not a repetition of these well-known formulas, but the way in which observation enables men to apply them with new force and vitality; for that, and not mechanical structure, is the aim of the present chapter. Not only does observation give the writer something to express, it aids him in the actual expression. A factory inspector presents a well-written report only when he knows what points to emphasize and what points to slur. Choice of words is one of the marks of a good style; yet how can the traveler choose the precise words in describing the color and shape of a foreign tree unless he has trained his vision to notice hues and forms? Only when the hitherto careless author has learned to visualize in his imagination the thing that he is talking about, to realize its significance and far-reaching effects — only then does he realize how inadequately he has passed the fact from his brain to his reader's by the first ill-chosen word that suggested itself. How can an author develop a paragraph by the method of examples or detail unless he has at hand the facts which are his examples? One of the chief virtues of Macaulay as an orator was his ability to buttress up any point by numerous illustrations from past history. It was the power of his mind in amassing facts that made him able to round out a convincing paragraph. In the arrangement and style of an essay, as in all things else, knowledge is power, and accumulated facts are knowledge.

One need not be a great author or traveler in order to find the above principles useful. Let any man walk with discerning eye through the slums, the museums, the art galleries, or the wharves of a great city, and then write his experiences. Proper variations of emphasis on his different points will come naturally from the varying intensity of his emotions; his paragraphs will round out spontaneously from the wealth of gathered material; amusement, indignation, and enthusiasm in alternation will give him words that sting and glow instead of the hackneyed vocabulary of textbooks; and if in the end he does not write well it will be largely because he has not yet learned to see well.

III

Next to facts gained by simple observation come those acquired by experiment. Of these, the most simple and conclusive are those derived from the laboratories of the physical sciences, where various ingredients can be tested first together, then separately, and the varying results noted. Such experiments have led to most of the great discoveries in chemistry, physics, medicine, and machinery. The results, like those of observation, are usually definite and unquestionable, and can be used in the same way to buttress a point or furnish an illustration. Moreover, an account of the experiment itself may become valuable reading matter for the public, partly because it suggests new lines of similar experiments, still more because of the appeal that it makes to the restless ingenuity and eager curiosity of the human mind.

A greater interest for the average man, however, is found in another field, where the elements to be examined are neither simple nor separable, but complex in themselves, and still more complex through the inextricable way in which they are twisted together. They must be examined, not in some simple combination arranged wholly by the investigator, but in an exceedingly complicated one made by nature and only slightly modified by the experimenter. Such are the problems of the social sciences, dealing with human passions, causes and consequences of war, of immorality, of race suicide, of economic success and failure. The simple pairing off of related phenomena and elimination of every other disturbing element, which is the chief feature of the laboratory experiment, become impossible. What man ever separated the intemperance of a drunkard from his other characteristics, and examined its reactions when combined or not combined with ten measures of will power? Chemistry makes a few perfect experiments under ideal conditions and arrives at certainty; the social sciences, finding this rarely possible, fall back on a great number of imperfect experiments which gradually approximate toward certainty with the increase in the number of attempts. The mental training developed by experiment in physical sciences is helpful to the social scientist. The methods of reasoning in the two fields are often similar, but must in the study of economics and government be supplemented by such a knowledge of life as no textbook can give.

Yet more vague in their details, but still depending at bottom on the old principles of elimination and comparison, are the experiments, not of any science, but of what is usually spoken of as human experience. All life is, in one sense of the word, an unending experiment in an eternal laboratory. Every test of a neighbor's temper is an experiment, every new device for entertaining a guest. All these become part of the tissue of life, part of what the writer must handle in either scientific or literary work.

Detailed directions for making experiments in either the physical or social sciences can be found in other books. Our present concern is with the use of such procedure for purposes of writing. In the first place, any fact gained by a trustworthy form of experiment — like the facts gained by observation — can be employed for purposes of proof or illustration, without reference to the methods by which it was proved to be a fact. The truth about human evolution is daily used to illustrate thoughts on widely differing subjects, and used by men who do not even know the experimental processes that Darwin followed. In addition, an account of the actual experimental procedure is often valuable for writing. It may strengthen an argument for or against the encouragement of certain experiments by showing how the very attempt now mooted wholly failed or partly succeeded before. It may further become a means of expressing exact truth by showing precisely how far a certain experiment was, how far it was not, convincing, and just what reservations we should make in accepting the results. The history of social reform is a never-ending study of partial success in man's ever varying attempts. Even for the most purely imaginative literature descriptions of scientific methods have a distinct value. Novels, tales, and dramas teem with imaginary experiments, not always possible in actual life, perhaps, but suggested by the methods of genuine science. Mr. Thomas's "Witching Hour" and Edgar Poe's "Strange Case of Monsieur Valdemar" both turn on experiments in mesmerism. A narrative of country life might gain excellent local color from the scientific testing both of provincial tempers and of farming machinery. Any man who desires to become a stimulating and forcible writer may well train himself to examine all phenomena of life with which he comes in touch, now separately, now together, now under one set of circumstances, now another, until he has thus gained insight into their true nature and causes and so laid up plentiful material for future writing which men will be eager to read.

IV

So much for facts obtained at first hand by the writer's own observation or experiment. It is somewhat humiliat ing to realize how small a part of any man's knowledge falls into either of these categories. At every turn one must depend instead upon facts gained at second hand, facts of which one knows nothing except what other men have told him. How do we know that there is a frigid zone? Most of us, certainly, have never been there. Why are we certain that the human race existed two hundred years ago? We were not alive then to see. Why shudder at the reported horrors of the Inquisition? We have no first-hand proof even that the water torture is disagreeable, much less that anybody was ever so tortured. Few of us have had any ocular proof that Europe during and after 1914 was not in a state of the most exemplary tranquillity. Why are our readers convinced that a plural subject requires a plural verb? They have not examined one one-millionth of the printed books in the language; they have not heard that language from one one-thousandth of the English-speaking world; — and half of that less than one one-thou sandth appear to follow another usage. Nearly all our knowledge, on which we depend for our code of honor, our present happiness, and our future salvation, is taken on trust from the statements of others.

More ominous yet is the fact that our limited experience does not inspire us with implicit trust in such derived knowledge. A large part of the human race will not tell the truth, and another large part cannot if they try. The history of cross-questioning in law courts shows that only a small minority of witnesses can give a consistently true account of what they have actually seen. King David said in his haste that all men are liars; and we may assume that in calmer hours he but modified slightly the numerical adjective. Even the works of our most erudite scholars are found by other scholars to be full of crass errors in fact. No textbook on geology fifty years old would be tolerated in a modern university. Warton's "History of English Poetry," which five generations ago was a masterpiece in the field of literary history, has now been almost annotated out of existence by the desperate efforts of recent editors to correct its multitudinous mistakes. If this is true of professional scholars, how frail is our dependence on the word of the untrained amateur, the immature undergraduate, the impulsive enthusiast; and below them on the drudging, unlettered masses.

It seems at first as if under such conditions one must despair of genuine knowledge; must accept the universe as a *terra incognita*, peopled with fictions, dreams, and delusions. Deeper analysis, however, shows that this is not the case. Most men may be inaccurate witnesses, but all their separate statements are not falsehoods; and truth may usually be sifted out of untruth if only the right process is known. Modern architects have learned how to build the most heavy sky-scrapers on foundations that are little better than shifting mud; and on a foundation of testimony equally unstable, man may rear a reasonably accurate body of knowledge, once he has found the method. This task lies especially in the province of the speaker or writer. As an author he is the transmitter of thought, therefore the custodian of truth. Every statement which he repeats without examination may be a lie which he thereby endorses. In the historian this may prove a gross injustice to the noblest of his contemporaries, or a libel on a whole people. In books on science and finance it may become a false beacon, luring misguided readers along dangerous paths to their ruin. The undergraduate who like a parrot reports an untested statement to a Discipline Committee may find himself the means of expelling an innocent man from college or of rendering an honorable amateur ineligible for a championship team.

How then is the writer to grasp and impart truth in this befogged and befibbed world? His first requisite is the power to repeat accurately to others what has already been told accurately to him. The man who does this becomes a benefactor of his race, one of a small and noble aristocracy at once honest and scholarly. Law courts either reject second-hand evidence entirely or discount it heavily. They do this because they have learned through the centuries that few people can reproduce accurately what some one else has told them. Error grows like a snowball in its passage from mind to mind. Not until a man has overcome this tendency has he any right to meddle with the thought of his age by entering into print. Swift tells us in his "Voyage to Laputa" that the commentators on Homer and Aristotle durst not come near these worthies, so wroth were the two great men at the way that they had been misinterpreted; yet the fate of Homer and Aristotle was mild compared with that of many a modern scholar, whose noblest thoughts, the result, perhaps, of years of labor, have been garbled and travestied and turned from truth into falsehood by the most morally irreproachable of our young college men, not in examinations only, but in conversation, and even in print.

What is meant by truth in the reproduction of another man's statements? Partly, the most rigid accuracy of detail. Any man may forget and omit; no man has a right to forget and garble. What is given at all must be given correctly. Details are often sacred things, no matter how small they seem. A young man in Europe writes home to a local paper that one thousand innocent people were killed in a recent massacre, when the real number reported to him was only ten. The difference in significance is great, for the larger the number of innocent dead, the stronger is the presumption that the brutal spirit accountable for their fate was national and not merely local. Had this man changed 10 to 1000 on a check he would have received five years at hard labor; yet is not a printed slur on a nation's honor more criminal than some slight pilfering from her coffers? In Grant's campaign of the Wilderness a careless dispatching officer, copying an order, inadvertently wrote a wrong destination, and thereby sent thousands of men miles from their proper position in the crisis of a great action. He made a slip of only a word; yet it almost decided a battle, and might have decided a war.

Mere accuracy of detail, however, is not reproduction of the truth. It is as if a thief who had stolen the Mona Lisa should return its mangled fragments as an honest equivalent for the purloined masterpiece. Truth in proportion and in subordination is just as essential as truth in details. Relative emphasis on different points, order, relation, the subservience of one idea to another, must all be preserved. Stevenson in "Pulvis et Umbra" stresses the brutality of man's origin and environment, but uses this point merely as a means to prove man's nobility in struggling so bravely under such a terrible handicap. The most accurate report of his paragraphs on man's origin and surroundings, separated from the main thought to which the author made them subordinate, would give an utterly distorted conception of Stevenson's meaning.

Two forms of writing which illustrate how the principles so far discussed can be applied are the book review and the *précis*. A reviewer does not necessarily give an orderly and logical digest of the book he is discussing; but it is frequently desirable to do so, especially with works on science or social and military conditions, where the conclusions are not disputed, the style is a minor matter, and the substance of the book needs to be widely diffused and justly understood. Such a review would bear the same relation to the book discussed as a miniature does to the human face it copies. The main points of the author must be accurately grasped and fairly worded; the reviewer should apportion his emphasis among them approximately as the author does. Detailed statements should be accurately reproduced in connection with the main points which they are intended to illustrate; and since all details cannot be reproduced in such limited space, those chosen should be typical of those omitted.

The *précis* is a condensation of a book, essay, or lecture, and aims to present the given subject matter as justly and fully as possible in limited space. Its practical value lies in the clearness of its outline and the saving of time for its readers. It has also a great disciplinary value as training for the man who makes it; and for that reason, at the stage which our discussion has now reached, every writer not already familiar with the *précis* should practice it until he feels that he is able to transmit facts to another at least as accurately as they came to him.[1]

V

If the whole world could be trained to reproduce facts and conclusions with the accuracy which we have just outlined, nothing more might be necessary. Unfortunately this is not the case. Trained, scientific, honest minds are always a little minority in the midst of the wilfully dishonest or the mentally confused. The lawyer or judge finds himself confronted by a vast mass of inconsistent and conflicting evidence, all of which cannot be true, and very little of which can be blindly trusted. Even worse, perhaps, is the situation of a Commission of Inquiry — such, for example, as the Bryce Commission which examined into the alleged

[1] For directions in writing a *précis* see Appendix I, p. 317.

atrocities of the Germans around Louvain. They find before them a chaos of contradictory statements, allegations distorted by hatred, exaggerated by hysteria, or concocted by deliberate dishonesty, truth suppressed by fear or misconceived through sheer stupidity. Accurate reproduction of these different stories in manuscript is an initial step toward the truth, but merely a step. The actual verity, the faithful picture of all that really happened, probably exists in no living brain, could not be obtained by bare recording of individual impressions if the members of such a commission were mind-readers; it must be toilsomely pieced together by testing, selection, rejection, and even then may be only imperfectly attained. For it must always be remembered that in the world of human experience — as contrasted with the world of pure mathematical reasoning — much of the time we can gain but a partial and broken conception of what happened; even the most rigorous and judicious method can frequently give only that as a result. We found our plans for business or battle alike on probabilities, not certainties; we exalt one man to the gallows and another to the presidential chair on strong but inconclusive evidence. Yet, although the wise man as well as the fool must proceed on guesswork, the wise man guesses shrewdly in the light of all obtainable evidence and nine times out of ten succeeds, while the fool leaps blindly and usually fails. In other words, though the systematic weighing of evidence may produce only fragmentary knowledge, such knowledge is often of inestimable value in practical affairs.

What then is the proper method of procedure? Let us illustrate its nature in a particular case. Let us suppose there have been labor troubles of a most serious type in a certain mining district; and a Commissioner has been sent by the Federal Government to ascertain the facts.

He hears lengthy statements from union laborers, strike breakers, capitalists, superintendents, innocent bystanders, and officers of the militia; reduces all these statements to writing, and then compares them. Immediately the manuscript begins to bristle with interrogation marks. The strikers declare that their pay was not a living wage. Was it? They say that they were forced to buy their groceries from the company's stores. Were they? The militia assert that one of their number was shot intentionally by strikers; the union men answer that he was the victim of a private grudge. Which is right? And so the dispute goes on. Let us assume that the systematic Commissioner gradually reduces the whole problem to a long list of such questions, each kept separate from the others; that with a pair of scissors he clips from the carbon copy of the manuscript all the answers to each, and ranges them, affirmative or negative, under their respective headings.

The first discovery resulting from this method is that there are several details on which all parties agree. Evidently at these points the truth is already attained. If men with adverse interests, hating each other, and giving each other the lie about most matters, agree on one certain detail, who shall say them no? Here are a few reliable facts that begin to loom through the confusion like hilltops through dissipating mist. They may be minor points; but if considered carefully they sometimes help to show the general contour of the landscape.

A further search usually reveals other questions as to which the evidence is overwhelmingly on one side; in which the weaker party disputes and denies without definite evidence, while the stronger piles up affidavits, statistics, and details. The contrast between the two sides, though not perhaps wholly convincing, is certainly impressive; and if the evidence of the preponderating party will bear the most rigorous tests — such as will be discussed in a moment — absolute certainty may follow.

There remain a large number of questions, each with a formidable mass of testimony on either side. Here the affirmative and negative statements must be weighed against each other in a mental balance, and as just a decision made as possible, though it avowedly decides what is probably, not what is certainly, right. The various devices for weighing in this balance involve the most intricate and delicate machinery of thought and vary so much in individual cases that they can be best discussed if the typical case of the Commissioner is temporarily laid aside, to be taken up again later.

Tests of evidence are frequently classified under the heads of honesty, prejudice, and mental competence; but many interrelations, many subordinate and possibly supplementary headings have to be considered in facing a practical problem. Honesty in the witness is exceedingly important; yet notorious criminals, Becker, for instance, have been executed on the testimony of men who acknowledged a past replete with falsehood. There is a stupid dishonesty which from sheer force of habit lies with verminlike persistency; there is an intelligent dishonesty which will lie atrociously for great stakes but tell the unvarnished truth when there is little or nothing to gain by falsehood. Also consistency is almost as important a test as is the witness's character for veracity. If all the details of a man's story are consistent with each other, and consistent, to the most minute detail, with the stories of several other men, he may have lied repeatedly in the past, but he is probably telling the truth now; so hard is it for even the most ingenious brain to evolve fictions that will fit in at every point with realities. Such testimony from an avowedly dishonest man, however, becomes worthy of consideration only when

c

it has been subjected to a searching cross examination, which would reveal any discrepancies that existed.

Mental competence is an important test; but mental competence is a vague term and needs defining. The same man may have great powers of judgment and remarkable weakness of memory; might judge almost infallibly on facts presented by others and yet be highly unreliable concerning events of which he had long ago been an eye-witness. Then, too, when we leave the courtroom for more literary arenas of thought, what shall we say of the imaginative temperament, which lives partly in a universe of its own fancies and may be constitutionally unable to separate the world of realities from its own superimposed world of dreams? Here arises a vital problem in writing biographies of geniuses or books on the history of art and literature. The very men who in some ways are the most competent judges are accustomed to think of external facts as the crude material which they may melt and reshape in their imaginative furnace; they are at once the most and the least reliable of witnesses. Again, there are problems in life which depend on sympathy as well as logic; and the dependable witness is he who has discerning sympathy — intelligent fellow feeling and not blind sentimentalism. Was Byron sincere behind his melodramatic pose, or was he an unhallowed compound of misanthropy and gigantic vanity? Mere logic could never answer; the only convincing answer can result from that harmonious action of the brain and heart which we have called discerning sympathy. Several of Byron's contemporaries, Scott among them, had this quality; and because we feel its presence in them we respect their testimony concerning the redeeming side of the passionate prodigal son of literature.

Associated sometimes with the question of the witness's honesty, sometimes with that of his mental dependability is a valuable supplementary test, the definiteness or vagueness of his account. The excess of hazy generalities in Dr. Cook's lectures on his Polar journey first awakened public suspicion. Some of the witnesses before an Inquiry Commission present plentiful statistics and masses of detail, while others deal in vague generalizations. To be sure, if the details offered are such that they cannot possibly be verified they may prove nothing but the speaker's imaginative powers. Gulliver gave unlimited details about the non-existent island of Lilliput because he knew that no one would sail there to expose him. If, however, the witness's details are such that an enemy could disprove them were they false, the mere fact that he dares to offer them is evidence of his truthfulness. Every definite statement then becomes a test; and he is voluntarily meeting as many tests as possible. If a man's honesty is admitted, the fuller his statement of concrete facts, the greater its probative value. Details and statistics show either that he has had unusual opportunities for acquiring knowledge or else that he has unusual powers for using such opportunities as were given — in either case that he is mentally an exceedingly reliable man.

The question of bias or prejudice is of great importance. If a writer's statements run parallel to his prepossession, they should be discounted; if counter to it, they should be given additional weight. Yet the amount to be added or subtracted — in the case of a man who, though biased, is thoroughly honest — varies greatly according to circumstances. Prejudice is exceedingly distorting in matters of opinion or inference; in questions determined by counting, by measurement, or by any other mechanical action of the hand or brain, it may become almost negligible. An honest but jealous woman would give a very unreliable verdict on her rival's beauty, but a reasonably trustworthy statement as to the latter's height and color of hair. The two largest stained windows in England are in York and Gloucester cathedrals. A conscientious verger of York, who had measured both, could be trusted as to their relative dimensions but not concerning their relative value as works of art. Also, the more intelligent the writer, the more the thinking man's instinctive love of accuracy will struggle against his bias and enable him to tell the exact truth, if he honestly wishes to do so. On the other hand, violent prejudice may at times develop into temporary dishonesty. Such overwhelming passions as patriotism and mother love may, under peculiar and transitory conditions, drag people of the noblest character into deliberate falsehood. *Dulce est pro patria mentiri*, says the sardonic proverb, "Sweet it is to lie for one's country"; and the statements of impassioned patriots, mothers, and partisans should always be taken only for what they are worth.

Another test of any statement presented is what is called its "antecedent probability," that is, the question whether our whole background of experience in related matters makes it seem probable or preposterous that such a thing could happen. "Who would believe," says a character in Shakespeare's "Tempest,"

> "that there were such men
> Whose heads stood in their breasts?"

The hearer's doubt in this case is due, not to any known dishonesty or bias or stupidity in the teller, but to the preposterous nature of the thing told. Yet here also a word of caution is needed. The rich do not always think like the poor, nor the Italians like the Anglo-Saxons, nor the young like the old, nor decadent criminals like healthy-minded jurists. "Put yourself in the other man's place," says the proverb; but to put yourself in his place when your whole attitude toward life is different from his and then to reason out what you would have done is to believe him when he lies and doubt him when he tells the truth., Especially should this caution be borne in mind when the question concerns the conduct of foreign races, or of social types with which the investigators are not familiar.

Such are the general principles for sifting conflicting statements on any problem. Now let this be applied to the Federal Commissioner, whose case was recently discussed as a typical one. Guided by the principles just outlined, he would go through his accumulated mass of evidence. He would encounter certain facts admitted by all; others denied by one side, it is true, but overwhelmingly established by their opponents; and many with much evidence on both sides where weighing and sifting showed one party to be apparently more trustworthy than the other. On the strength of this he would be in a position to give a final verdict, obviously not infallible, but as righteous and intelligent as the limited human mind can hope to achieve.

Having fulfilled his duty as judge, the Commissioner would next face the problem of authorship, in this case the writing of the report embodying his verdict. Such a report is intended, in part at least, for the public, for readers not only ignorant of many facts but also woefully confused as to the issues involved. To meet their needs, the pamphlet would naturally open with a clear definition of the problem and the main questions connected with it. Then the discussion of these questions should follow in coherent order, usually *seriatim*. The subject matter under each heading presents a problem in selection and rejection. The public wish to know not only the final decision but also the general nature of the grounds on which that decision was based. On the other hand, they cannot and will not traverse all that dreary chaos of controversy from which it is the business of the Commissioner to evolve order.   They wish a few brief typical examples of the evidence considered, some general statement as to the nature of testimony not quoted and as to the line of reasoning followed by the judge.   Moreover, the majority of them have little idea of the relative importance of the different questions involved.   It is the writer's duty by varying the stress on different aspects of the problem to distinguish the more from the less important;   otherwise he may give a distorted caricature of truth instead of the truth itself.   Many incidental stumbling blocks will necessarily be met with which cannot be prepared for in advance.   However, both in sifting material and in writing the final pamphlet the following items are always essential: a clear conception and definition of the questions involved;   a systematic division of material, so that each problem may be analyzed and discussed by itself; accuracy in the handling of detail;   honesty in the weighing of evidence;   fairness in the sense of proportion.

The above method of reasoning and writing is not confined to industrial problems.   Any one who wishes a more literary subject may sift the many and conflicting statements as to the character of Coleridge or of Byron.   If he is a sportsman he may winnow the seemingly irreconcilable testimony as to a certain athlete's ineligibility, or as to the exact extent of professionalism in amateur sports.   Wherever witnesses disagree and a public desires to know the truth, the procedure which has just been outlined can be applied.

The usefulness of such procedure as we have discussed is not confined to the production of a *précis* (including the related book review) and the report of an Inquiry Board. Neither is it confined to the training which enables an author to gather a wealth of material and to use this in rounding out and vitalizing the framework of his projected essay.

Beyond all that a rich store of gathered facts has other influences, far reaching, although indirect. By the emotions and mental attitudes which it produces, this wealth unconsciously enriches one's style. The emotional residuum of uncounted observations, experiments, and experiences molded the noble language of the old Hebrew writer when he said · "I have been young and now am old; yet have I not seen the righteous forsaken, nor his seed begging their bread." By the same wealth of knowledge, though pessimistic instead of cheerful, Swift gave edge to the trenchant satire in which he declared that the past history of England "was only a heap of conspiracies, rebellions, murders, massacres, revolutions, banishments, the very worst effects that avarice, faction, hypocrisy, perfidiousness, cruelty, rage, madness, hatred, envy, lust, malice, or ambition, could produce." Lastly, as will be shown in the next chapter, this accumulated knowledge of details becomes the fertile soil out of which ideas generate and a wise attitude toward the universe becomes possible.

CHAPTER II

THOUGHT

I

UNTIL a fact is put with other facts and built upon, or until it is seized by the emotions and utilized by life, it remains just a fact, a dead, cold thing, uninspiring and not valuable. Thinking and feeling make use of facts. Thinking especially, as has been made clear in the last chapter, tests facts, arranges and compounds them into true conclusions. There is not much of value to be done with facts unless one is willing to think about them.

This, however, is not the only way in which thinking is connected with good writing. Sometimes the man about to write begins with an array of facts; but quite as frequently the germ and first form of that which is to be written is a thought, a thought complete as a cell is complete, and needing only the test of truth and a logical development. This is what is meant when it is said that a man has an "idea." It is not a fact that he is possessed of; it is a thought; a thought that must be tested — so far as it is possible to do so — by facts; which must be developed by logical processes. The brain, so psychologists tell us, acts with kaleidoscopic rapidity. It shakes together an "idea" with a single twist — and there is a thought ready to be tested for its worth. Such a rapid mental operation, for example, in the brain of the French philosopher Rousseau, may have produced the idea that there should be essential equality among men. The fire and slaughter of the French Revolution tested it by facts.

Some men sparkle with ideas whenever life surges high for them and energy pulses through the brain. Most of us are favored now and then by something that may be called an idea, or at least a new and personal thought. Some unfortunates never have a real idea from one week's end to another. But every man who speaks or writes must handle thoughts, must test them, must develop them, precisely as he must handle facts — if not his own thoughts, why then another's. A thought after all is merely a relationship. When I connect the idea of food with the idea of time, the thought "It must be lunch time" flashes across my nervous system. This is an interesting idea, but scarcely an original one. When I connect the idea of war with that of death, and these two with the loss of so many willing hands made idle forever, the thought "War is waste" burns itself into my mind. This too is not highly original; but it is valuable; it is worth trying out by the facts; it is worthy of development.

Here then is the essence of this discussion. Given a relationship brought forward by the brain, an idea as we call it, how can the truth of that thought be tested, how can it be developed so as to be useful for thinker and reader alike?

The first moral to be drawn is painfully obvious. Just as it is idle to handle facts until one is certain that they *are* facts, so it is a waste of time to develop a thought until one is sure that the thought is worth developing. Why are so many "themes" worth just the price of waste paper in a glutted market? Because they are deficient in fact or weak in thought. It is worse than useless to spend time in learning to write unless one is willing to search for and capture thought. But granted that eager stir of the mind in the midst of which real ideas are born, granted an idea at least once a week, which is quite often enough for the purpose, how is the infant to be raised and put to work? That is the question.

An idea, as it has been described in the previous paragraphs, is really a hypothesis; that is, a tentative statement whose truth remains to be proved. For example, many thinkers, from the Greeks down to Goethe, had put forth the idea, which was really a hypothesis, that life proceeds by evolution, from lower forms to higher forms, from beast to man, from savage to civilization. It remained for Charles Darwin, in his "Origin of Species," to test this hypothesis by laboriously gathered facts, and by reasoning based thereon. Indeed, nearly every great advance of the human intellect has begun with an idea, and has proceeded by means of a trying-out according to reason and according to the facts. So with the lesser steps of personal development. It occurs to a teacher in a moment of illumination that the average undergraduate would learn more if he did more thinking and less listening in the classroom. Is this true? There is no way of discovering except to try it out by the facts and to use reason where facts fail. That the stars are formed of compacted nebula, and that education is not the same as information, are both hypotheses. The first might make a book; the second an editorial; the first is a subject for a lifetime of study; the second for a day's thinking; but the same principles of test and development apply to both. What are these principles?

Let us begin with a simple hypothesis such as one meets with in any study of scientific method. Let us endeavor to prove that an acid and a base will unite to form a salt. Given a test-tube, some hydrochloric acid, and a copper cent, the test can be made and made successfully. When the facts are recorded the hypothesis has been made good.

But few thoughts that men have to deal with in the course

of everyday experience are as simple as this one. When the idea involves life values as well as the attributes of dead things, it becomes more complex. Let us choose a thought whose working out will require more than an experiment in elementary chemistry: "The best way to prepare for war is to prepare for peace."

The first step is to test the truth of this proposition. But the term "truth" is not so simple as it looks. "'What is truth?' said jesting Pilate, and did not stay for an answer." There is truth to facts; there is truth to reason when facts fail us; and there is emotional truth, which is quite a different matter. Truth to facts usually deserves the first consideration.

What are the facts which may be used to support the assertion that the best way to prepare for war is to prepare for peace? They may be sought for and obtained by a series of questions. What is required for a successful preparation for war? One answers, an adequate army and navy; sufficient armament and munitions; military skill to direct the whole. A little more thinking brings the further answer, an industrial and economic system that will support the enormous endeavor necessary for modern war. These one may fairly call facts. And now what is preparation for peace? Efficiency, organization, the development of trained brains, an emphasis upon self-dependence rather than upon aggression, a preference of conquests over nature to conquests over man. These also are facts. Finally, what will be the effect of a preparation for peace upon the possible enemy? In measure as the peaceful nation is unaggressive though potentially powerful, desirous of peace though efficient for war, in like measure, or at least in some measure, the enemy will be slow to attack. This also is a fact. Grouped with the others, does it or does it not support the hypothesis?

The truth of the matter is that there are not facts enough here either to prove or to disprove the proposition; and it is doubtful whether, as the world stands at this time, enough could be gathered. If we are to come to any conclusion we must trust to a further process, reason, the power of convincing ourselves by logical processes of thought, the power which, when all the facts available have been obtained, will put two and two together to make four. For example, as regards the question of peace and war, what can be de duced from the experience of other nations where the facts cited above have existed and have led either to peace or to war? What inductions can be made from these facts as regards the situation here in America? What analogies can be found to this problem in man's experience in other fields than war?

It is a very difficult problem. The testing of all real thought is difficult; if it is easy there has been no real thought! But this, at least, has been established by these preliminaries: the first task of the man with an idea is to get the facts available, the next is to apply his reason to the handling of these facts. It may be well to begin again in this discussion, with another hypothesis.

As a result of his experience with patients suffering from hysteria, the Viennese doctor Freud conceived the idea that dreams, instead of being merely wild vagaries of the relaxed brain, were, in their own way, coherent, logical, and susceptible of interpretation. His idea was that a man's dream contains a suppressed wish. The many de-sires for things unobtainable by the will in the daytime find vent in dreams, and under strange disguises make stories of their own in sleep. The facts to be handled in endeavoring to prove this supposition were many. He collected them. There were the facts as to what men and women actually dreamed. There were the facts as to what these same men and women had done the day before the dreams in question. There were the facts — most difficult to secure — of the secret desires his patients had suppressed, had forced, as it were, below the level of consciousness. This was but a beginning. The next step was to connect the three sets of facts. If a given lawyer, let us say, had talked in all friendliness with a rival whom he admired, but envied; if he had professed his admiration, but concealed, even from himself, his envy; if in a dream that night he had seen his rival conduct a case with such stupidity that the court was dissolved in scornful laughter, — why then, what inference was to be made? Freud, by a process of simple deduction, decided that the envy suppressed in the daytime, revealed itself, disguised in a story, at night. Then adding to this case a hundred others he was able, by reason again, to generalize upon his facts, to say that such a relationship among them was generally true. And so he maintained that his hypothesis was verified.

Whether he was right or not, whether anyone is right when, after gathering his facts and applying reason, he asserts the truth of his hypothesis, depends upon the worth of the facts and upon the soundness of the reasoning. If the facts are insufficient, or if they are not facts, the hypothesis falls. If the reasoning is fallacious, the hypothesis remains a hypothesis merely. I can prove with much effectiveness that religion is merely an inheritance from ghost fear. The study of every primitive race gives facts to support my conclusion. The tracing back of every religious ceremony confirms it. The line of evolution, proceeding from the savage afraid of his friend's ghost to the prophet in awe of Jehovah, is direct and whole. But beware of fallacies. Man, chemically considered, is a compound of a few simple elements only, and yet one learns little of man by knowing what he is made of. Fear is only a muscular contraction plus

a mental image, but the combination wrecks lives and king-
doms, shakes beliefs, and gives rise to philosophies. And
so with religion, which the facts of origin alone fail in any
way to define or explain.

And thus the first step in the testing of the truth of thought
is to get the facts, and the second is to apply these facts by
sound reasoning. Common sense will take the place of
elaborate reasoning processes, when only common thoughts
are in question; for common sense is precisely the application, by means of short-cut reasoning, of our own experience
to the case in hand. But common sense is not a safeguard
in all questions unless it is really uncommon sense of a very
high order. Few men under middle age have had sufficient
experience to enable them to judge fairly of thoughts that
transcend their own narrow field. "There aint no sech
animal," said the country bumpkin of the giraffe. "There
is no such woman," says the undergraduate of Ibsen's
Hedda Gabler, trusting to what he calls his common sense.
And ideas are no more exempt from such misjudgments
than women and giraffes. Only reasoning, and clear and
sound reasoning, will follow the uncommon thought, which
means the new, the valuable thought, into airy regions
and bring it back to earth.

If the world were made up entirely of mathematics,
chemistry, physics, and economics, the foregoing explanation of what thought is and how it must be proved in writing,
might conclude with advice to wrestle with the next idea
that comes and learn by experience the truth of what has
been said. But life is not all mathematics; the brain
uses reason, but is seldom governed by it; intuition has
more practical importance sometimes than logic; and when
a man makes up his mind to do a thing, it is nine times
because he "feels like it," to once because he has reasoned
it out. As psychologists and philosophers alike have shown

us, we decide upon our course of action first and find our reasons afterwards; we choose a college, vote the Republican ticket, or select a friend, and then and only then reason out the wherefore and the why. Back of the reason, indifferent often to the facts, lie our emotions, our prejudice, our tendencies of mind, which will usually determine in advance whether in any question the conservative or the radical, the pessimistic or the optimistic side will win the day with us. In the least decision of the will, influences figure that come from the hidden springs of ancestral life itself. Upon all such influences reason acts as a partial control, but it cannot do away with them; for logic, which is certainly the law of matter, is not always the law of life.

Therefore a new problem presents itself to the man who would learn to write — one too little considered in formal textbooks on composition. Truth to facts, truth to reason have been defined; but what is emotional truth? For clearly there will be many questions where the way men feel about facts is quite as important as the facts themselves; and just as many where the way one feels is no less important than the way one thinks.

Suppose that one chooses for consideration the not very radical idea that poverty is at the root of inefficiency and crime. Bernard Shaw, in his "First Aid for Critics," prefaced to his play "Major Barbara," discusses this thought with convincing force, backs up his proof with an abundance of facts, turns and twists it by means of clear reasoning until it is made to apply to many ills of modern society, and afterwards drives home the principle concretely in the play. Is it true? For *him*, for the problems he discusses, one can scarcely deny the validity of the statement. It survives the test of fact, the test of reason; it is emotionally true also, for men who view the world as Shaw views it must feel that his idea is right.

But what about St. Francis of Assisi who courted "Our Lady Poverty," who "professed poverty before God and before men" as the nearest road to humility of spirit, simplicity of soul, and true usefulness! What of the hundreds of thousands of men and women who, not necessarily condemning wealth in others, have for themselves followed the precept, "Take no thought for your life, what ye shall eat; neither for the body, what ye shall put on." Facts, the facts of history, prove that their influence upon the world has been invaluable; for if they have not contributed to industrial efficiency they have certainly helped to save civilization from a brutish dependence upon mere subsistence as a chief end of life. Indeed, reason proves that there must be such individuals and such a point of view if we are not to sacrifice pity, humility, love, and all the most human of the virtues to a soulless efficiency that will give a man all the comforts of life without the character to profit by them.

Now what is the *truth* as to these two proposals? It is not enough to say that Shaw is right for industrial efficiency and St. Francis for spiritual efficiency, since the material and the spiritual cannot be arbitrarily separated. Both are involved in the question as to whether poverty — or at least the will to live poorly — is good or bad for the morals of man. The answer depends, does it not, to some degree at least upon the individual. The truth of either proposition depends in some measure upon who says it, and for whom it is said. Poverty would probably not be very good for Bernard Shaw. Riches would certainly not have been good for St. Francis. He spoke sincerely, he spoke truly when he said that for many men poverty was best. So was Bernard Shaw sincere. He saw that for men who held his idea of life and its value in this world, and for many men with no ideas on the subject whatsoever, poverty was bad. The truth in either case is more than truth to facts; it is truth to the character, to the experience, to the feelings of the speaker. Each of the two conflicting statements that we have been discussing was emotionally true.

Many hypotheses of course, especially those in the fields of science, can be absolutely validated or exploded simply by seeking the facts; but the instance above is typical of many more where the personal feelings, the character, the innate tendencies of the writer or reader count at least as much as the facts, which, incidentally, in such examples are never complete enough in themselves to justify a decision. Who was wrong as to the theory of states' rights and the idea of government by an aristocracy, the Virginian of 1860 or the New Englander of the same period? The New Englander thought that the democracy should rule and the state be subordinated to the nation. The Virginian believed in control by the "quality" and a sovereign state empowered to satisfy its own needs rather than those of the central government. Legally the Southerner seems to have had the right of the matter; judging by his earlier history he may have been right, for although we know the results of the Civil War, we do not know what might have happened if the South had got its way without a conflict; emotionally he was certainly right. The theory of govern ment he supported was the true one for *him;* so true that when it was defeated, he and his type of mind began to disappear along with the theories of living which they upheld.

All this explains why emotional appeal is so much more powerful than pure reason in writing or speaking. The man who wishes to persuade must show his readers not only what may be true in the abstract, he must also show what is true for them. As an example, race prejudice is a universal human heritage that is seldom altogether reasonable. We

D

cannot feel in the same way toward a Japanese as toward an American, not because we despise him — we know him now too well to do that — but because he is not of our race. Now if you disregard this feeling in an argument for closer relations with Japan you are simply not being true, — no matter how far the abstract truth that men work best in brotherly understanding may support you, no matter how reasonable it may seem that racial feelings should be suppressed. As a man thinks so he is, might be more truly written, as a man feels so he is.

Of course all this is not advocacy of prejudice. Prejudice is simply feeling that runs dangerously counter to reason, although at times it may come very close to emotional truth. Prejudices should be fought against, argued with, suppressed when possible. In the search for truth they must be comprehended and allowed for; but they cannot be denied. They are excessive indications of the particular feeling toward life that in the long run determines our course in every action as much as, if not more than, reason and the plain facts.

And therefore, if the thought to be developed is personal, or if it involves emotions such as love, hate, or prejudice, or if it touches upon character or morals, reason of course must not be neglected, nor whatever facts may be found to bear upon the subject. Both must be pushed as far as they will go, and, if possible, the seeker must abide by the results. But it is not safe to stop here. The idea will seldom be completed, the hypothesis will seldom be fully tested, until one has determined whether or not it is absolutely true for the writer himself, or for his audience — whether it is emotionally true. In that wide field where are to be found, among many other subjects, war, philosophy, politics, honor, morality, love, and religion, the human, the emotional element cannot be left out. There one finds no absolutely verifiable truth. (Sincerity to what the writer feels, to what he thinks his readers can be made to feel, is the nearest approach to a final test.)

If a college professor wishes to explain the charm and the value of the academic life, he cannot be content to reason about its usefulness, or to present facts to prove that the study has influenced the world as much as the business office and the senate chamber. He must go deeper. He must make his readers feel the infinite value of such a life for characters like his; he must get his love of thinking, his belief in thinking, into his words, or those for whom he writes will remain unconvinced. Furthermore, since he is presumably not writing for other professors, he must remember that his readers will be more familiar with the active life than the contemplative, and that they will not *feel* as he does about an activity purely intellectual. He must allow for the difference between their emotional attitude and his, as well as the difference between what they know and what he knows of the academic life, if he is to give his words due weight. He must reason truly, give true facts, but most of all recognize a divergence of feeling that facts and reason alone will never reconcile. Emotional truth, to sum it all up, is gained by a sincere depiction of the emotions that lie behind and beneath thought.

II

When it comes to testing a thought much depends, as has been demonstrated above, upon the nature of the thought. But when it comes to developing a thought, to putting the results of the testing clearly and simply and directly before the reader, there is only one general procedure, though with many different applications. It is true that an idea can be brought home indirectly to the reader by making a story or a play about it. That method will be discussed in the next chapter. But for direct explanation or persuasion the writer must follow the natural laws of the human mind — called logic — or fail in his attempt.

These laws apply as much to the setting forth of facts as to the development of thought. They codify, when all is said, merely the best ways of putting one man in complete possession of what another man is thinking. And which of these ways is to be used in a given instance depends always and entirely upon the nature of the thought, or the kind of facts that have been collected. No one relies upon the same stroke in tennis to return every serve; he must know all strokes, and choose according to circumstances. Just so with the logical development of thought, or the logical presentation of facts.

The best way to make clear this highly practical subject, which lies at the heart of construction in writing, is to take a topic and work it out. Let the subject be an idea for a brief essay: "A college course should first of all develop broadmindedness."

Such a topic as this one is a germ cell. It is capable of development by the proper means, but its true nature will remain unknown until careful thought has been expended upon it. Of precisely what developed thought is this idea the germ?

The biologist applies his microscope. The writer applies his brain. The biologist differentiates the germ cell — when possible — from other germ cells by characteristics of structure, size, and general appearance; and then and only then can guess the conditions that will govern its development. The writer gets acquainted with his idea by studying it, by asking himself in this case precisely what is meant by broadmindedness.

Now there is only one way to discover what is meant by a word, a term, or a statement, and that is to define it. Logical definition is a simple process. The subject, a dog for instance, is placed in its class, its *genus,* in this instance the genus quadruped; and then its *differentia,* that is, its differences from other members of that class, indicated. By this process it is easy to define the term dog with scientific exactness. And definition can perform the same service for less concrete terms, with not so much precision, but greater profit.

What does one mean, for example, by broadmindedness? Clearly some form of "improvement of the mind" — and that is the *genus* to which the term belongs. But what does one mean by *broad*mindedness? How does it differ from deepmindedness, from keenmindedness, from disciplining, from informing the mind? What are its *differentia?* A dozen questions must be answered before one can define the term; and until they are answered the proposed essay will not be worth the time it takes to write it. Does breadth of thinking consist of knowing a little of everything, or a few fundamental things well? Or perhaps it is no matter of knowledge at all, but rather the way one thinks? Is broadmindedness a quality that belongs to character quite as much as to intellect? Or does it come from the reaction of tolerant, intelligent thinking upon character? So much is merely a beginning toward a definition of breadth of mind. And now, what is meant by a "college course"? Any higher educational process, such as that of a technical or professional school? Or a strictly undergraduate training in what are called the liberal arts? All these questions must be satisfied and the subject exactly defined before one is ready to go ahead with the development of the thought. Otherwise, one gets not real development, but muddle — and we do get muddle in a disgracefully large proportion of the so-called thought developments inflicted upon a patient but none too clear-headed public. Definition, in

42080

the sense used above, is a very necessary part of prepared-
ness in writing.

This is one step. Another immediately suggests itself.
By what end are you to grasp this ticklish subject of broadmindedness, once you know just what it means? Where
does one begin to write, when, after due consideration,
one discovers exactly what it is that he proposes to write
about? If every subject were as simple and indivisible
as the familiar proposition in logic, "All men are mortal,"
there would be no more to do than to define mortal and let
it go at that. But even the simplest subject is ordinarily
divisible. The child who writes on "My Dog" begins with
dog morality, he is a good dog; continues with dog nomen-
clature, his name is Bounce; and concludes with dog physique, he is small and curly. The man is but a complex
child, and a man's thought is but a complex child's thought.
For easy reading both must be divided.

The difficulty in division comes simply because the thought
is complex. One laughs at the child's naïve essay on the
dog and then proceeds to commit one or both of the two
cardinal sins of division, overlapping or incompleteness.
For example, here is a discussion of the minimum wage
law under the quadruple heading: "Effect on the laborer;
effect on the employer; effect upon capital invested; effect
upon the community." The writer never noted that his
fourth item overlaps all the others, and as a result his essay
is repetitive and confusing. And here is another upon scientific management, which is developed under the headings:
"Increase in output; effect upon wages; effect upon profits."
This writer did not observe that the possible effect of the
"speeding up" of scientific management upon the human
material employed has not been touched upon at all. He
traveled through· three arcs of the circle of his subject,
but never entered upon the fourth. His topic was not

thoroughly developed because his division was incomplete.

The method by which one divides any subject in advance into natural parts is so simple and so efficacious, that one wonders that it is so seldom done consciously. Most writers do it unconsciously — by instinct seemingly — whenever they write. But so long as the process remains instinctive, unreasoned, uncontrolled, it may fail to work when most needed, or may, as above, work imperfectly. Think of the thought to be developed, or the group of thoughts to be explained, as a circle inclosing the subject matter. Divide the circle-subject into arcs, following the natural lines of cleavage. See that the divisions do not overlap. See that all the circle is divided. Then lift out the division that can best be handled first and begin. This advice is thoroughly conventional. One can find such directions in any book on logic. Indeed, they are so obvi ous that most writers do not heed them — and as a result pay a price in time and effectiveness.

Equally obvious but far less neglected is the next step in logical presentation. Specification, as it is commonly called, is really a rough kind of definition, which enlarges the meaning of the topic. When a subject has been stated, it is usually necessary to present the details, to elaborate it, to specify the circumstances that it involves. If it is a group of facts that is to be handled, one must describe them, turn them over, give the details, the specifications, until all that is implied by the subject is made plain. I am writing, for example, of the benefits of compulsory service in a democracy like the United States. After I have defined what I mean by compulsory service; after I have divided the subject into, let us say, objections and benefits; why then I must specify the precise nature of each objection and each benefit; I must elaborate; I must give the details. This is specification, a somewhat loose process, but so natural that it needs no further discussion.

It is not easy to develop a thought without division, definition, and specification, but the fourth method of presentation is not so generally applicable. Comparison and contrast require on the part of the writer some imagination; they are adapted, furthermore, only to subjects where comparison and contrast are really valuable. And comparison particularly is tricky, for there are more false analogies in the world than true ones. Nevertheless, the writer who can reach the mind of another by an apt comparison makes quick strides toward his goal. If the undergraduate can be made to see that when he measures service to his college entirely in terms of athletic prowess he is like the statesman who measures service to the state entirely in terms of oratory, conviction of a possible narrowness is much more likely to be brought home to him. Likewise, if I can set the initiative of the American pioneer, his inventiveness, his adaptability, in contrast to the inflexible mind, the timid spirit, the helplessness in crisis of the peasant in a despotic Oriental state, I have done much to explain the blessings of residence in a land still rich in new careers.

Unfortunately, if the comparison is not accurate or the contrast unjust, this method of thought development is perhaps the worst. The war, for example, has spawned a multitude of false analogies that fill the daily press. It was effective to compare the defenseless United States to defenseless Belgium; but the comparison left out of account a difference in geographical location so great as to destroy the analogy. In 1914, every move of the belligerent armies was explained by comparison with the war of 1870-1; but by 1915 that analogy was seen to be false. The Franco-Prussian war disappeared from military comment except as in contrast to current battles. An extraordinary amount

of bad arguing comes from thinking that Tweedledum is
just the same as Tweedledee. But an accurate use of
parallels in explanation or persuasion makes strong, effective
writing.

Only one possible form of subject development remains,
the use of reasoning. Reasoning is not quite the same as
argument, although the two are usually confused. Any
form of statement used to persuade becomes argument —
whether a mere assertion of facts, or an analogy, or reasoning
itself. Argument uses whatever weapon lies handiest, and
— to revert to the conventional terms of rhetoric — at
least half of all argument is pure exposition.

Reasoning is the use of facts and thought in combination
in order to reach a definite conclusion. If the methods
employed are analyzed, it quickly becomes apparent that
they fall invariably and necessarily under two heads. The
thinker finds some general principle that he knows to be
true, and fits into it the facts of his particular case. This
is deduction. Or he begins with the facts; that is, having
a definite effect he may seek for a possible cause, or vice versa;
or having a sufficient number of observed facts, he may
attempt to base upon them a general conclusion that will
seem to be generally true. This — whether cause and effect
reasoning, or generalization — is induction. He may use
either deduction, or induction, or both; but in a vast
majority of cases writers and speakers use both in such close
coöperation that only thought analysis can disentangle
them. This is as it should be, for the purpose of reasoning
is not to display rhetorical forms, but to use them so as to
get a result. Indeed, it is far more important to decide
whether this final conclusion is just than to separate the
methods of development, although by analyzing arguments
it is often possible to detect fallacies and to discover when an
assertion is not supported by the facts.

In thought development reasoning is often a last and necessary resort. For instance, even though in the essay proposed above I may have defined compulsory service to the state, and may have listed the objections against it and the possible benefits, the nature of the question is still at best made clear and the answer is still doubtful. Remains the final effort of pure reason. Is it true as a general principle that democracy and universal service are compatible and mutually helpful? If so, it is easy to bring the special case of the United States under this law, and so take a step forward in the argument. This would be deduction. And again, can the reasoner present desired effects upon our social life of which compulsory service would be the only cause? And does the available evidence as to what Americans have accomplished under discipline, and in public affairs, permit him to generalize, to say that compulsory service in the United States would work? These two arguments — both the cause and effect and the generalization — would be induction, and further steps toward the conclusion he seeks. In practice he would not argue so simply. He would probably combine his methods, getting a general principle by induction and then using it to deduce. He would think, and rightly, much more of the proof desired than of the particular form of reasoning employed. But reason he would certainly have to use; and this is the fifth means of securing a complete and satisfactory development of thought.[1]

These five means of thought development sound fatally like a set of rules guaranteed to fit any subject and produce a perfect writer after fifteen minutes of memorizing. Nothing, unfortunately, could be further from the truth. To

[1] For a more detailed discussion of the special problems of reasoning and argument see "English Composition in Theory and Practice," The Macmillan Co., Chapters VIII and IX.

understand them helps; to know that in any thought development, as in any presentation of facts, one or two or all of them must be used and that there are no others avail able for direct presentation, also helps. But each in itself is really valuable only so far as the writer's thinking is clear and accurate, his grip upon fundamental facts sound and true.

And again the real problem is not how to develop thought, but how to develop *a* thought. Some ideas need defining; others do not. Sometimes the most intricate processes of reasoning are necessary; again a straightforward specifica tion of what is known about the subject is sufficient; or a cogent analogy will serve to do the work. The brilliant idea that since war has its virtues as well as its defects, there may be found somewhere in the social realm a moral equivalent of warfare, was struck out from the mind of William James in his "Varieties of Religious Experience" some years before the essay included in this volume was written. "What we now need to discover," he wrote, is "something heroic that will speak to men as universally as war does, and yet will be as compatible with their spiritual selves as war has proved itself to be incompatible." In the chapter on the value of saintliness of which this sentence is part, he had no room to develop the thought. Contenting himself with a brief definition of the moral values of war, and specifying that discipline of voluntary poverty, which many a saint has practised, as a possible substitute, he passed on. But the idea worked in his mind, sought a development entirely apart from any arguments for or against saintly poverty, found it, and was expanded by new processes of reasoning into essay form. The other essays appended to these chapters will also illustrate the truth that every thought has its own best development. Practice with expanding ideas will quickly confirm it.

Practice in writing consists in getting ready to write, even more than in covering paper. As Hamlet says in a somewhat more important connection, the readiness is all. And the best form of readiness for composition is a clearly grasped, clearly developed thought, whose outlines may be jotted down in the form of a plan. The first draft of an essay, or an article, or a report written from such a plan should be an experiment merely. When it is done, the incompleteness — the crookedness, the inadequacy of the thought development, if such defects exist — is rendered manifest. Then is the time for more and straighter thinking, for replanning and rewriting. Recopying merely is a waste of time; revision — a word that means reseeing, and thus implies rethinking — frequently turns a weak page into a strong one.

Learning rules for writing is a disagreeable task, and sometimes an unprofitable one. But the attempt to turn a thought that really means something to the writer into a piece of writing that does its work, that touches the brain or reaches the will of the reader, is one of the major sports of the intellect. To speak of such endeavor as learning to write is much too narrow a statement. Learning to think and learning to know are heavily involved, as these chapters have indicated; learning to utilize the imagination is also included, as will be made clear in the chapter to come.

CHAPTER III

IMAGINATION IN THE SERVICE OF THOUGHT

I

IN the preceding chapters much more has been said about matter than about manner. This is as it should be. Accuracy of fact, soundness and clearness of idea, are essential to any writing that is to be more than momentarily amusing; the graces of presentation are valuable but subsidiary aids. Readers of our oldest and most respected periodicals know only too well how often articles make their way into print by brute force of the valuable material they contain. It is undeniable that a new and true idea or a fresh and significant observation of fact will usually win a hearing, let the presentation of it be ever so unattractive. On the other hand, the art of the *jeu d'esprit*, the cleverness that lends charm to the trifle, is not to be learned from books.

Nevertheless, the ordinary man can ill afford to neglect anything that will help to attract a possible reader. The compiler of an engineer's report may be happily certain that his work will be inspected by some superior official; the student who composes a theme may be unhappily certain that even his dullest production will receive the blue-pencilings of an instructor; but the great mass of writing must make its own way, must — if it is to succeed at all — gain and hold the attention of those who are free to refuse it. Such writing must be interesting or unread.

Interest is often, of course, an inherent quality of the facts or ideas to be handled. An essay which presented a certain means for assuring permanent international peace could scarcely be made so dull that it would be wholly unnoticed. An article announcing the discovery of a cheap and satisfactory substitute for gasoline would be eagerly read even though it lacked every recognizable device for awakening interest. A keen appetite needs no sauce, and for a few things the public appetite is keen. But not everyone who finds himself impelled to write is the happy possessor of material which will of itself make this immediate and general appeal. The attraction of most ideas, like that of most women, is obscured by an unattractive or ill-designed dress. Not even Cleopatra despised the aid of silks and jewels, and for even the best thought there is a worse and better form.

Now and then there appears a man with an inborn ability to present his ideas in the most interesting way possible, one who could give to the multiplication table the fascination of romance. Others, in spite of all their pains, would be dull even if they were allowed to report the Day of Judgment. But nearly everyone who will force his imagination into the service of his thought can give his work an interest which it would otherwise lack; for, more than upon anything else, interest is dependent upon imagination.

The word imagination may properly be used to denote the power of constructive thought which has been discussed in the preceding chapter. It may also mean, as here, the power that the mind has of picturing to itself the unseen, of translating the abstract into vivid, concrete terms. A psychologist might easily cavil at the attempt to differentiate sharply between thought and imagination; but a man may think clearly about battles without once imagining the blood and filth of the trenches, the stench of the wounded, the continuous, maddening roar of artillery. The distinction between these two mental processes is certainly a serviceable one, and when a man makes use of such mental pictures he may be said to put his imagination into the service of his thought.

One way in which the imagination may thus be used appears at once when the writer considers the desirability of conceiving the character of the audience which he is to address. A speaker, having his hearers before him, can easily adjust himself to them. He can discover from Mr. Brown's puckered brow that a supposed explanation does not explain, or from Mr. Smith's ill-concealed yawns that a less ample presentation of the subject would be more acceptable. The writer, though he lacks this ocular aid, must none the less adjust his manner to the wishes and capabilities of those to whom he would appeal. A dramatic criticism admirably suited to the pages of "The North American Review" might easily bore the readers of "Vanity Fair." For the one audience the critic might well stress the construction of the play; for the other he would do better to remark on the construction of the players.

Perhaps the chief reason why the majority of college themes are hopelessly dull is that their authors have in mind no specific type of reader. By addressing everyone in general the student fails to interest anyone in particular. At one moment he takes for granted too much knowledge; at the next, too little. Here, as in every other kind of writing, it is necessary to adapt both matter and form to the needs of some definite sort of person, some definite degree of intelligence.

But to do this successfully the imagination must be employed. Only by summoning before the inward eye the type of person whom he hopes to reach is the writer able to decide wisely what he had best say and how he had best say it. The man who, as he writes, sees a pudgy commercial traveler in a stuffy smoking compartment is obviously more likely to say that which will awaken such a person's attention than he who merely shoots his words at random. Many a man who has prepared an article without conceiving the effect it would be likely to have upon any specific individual has found to his cost that he has painfully squared a peg for the roundest possible hole.

Moreover, the more vividly the imaginary audience is seen, the more personal and characteristic will be the utterance. With total strangers people are commonly stiff and repressed; with friends they reveal their actual selves. No one is willing to let himself go so long as he fears to be misunderstood. Similarly, no one will write freely, easily, and — in consequence — interestingly, unless he feels that he knows those by whom his words will be received. Compare on this score the letter that a lad visiting Paris for the first time writes to his brother with the letter the same lad writes when forced by his family to describe his experiences for some forlorn female cousin with whom he is scarcely acquainted. The one is usually fresh, entertaining, attractive even to a person who has long been familiar with the scenes described; the other is likely to resemble an exceptionally bad guidebook. The reason is simply that the former conveys an impression not only of the city, but also of the writer — that the charm of the one is inextricably mingled with the charm of the other — in short, that the letter written to the intimate friend has personality. And in all work that is not wholly scientific or technical the free expression of personality counts for much. If Stevenson's essays are read to-day when those of other contributors to "The Cornhill Magazine" are forgotten, it is not because Stevenson was so much wiser than they, but because he knew better how to make his work an expression of himself.

The most interesting essayist is usually, moreover, not only one who expresses himself individually to a concrete audience, but also one who sees his subject concretely. Just as our interest in mankind is inevitably less vivid than our interest in Tom or Dick or Mary, so an abstract proposition rarely grips us as does a concrete instance. A man who is very mildly enthusiastic about the maintenance of national honor will forget his pacifism and clamor for a gun if an injury to his missionary sister is unavenged by Washington. The best theoretical defense of a protective tariff has won a single vote for the Republican party where the alleged relation between such a tariff and the full dinner pail has won tens of thousands.

The skilful writer seizes upon this psychological fact and uses it for all it is worth. Take for instance a paragraph by G. K. Chesterton in which he is discussing the supposed "need for 'scientific conditions' in connection with alleged spiritual phenomena." Instead of putting his point abstractly he makes it as follows: "The fact that ghosts prefer darkness no more disproves the existence of ghosts than the fact that lovers prefer darkness disproves the existence of love. If you choose to say, 'I will believe that Miss Brown called her fiancé a periwinkle or any other endearing term, if she will repeat the word before seventeen psychologists,' then I shall reply, 'Very well, if those are your conditions, you will never get the truth, for she certainly will not say it.' It is just as unscientific as it is unphilosophical to be surprised that in an unsympathetic atmosphere certain extraordinary sympathies do not arise." A Freshman, writing on Thomas Hardy's point of view, brightened a dull and commonplace theme by remarking that " Hardy is the kind of man who believes that if you drop a piece of bread and butter it will always fall buttered side down."

The value of concrete illustration as a means of develop-

E

ing an idea clearly has already been pointed out in the preceding chapter. It is necessary to recur to it again partly because it is one of the most effective means of gaining interest, and partly because one's success in hitting upon or devising such illustration is generally directly dependent upon one's success in putting the imagination to work.

Of course, when a principle or a theory is the result of a direct induction from facts — as, for example, in an account of scientific investigation — it is easy enough to reverse the process and instance the facts as illustrations of the theory. More often, however, the affair is not thus simple. A writer starts with a theory about some general topic, such as the unifying force of war upon a nation. It is only as he makes himself see the effects of war upon definite sorts of people, upon the reformer and the office-seeker, upon a Mr. Rockefeller and a Mr. Gompers; it is only as he brings his imagination to bear, that vivid, specific illustrations flash into his mind.

Even more is this the case when the illustrations are drawn, not merely from the field under discussion, but from other, often widely different fields. It is not by chance that the poet more often than the writer of prose illustrates his idea by comparison, by the use of metaphors and similes. It is because the imagination of the poet is more often actively at work. But only the prose writer who is content to be uniformly dull can afford to despise the aid of such comparisons. The border line between them and the concrete instance is not always easy to draw; the distinction is in any case immaterial. The only important question is whether the illustration is or is not of real service. When Chesterton characterizes a certain type of man by saying that he was born, not with a silver spoon in his mouth, but with a silver knife in his mouth, he not only produces an effect an unimaginative writer could not produce, but he produces it much more economically. A single sentence of this sort can do more oftentimes than a page of abstract discussion.

A good figure, then, is no mere adornment, no piece of merely feminine finery. But a figure introduced only because figures are supposed to "improve the style" is not a good figure. If we are weary of reading about ruby lips and pearly teeth, it is not simply because these are hackneyed metaphors; it is rather because they are the counterfeits of imagination — wretched and conventional substitutes for the real thing. They suggest no clear and fresh vision of a beautiful face; they indicate only the lazy borrowing of an empty phrase.

Such figures as these are scarcely figures at all. When one reads them he has no momentary vision of the cloudy pallor of pearls nor of the gorgeous radiance of rubies. Thus used, ruby and pearly are merely outworn adjectives. But a single adjective may display as much imaginative power as an elaborate comparison. When the domestic arrangements of an English household are described as being — from an American point of view — "sketchy," we get a real figure, the apt suggestion of which grows upon reflection. Imagination can suggest the vivid word as well as the vivid phrase. By its aid one realizes the power latent in some words and lacking in others. Nine times out of ten good diction is imaginative diction.

Even in connection with the best illustrations, however, two dangers present themselves. The first is that by their abundance and interest they may distract the reader from the point really at issue. He may become so fascinated by the illustrations as to forget what it is they illustrate. Any good teacher who has inspected his pupil's notebooks has more than once found recorded there only these sparks thrown off from the central flame, these fringes of his thought, with no trace of the main point from which they depended. More than one essayist has been considered a shallow thinker only because the blaze of his fireworks has been too dazzling. It is always possible to lose the forest in the trees.

This danger is scarcely one to terrify the average writer. Few imaginations are thus active. A much more common tendency is that which uses an illustration as an ineffective substitute for proof.[1] A comparison is seldom so perfect that it can replace logical reasoning. A specific instance almost never makes an impression so profound as to beguile a thoughtful reader into forgetting that it is only a single instance, and that a sound generalization demands more than one case for its support. Mathematical demonstrations are to many people dull, but they are conclusive to a degree that nothing else is. Most sentences devoted to gaining or holding interest replace others that might be devoted to gaining assent. The best illustrations serve both purposes, but they can nevertheless be overworked. The course between dullness and soundness is a narrow and difficult one, but the successful writer must and does keep clear of either rock.

II

Such uses of the imagination as those just discussed are everyday affairs; they appear in most good writing, in most good talk. Consciously or unconsciously any competent writer adjusts his material to his audience and presents it with reasonable concreteness. But the possible service of the imagination is by no means limited to such matters of detail. In other ways, more frequently available than an inexperienced writer suspects, the imagination may be

---

[1] Analogy has evidential value, as has been shown in the preceding chapter. To overwork analogy, however, is not to make imagination serve thought, but to let it replace a more forceful means to the desired end.

used to arouse and compel a reader's attention. It is often of the greatest value when it determines the form in which ideas or facts are presented.

Anyone opening a magazine or weekly periodical is likely to find himself immediately confronted by the figure of a forceful-looking man who points his finger at the reader and says: "Now listen! I'm Slippery Jim, and I know more about making good pipe tobacco than anyone else. I've been making smooth-cut for forty years, and I can promise you" — and so on. One knows that this is an advertisement, that Slippery Jim is a wholly mythical person, yet one can scarcely avoid reading what Jim has to say, whereas an impersonal exposition of the merits of the article in question, however carefully phrased, would be passed over with scarcely a glance. The advertising managers who devise such traps for the public attention know very well what they are about. They know that the average human being is much more influenced by persons than by ideas, that he is much more easily interested in the opinions of John Jones than in the greatest abstract thought. Hence they create an imaginary character and put into his mouth what they have to say.

Such advertisements are new applications of an old method of the essayist. If, in the days of Queen Anne, the "Tatler" or the "Spectator" was to be found on every breakfast table, it was due in no small measure to the fact that the editors of these periodicals created such figures as those of Isaac Bickerstaff and Sir Roger de Coverley, into whose mouths they put their opinions. By means of such imaginary personages they could present subjects from various points of view, in various manners, and give to their thought a life and interest hardly attainable otherwise.

The essayist, of course, has one difficulty not felt by the advertiser. The latter calls in the aid of an artist to give

reality to the fictitious character. The essayist must do
this unaided. He has not only to maintain the consistency
of his character, to put into his mouth only such words and
opinions as might naturally be expected there; he has
also to add such strokes as will suggest a real and attractive
personality. Unlike the novelist, the essayist cannot depend upon incident or action for revelation of character;
unlike the dramatist, he has no assistance from living actors.
Nor can he safely delay his points too long by pausing to
give an elaborate character-sketch. If he is skilful he will
gain his effect by a few suggestive strokes such as those of
Charles Lamb's essay entitled "Mrs. Battle's Opinions on
Whist" · "'A clear fire, a clean hearth, and the rigour of
the game.' This was the celebrated wish of old Sarah
Battle (now with God) who, next to her devotions, loved
a good game at whist." In a sentence or two this old lady,
"who was none of your lukewarm gamesters . . . who
affirm that they have no pleasure in winning," is made a real
personality about whose opinions one is eager to know.

Lamb employed an extremely effective variant on this
method in his essay "Dream Children," where he speaks
at first in the character of a widowed father and then later
reveals himself as the bachelor who is writing only of the
might-have-been. Thus the fictitious character may be
used for only a part of the essay, possibly as an opponent
or defender of the ideas to be conveyed.

From the single figure to the group, from the monologue
to the dialogue or conversation, is an easy step. When
Mr. Lowes Dickinson wished to discuss various points of
view toward English social and political conditions, he cast
his essay in the form of a series of speeches made by men of
strongly contrasted types, and by naming the result "A
Modern Symposium" called attention to the fact that he
was using a device as old as the Socratic dialogues recorded

or imagined by Plato. As we read in Mr. Dickinson's pages that when the preceding speaker had concluded, "MacCarthy, without waiting my summons, had leapt to his feet and burst into an impassioned harangue . . . his Irish accent contrasting pleasantly with that of the last speaker," we are already much more eager to know what this anarchist has to say against the socialist point of view than we could possibly have been had the two positions been presented directly and impersonally by the author himself.

The fact that the use of the monologue and dialogue as means of conveying thought has been illustrated by the work of distinguished essayists in no way implies that such devices are valuable only to those who have literary ambitions. As a matter of fact, many a reasonably truthful person when compelled to give a disagreeable bit of advice has coated the pill by beginning, "Well, a chap I once knew got himself into a peck of trouble that way. He thought —" and so on. The fact that such an unfortunate never existed does not in the least reduce his value as a means of administering opinions otherwise unpalatable. From an ethical point of view one may possibly object to such a practice, but its utility is attested by its common use. In writing, moreover, the question of actual deception rarely arises. Criticisms, suggestions, opinions — whether they have to do with local conditions and activities or any of a thousand subjects — may often be put with advantage into some one of these personal forms. Which one is best applicable to the individual case is a question easily determined; the possibility of using some such form is always worth considering.

So long as a writer merely enlivens what he has to say and intensifies its interest by putting his thought into the mouths of personalities not his own he remains an essayist, primarily concerned with the clear and forceful exposition of his ideas;

the depiction of character remains a subordinate detail. But when he goes one step further and attempts to make use of characters in action, he gets into the field of the story or the play and is confronted with quite different conditions.

III

The attempt to convey a thought by means of some form of narrative is one of the commonest efforts at expression. The giver of disagreeable advice referred to a few paragraphs back is even more likely to tell a story about his imaginary instance than simply to report his opinions. Not only the teacher and the preacher, but also the man talking to you across the table is likely at any moment to say, "Now I can tell you a story that will show you what I mean."

In a sense any story that does more than merely thrill or amuse the reader has back of it a similar purpose, the effort to convey effectively some kind of idea. Any writer of fiction who takes his work at all seriously is attempting to record his impression of life, the way in which he believes men or women react to one impulse or another. The author may not consciously have formulated any conclusions from the incident he relates; he may not wish to; he might even be unable to do so if he tried; but the very fact that he has written as he has implies that he would answer, Yes, to the perennial questions, Is this true to life? Do people really act in this way? Although Kipling, in his story "Without Benefit of Clergy," did not intend to propose or prove any thesis about the relations of Englishmen in the Civil Service with Indian women, although it would probably be unfair to say that the story illustrates any definite theory about such relations, nevertheless Kipling believed that he had something to tell about such conditions or he would never have written the story.

It is a natural corollary that the writer of any story which pretends to tell the truth about life needs to test the accuracy of his observations and conclusions just as much as does the author of any essay or report; and similarly the reader owes the writer such careful attention as is necessary to discover exactly what impression the story is intended to convey. To ask whether the author has really conveyed any true and fresh impression at all is a test which will speedily disclose the triviality and often the worthlessness of a vast multitude of the stories printed in the cheap popular magazines and in some of the more pretentious ones as well. It is by no means the only touchstone of judgment, but it will usually serve to show whether or not a story is anything more than a means of whiling away an otherwise emptier hour.

It is, however, with a much more limited and commonly inferior variety of story that we are specially concerned here, with the story that is the embodiment of a definite idea, with what is often called the thesis-story. This idea may be of a very simple sort — an idea, for instance, about some historical person — or it may be of a very wide scope, a theory about the marriage relation or about religion or about the treatment of labor by capital. Stevenson's story "A Lodging for the Night" is an example of the first sort. Some time before he wrote it Stevenson had published an essay about François Villon the title of which described this great rogue and great author as "Poet, Student, and Housebreaker." A comparison of the story with the essay shows that in the former Stevenson embodied in concrete incidents exactly the conception of the poet's character that he had set forth in the latter. In writing the story he drew upon his imagination for such situations as would make the reader feel the traits which he had attributed to Villon in the essay. Consequently the reader may properly ask about it as well as about the essay whether the author's representation of Villon is historically correct. In this particular instance, however, the story is so vivid and true to the type of life depicted that it has a value quite independent of its truth to fact in the specific case.

Where a story embodies a general thesis, on the other hand, the author cannot escape so easily. The primary reason for the general contempt in which "Sunday-school books" are held is that the theories of life which they convey are not true. Very few people are able to take seriously the belief that little boys who tie tin cans to the tails of unfortunate dogs, or who smoke surreptitious cigarettes behind the barn, inevitably end in prison or some other undesirable place. Nor can the model infant who is always neat and clean and who never plays truant always be certain that he will ultimately be the heir of a rich uncle who will be kind enough to die at the most convenient moment. No graces of style, no mastery of construction could save such stories; for the ideas which they embody are silly and false. The man who starts out to embody an idea in a story must first catch an idea that is worth embodying.

This statement is one with which everybody will agree theoretically; indeed — like several other points to be made in this section — it is so obvious that it might seem to need no discussion. Nevertheless, the majority of those who try unsuccessfully to present their ideas in narrative form look for the fault in the wrong place. They attribute their failure to some mysterious flaw in their "English," when the real difficulty is that their thought is either utterly commonplace or untrue. Nor is the truth of this point a matter which concerns only the professional author. As a matter of fact, many a story is the more salable because it lies about life. Its popularity is often due largely to the fact that it represents what people would like to believe rather than what they do believe. But such success is failure for the man who is really trying to convey an idea. He must make his audience feel that his story represents what they ought to believe.

The problem we are considering, then, is certainly not exclusively or even primarily that of the professional author nor that of the student who wishes only to write something which will appease an instructor who demands a story. It is that of any man who desires to make any other person see some point as he sees it and to utilize for this purpose the fact that most people are much more readily interested in narrative than in the direct presentation of ideas. That certain of our weekly and monthly periodicals are more and more employing this means of influencing public opinion is good evidence of its value, evidence of interest to others than the makers of magazines; for, on the one hand, that which works in magazines will work equally well with the smaller audience of college, society, business, politics, with which the ordinary man is concerned; and, on the other hand, the man who reads or hears such stories needs to be able to read them or hear them intelligently so that they will have only the influence they deserve.

It is by no means the purpose of this section to give a series of directions supposed to enable anyone to write a successful story. Such directions are about as valuable as a set of precepts on how to choose a wife. The good results of advice in either case are commonly negative rather than positive. Besides, the technique of story writing is a subject which cannot profitably be discussed in a paragraph or two. It is possible, therefore, only to suggest some general principles of use to one attempting to convey his ideas by means of narrative, and also, perhaps, to the reader of stories who has thought of them only as a variety of entertainment.

The man who puts narrative into the service of thought must not only have a real thought, but must also embody that thought in a plausible situation. It goes without saying that no one will be convinced of the truth of a general proposition by a highly improbable case or one which is plainly an exceptional one. It is quite true that the United States should have a more adequate army and navy, but very few sensible people would be convinced of this by a story which represented any foreign power as landing on our shores within a month an army of a million men fully equipped with horses, motors, ammunition, and big guns.

On the other hand, the more the incidents of a story can be made to seem at once plausible and typical, the greater its effect as a means for propagating ideas is likely to be. One of the main reasons why "Uncle Tom's Cabin" influenced the minds of large numbers of people was that Mrs. Stowe made her readers feel that the misfortunes of Liza and Uncle Tom were of a sort likely to occur to thousands of slaves under conditions then existing. If these misfortunes had seemed merely those of two individuals, one might have felt regret and let the matter drop there; but, being typical, they aroused widespread hostility to the system that made them possible.

This particular book is an admirable illustration of a point which must not be overlooked. The popular success of a story as a means for presenting an idea is not necessarily an indication of real value in the idea or in the story. If "Uncle Tom's Cabin" is not now commonly considered to be a great novel, it is largely because the situations and characters are neither true to life in general nor fairly typical of conditions existing in the South of 1850. The fact remains, however, that they were plausible enough to seem true to many people at the time, and hence to convey Mrs. Stowe's ideas about slavery. They served their purpose, but one may now smile at the author's reported remark that "God wrote the book."

Another point often disregarded is that the incidents chosen for the story should properly be such that they will in themselves carry the author's meaning. Dozens of stories and plays have failed because in them the imaginative conception of the theme was only partially complete. It is not enough that the author should imagine a group of people to whom something happens which he can make the text of a discourse, or who for one reason or another get together and discuss at length the problem in which the author is interested. It may occasionally happen, as in the case of Bernard Shaw's plays, that the author's ideas are so interesting or the expression of them so brilliant that they will hold the attention of the reader or playgoer without further aid. But the success in that case is not that of the narrative but that of the discussion; the ideas carry the story rather than the story the ideas. Besides, there are few Shaws, and it is safe to say that the effect of the average story or play intended to convey an idea is in inverse ratio to the amount of abstract discussion of the theme. In plays like "A Doll's House" or "Justice" the incidents and characters speak for themselves and make their impres sion unaided. Nora and Falder are no mere mouthpieces for Ibsen and Galsworthy. What they say is not merely what the author's purpose demands, but what such people would say under such conditions.

Finally, it is not enough that the story shall really embody the author's idea; it must also be interesting in itself. It is not enough for a man to say to himself, "It makes me sore to see the way a man is misjudged on the basis of one characteristic. I'll make a story about a chap who really likes people and the place he's in, but who is a failure socially and gets himself hated as a knocker because he never hesitates to speak out when he thinks something is wrong or going to hurt the place." Unless the writer devises a really interesting series of incidents which will arouse the reader's sympathy, he loses the persuasive power of direct argument without gaining anything in return. For it is clearly true that an idea embodied in fiction is less intellectually convincing than one supported by a mass of cold facts. If the imaginative treatment does not arouse interest, it is useless. One of our successful playwrights remarked not long ago that he had for years wanted to write a play dealing with woman suffrage. When asked why he had not done so, he replied, "I can't hit upon an interesting story that will really carry my ideas. I must have that first of all."

IV

To the experienced author of short stories or novels or plays such a lumping of them together as is to be found in the preceding section would seem confusing. To him the differences between these various literary forms are often more apparent than their likeness as imaginative vehicles of ideas. And certainly these differences are not to be ignored. Stuff that would make a good novel might make an uncommonly bad play, and vice versa. An idea which can be clearly and effectively conveyed by a single scene will look excessively thin if it is stretched over four acts or four hundred pages. Such a study of the effect of environment on character as appears in Hardy's "The Return of the Native" could scarcely be transferred to the stage.

But to discuss adequately what form is best suited to a given idea would lead us far afield. To attempt the task would be to fall short of any save the vaguest of conclusions; for the choice between dramatic and narrative form is not infrequently determined solely by the writer's turn of mind. And such a discussion would inevitably raise technical problems of construction which are outside the scope of this book.

All that has been said in the preceding sections applies, however, as well to one form as to another, to the simple narrative or the one act play, as well as to the novel in three volumes or the dramatic trilogy. Suppose, for instance, a man bitterly opposed to capital punishment who determines to win sympathy for his point of view by presenting it in an imaginative form. He needs first to ask himself very seriously whether or not his idea is really sound. Suppose he determines to awaken interest in his thought by means of a concrete example of the wrong capital punishment may work. After casting about for such an example he finally plans to tell of a traveling salesman accused of murder, entrapped by the third degree into incriminating admissions, convicted, sentenced, executed, and too late proved innocent by the confession of the real criminal. Are these incidents plausible and typical? Do they really embody the idea? Will the narrative be of interest in itself? Such questions the author must ask himself, whether he proposes to write a play or a story, whether he intends to treat his idea briefly or at length. If he is to write a really good story or a really good play, he must also solve, consciously or unconsciously, the peculiar technical problems imposed by the chosen medium; but these general problems are raised in any case.

Whatever the form decided upon, such use of the imagination in the service of thought is not limited to the makers of great literature. It is not limited to the telling of tales, dramatic or otherwise. It means, in the widest sense, no more than to think and to express one's thought, not in terms of x and y, but in terms of John and Jenny — not merely in terms of The Duty of a Fraternity to a College, but also in terms of the duty of a particular fraternity to a particular college — something that requires neither genius nor any remarkable quality of mind.

Forcing oneself to think thus concretely has a very practical value. To do so is to get back through thought to the facts of life. Abstractions are often convenient, but they are also dangerous; for they do not conform completely to the truth of things as we know them. It is convenient to talk about Man; but what we really know is not Man, but men. We speak glibly of Nature acting in this way or that, but do we know whereof we speak? If there were less said about the College Student, a non-existent abstraction, and more about the infinitely various individuals who actually go to college, we should be spared many dull and foolish words. If there were less thinking in terms of Labor and Capital and more in terms of such very human figures as Tom Poulos, who works in the smelter, and Stephen Forman, who owns it, the general interest in the questions involved would be greater and the answers to them nearer at hand. To put the imagination into the service of thought is to put it into the service of truth.

Hence imagination, which may serve to awaken and retain the reader's interest, may also serve another and still more important purpose, that of making the thing written worthy the reader's assent. Writing that is interesting, that is powerful, that is true — in other words, the best writing — is the product of imagination as well as of facts and thought. Other factors may conceivably contribute to the desired result, but it is out of these three that good writing is essentially made.

PART II

ILLUSTRATIONS

GROUP ONE

(To accompany Chapter I)

HABIT FORMATION AND REFORMATION [1]

Eliott Park Frost

RECENT experimental investigation has established much of the mechanism of our mental life. We are beginning to understand how our minds work. It once was thought that animals alone act from instinct, and that their behavior is therefore predictable; but that man acts from a will directed by wisdom and reason, and behaves in ways unpredictable and free. This poetical distinction is on the highroad to oblivion. The more the psychologist studies the mind and the way it works in normal daily life, and the more the psychiatrist studies the mind and the way it works in the insane and abnormal, the more each is wholly convinced that the nervous system is a mechanism or machine: wonderful and complex, but none the less a machine.

Now the significance of a machine is that it works infallibly: when energy of a certain sort is put into it, this energy is transformed into energy of a different sort and the job to be accomplished is done. Throughout it is assumed that the amount of energy necessary to do the particular work can be calculated and regulated, and the machine and its

[1] Reprinted from "The Yale Review" for October, 1914, by special permission of the editors.

product controlled. That the human body is this kind of machine every one now admits. It requires a certain amount of meat and bread and water to run it efficiently; if it gets more or less than this amount its efficacy is diminished. Among psychologists and nerve specialists precisely the same attitude is taken towards the mind. Laboratory investigations upon mental processes, animal and human, are indisputable. If you will allow me the same nice control of your nervous system that I have of my gasoline engine, I will guarantee to develop in you behavior as explicit in quantity and quality as I get from the engine.

To a degree, I can already regulate the behavior of others. Practically, I know very well that if I offer a certain man five dollars he will come to work for me for a day. Practically, I know that if I offer a certain other type of man twenty-five dollars he will steal, or set a fire, or do some other criminal act for me. Practically, I am sure that Mr. Brown, the wealthy banker, will probably do none of these things for any price. Practically, I know that if a group of people are herded together in a narrow building, and I cry "Fire!" there will be a panic, or that if I scatter gold coins in the street, I can in this way block traffic so long as the money lasts. I am as sure of these things, as sure that people in general will behave in these ways, as I am that a kitten will chase a rolling ball. I know that behavior is determined in the long run by factors that are as invariable as the tides of the sea.

Not only can I thus naïvely anticipate the behavior of my fellow men, but from my individual experience and observation I can trace at once the causes of many of the variations in their demeanor and my own. What we eat and drink, the amount of sleep we get, the exercise we take, the people, things, and ideas that surround us, — these restrict and mould us in ways of living. We are a distinct person at 7 A.M. and quite another at 7 P.M. We seem different, even to ourselves, as we till our gardens in old clothes and slouch hat, from that immaculate host who in the evening greets his guests at dinner. A touch of sea-sickness, and the man we were has shrivelled to the least possible denominator.

No earlier than yesterday floods, famine, disease, pestilence, and insanity were regarded as evils common to the human lot. But to-day one has ceased to censure angry gods, and men are busy looking for dirt, and germs, and ignorance, and human greed to explain these things. Yet precisely the obsolete notion of our bodies and material conditions that once obtained, still obtains among laymen regarding the mind. Too many men are still petitioning for powers that really lie resident within themselves — and they do not know it.

Whether consciously or unconsciously, the business of life can be done only in obedience to nerve laws. To pray for strength to fight the devil, and at the same time to over-eat, under-sleep, to worry, to loll about in stuffy rooms, to force the brain to action when the stomach is replete, to deny oneself the natural cathartics of play and recreation, — this is to disinfect the house against yellow fever and leave the windows open to the deadly mosquito and its poison. Just as knowledge of the plain facts of sanitation is saving lives and health of body to-day, so will knowledge of nerve laws save lives and health to-morrow. For our splendid nervous systems, complex as they are, work with the precision of fine-wrought mechanism. To comprehend this mechanism is in part to control it. Psychology and physiology are explaining and describing in simple terms what heretofore has been thought mystical and supernatural.

An experiment will illustrate the simplest act that our nerves can execute. Sit down and cross one leg over the

other, then tap sharply just below the knee-cap of the sus-
pended leg.   The foot will give a sudden jerk.   It has moved
"reflexly" or "automatically."   At the tap, a nervous
impulse is released and travels at the rate of some four hundred feet per second up a so-called sensory nerve to the
spinal cord.   There, in the region of the small of the back,
this nervous impulse passes over to another nerve, a motor
nerve, and is reflected back to the muscle, causing the foot
to jump.   The jump seems instantaneous, but it is not.
Time enough has elapsed for the trip of nervous energy up
and back.   If any obstruction be placed in the circuit the
reflex jerk will not take place, however severely the knee
be struck.

The technical name for this path of nervous impulse is
"sensori-motor arc."   Sensori-motor arc is a functional
term; it describes, not a structure, but a typical nervous act.
The structure upon which it depends consists of three dis
tinct paths: a sensory or ingoing nerve, a central or con
necting nerve, and a motor or outgoing nerve.   It thus acts
like a telephone system: the message goes in to the switch-
board, is at this central office transferred, and passes out
finally over another wire to the distant friend, whether next
door, or in another State, — in short as far as the wires may
reach.   In a human adult there are some eleven thousand
million of these "wires" or nerve elements; but every act
we perform, thought we think, or emotion we feel, makes
use of this single principle of the sensori-motor arc: an
ingoing, a central, and an outgoing nerve path.

Another conspicuous illustration of primitive nervous
action is found in the ordinary garden-worm.   One cannot
afford to scorn this humble creature.   Not only does he
beautifully display nerves in their elemental behavior, but,
unlikely as it seems, he is an undoubted ancestral type of
man, a few score of thousand of years removed.   His ner-

vous system is very like the human nervous system, only simpler. If sometime after a heavy rain, when these worms are crawling about over the ground, one cuts the creature in two he will find that while one portion squirms and writhes as if in pain, the other part (and this the head end), will crawl off unconcernedly, the loss of half its body appearing as it were a most indifferent affair, quite beneath notice. The explanation for this curious behavior is that the nerves which connect the various longitudinal muscles of the worm conduct nervous impulses in one direction only, and that backwards. The head end of the worm is not informed that its tail is missing. When one goes fishing and finds that his worm resents being strung upon the hook, turning him end for end will have an extraordinarily soothing effect.

As in the worm, so also the impulses in our own sensorimotor arcs must go in a prescribed direction. Sensory nerves always carry impulses towards nerve centres (as for instance towards the spinal cord), while motor nerves always conduct impulses away from nerve centres towards muscles. Neither sensory nor motor nerves ever act in the reverse direction. The reason for this peculiarity of nerves will lead us into the heart of the problem of habit formation.

But the worm has other characteristics that anticipate human behavior to an even more remarkable degree. In the first place, the worm is made up of segments, and each segment is much like every other segment. In man there are still traces of this old segmented structure, now only vestigial ruins of a vanished biological past. Already in the worm, however, the forward or head segment is dissimilar to the other segments — larger, for one thing, and containing more nervous tissue. Well, human heads with their big brains exhibit just this same unequally distributed nervous tissue still further developed; and developed, too, exactly where it was most needed, at the head end of man's ancestor; for one must remember that, geologically speaking, man has been walking upright for a comparatively few years only; and in quadruped days, or still earlier when he crawled, this head was naturally the first part of him to come in contact with things.   By no means is it therefore mere chance that most of the senses are grouped in the head. Ears, eyes, nose, mouth, and sensitive lips represent the front or business end of the body.   As man's ancient relative crawled towards and into his new environments, it was obviously necessary, if he was to live in a hostile world, that he should acquire an ability to sense the presence of food and water and good things generally, or to detect the presence of enemies and trouble.   And equally it was necessary that he should be able to send the information thus acquired to the segments following after; otherwise the head segment, however keen its sense organs, might, while perceiving the danger in front, nevertheless be thrust willy-nilly into it by pressure from the uninformed segments following in the rear.   The animal, in short, must be able not only to sense its world, but to act as a whole in response to these findings.   This much ability the worm has; and this much ability, in still primitive fashion, human centres possess automatically, independent of the brain.

The nervous system is really then a long bundle of nerve fibres called a cord, spinal cord, with a big enlargement at one end, the brain; and the whole system acts like a gigantic switch-board, ever translating incoming impulses from the outside world back again to muscles, and so finally into movements and behavior.   The simplest of these impulses like that of the knee-jerk is translated at once and directly in the spinal cord, but the more complex impulses are sent up to the higher centres of the brain.

The functions of the spinal cord are two in number.   One

is to transfer a sensory impulse directly into a motor impulse, as in the knee-jerk, or in the instinctive withdrawal of the hand at the touch of a hot iron; and the other is to carry to the brain those impulses which it cannot itself take care of, and to bring back therefrom the proper message to the muscles. This latter type of activity constitutes the conscious or willed acts.

All those movements performed by the spinal cord alone are unmodifiable by any conscious volition on the part of the individual. They are common to the species. All normal human knees behave in just one way when tapped sharply. Only disease or grave impairment of the body will change this action. The nerve paths which such impulses use are formed before birth. If all habits were of this sort, the problem of habit reformation would be answered just here, and one could look upon himself as a helpless spectator of the processes of life. One cannot modify the simple reflex acts of the body. We cannot train our knees.

Fortunately, most acts are controlled not by the spinal cord, or not by the spinal cord alone, but involve a greater circuit, namely the brain. It is in the possession of an extremely developed brain that man surpasses the lower animals. Many creatures have keener senses than has man. Dogs probably live in an atmosphere of odors that humans never sense at all. Some species of moths can scent a mate for three miles. Vultures can see their prey for twenty miles. But in ability to combine and use the data that the senses give, man has no equal.

Yet brains are not only the great switch-board for myriads of nervous interconnections, allowing the combining of any one of thousands of incoming impressions with any one of thousands of motor channels, but they are also the seat of memory. That is, by their mechanism every impression that comes in is not alone sent out again in some fashion, but an account is kept of the transaction, so that a subsequent impression has a chance to be modified by the results of former favorable or unfavorable experiences. The old sensori-motor arc is nevertheless still in function. In the brain circuit there is as before, an ingoing path, sensory to the brain, and an outgoing path, motor from the brain. The significant difference is in the central path, the brain itself. This mass of central or connecting nervous tissue of so simple a sort in the spinal cord, is become in the brain very complex indeed, so that the entering impulse has no longer a predetermined path waiting to take it out to a predisposed muscle. Rather its exit is here determined by many factors. The problem of habit, in a word, is the problem of the control of these several factors. What information the senses impart depends in the large upon environment. Any ability that man possesses is to reject or accept, to ignore or attend to these impressions. Each impression represents just so much chemical or physical energy that is bound to find outlet somewhere, somehow. Can one control these paths of exit so that the resultant movements and behavior shall be of one sort and not of another? When the knee is hit the foot jumps. One is powerless to prevent it. When presented with a glass of beer, is one equally powerless to govern his action? Is the path "to take," or the path "not to take" a controllable one, and if so how is it to be controlled? Here is the nub of the problem of habit. If one can find out just what factors specifically determine the taking or the rejecting of the beer, a long stride will be made towards solving the mechanism of habit control.

To go back for a moment to the figure of the telephone. The message comes in over a single wire. At the central office connections can be made for any one of thousands of other wires, over which the message may go out. To the casual onlooker it would be difficult if not impossible to predict in advance the connection that "central" will make. Nevertheless for each connection made, there is some adequate reason. For some cause or other, one combination is secured and all other possible connections are rejected. This done, the message goes out over its particular wire as mechanically and fatally as it came in to the central office. The central office alone holds the reins of discretion, the reins of power.

Now this exquisite function appears to be performed in human nervous systems by a microscopic mechanism found in every sensori-motor arc. Its discovery has been only recent. The name given it is "synapse." By synapse is meant the point of junction between ingoing and outgoing nerve fibres. To get from a sensory nerve to a motor nerve an impulse must cross a synapse, or switch-board, and its path may include an indefinite number of them. The synapse is the telephone central, and upon its action depends the fate of the impulse: whether it shall be allowed to pass out to muscle A or muscle B, — for instance, whether one shall take or shall refuse the proffered glass of beer. In this minute mechanism, then, the very issues of conscious life, and so of character, are determined.

By a series of experimental investigations it has proved possible to expose the mechanics of this synapse or switch-board, to show how it works, and under what conditions its action can be modified. For the layman to comprehend these conditions, the sensori-motor arc or circuit must always be kept clearly in mind. In simplest terms there is an incoming impulse, — say, the sight of a glass of beer; this impulse may be drained off through synapse a into one set of muscles, or it may be drained off through synapse b into another set of muscles. In one case the man takes the beer, in the other he refuses it. The nervous impulse will act precisely like an electric current, following the easiest path. The impulse, that is, will pass over that synapse that offers the least opposition. Of an habitual drinker one can then affirm that, other things being equal, the synapse at *a* offers the least resistance; of a total abstainer, on the other hand, one can say that the synapse at *a* offers a resistance greater than the resistance at *b*.

The general statement may now be made: the formation of habits is nothing more nor less than the breaking down of the natural resistance offered at one synapse, and the raising of resistance offered at another synapse; and the re-formation of habits is the reversal of this process, where a synapse of great resistance is broken down, and a synapse previously weak is strengthened. In short, physiology has established the fact that the problems of habit formation and reformation find ultimate solution in the readjustments of synaptic resistances.

The way has now been cleared to ask: how, then, are resistances at the synapses varied, so that at one time, or in a given nervous system, a certain path readily takes an impulse out, while at another time, or in another nervous system, that same path is blocked, and the impulse must seek exit elsewhere? Why does one man act foolishly, another man wisely? Why at one time does one seem to be endowed with power to withstand a temptation, to which at a subsequent time he yields so easily? The answer to this question can only be that there has occurred meantime a readjustment at respective synapses: paths that formerly offered austere resistance have been weakened to permit the passage of the impulse, and paths that were once broken down have now been built up, and thus check the ready passage of the impulse. In popular phrase, the man has formed good or bad habits.

Nerves are practically unfatigueable. One speaks of

"tired nerves"; "nervous prostration"; of being "nervously worn out." Nerves do not fatigue. These phrases are inaccurate. It is these switch-boards, these resistance-boxes, these synapses that become fatigued and prostrated. A nerve is perhaps the last portion of the human body to show wear. Muscle tissue breaks down at an alarming rate, but nerves exhibit extraordinary resiliency. After hours of continuous stimulation, provided it be not beyond the capacity of the particular tissues involved, nerves will show no appreciable effect. In this respect the nerve trunk is a conducting wire, neither more nor less. It appears to possess perpetual youth. In striking contrast to the almost literally unfatigueable nerves, the synapses very promptly show fatigue when successively stimulated. Their fatigue is instantly marked by an increase of resistance offered to any impulse, so that either the stimulant must be constantly increased or the resultant movement in the muscle will grow less and less.

In the second place, it has been proved that in the nerve proper an impulse can pass in either direction, while on the contrary just so soon as a synapse is crossed the nervous process becomes irreversible. Synapses, that is, act like trap-doors, allowing nerve currents to pass in one direction only. Still again, experiment has established the fact that these "trap-doors" will not open when a weak impulse presents itself, but will dam back the energy in such an impulse, resisting it until several such feeble currents have been summed together. This resistance is then broken down by the collective energies thereby accomplishing what one or two impulses alone could not do: that is, move the muscle. Finally, it has been made clear that these synapses exhibit the liveliest effects of toxic poisons carried in the blood, such as drugs, opiates, and anæsthetics, whereas the nerves proper are relatively immune to both stimulants and narcotics. .

There are, then, four remarkable peculiarities in the action of the synapse, demonstrable by experiment, that do not appear in the behavior of simple nerve fibres. In one word, it is in the action of the synapse only that the chief modifications attributed to the nervous system, and so attributed to consciousness, find expression.

All these discoveries have led to the astonishing conclusion that the seat of consciousness, at one time thought to be the pineal gland, is really, so far as one may speak of a "seat" at all, resident in the millions of synapses of the nervous system. Whatever one may say of the action of the synapse, may equally well be postulated of consciousness itself. For instance: the mental processes readily exhibit fatigue (one feels "mentally tired"); consciousness is irreversible (time always appears to go forward, never backward); consciousness is aware of minute stimuli only when they are summed together (as in the falling of rain-drops, or in the buzzing of insects); and finally, consciousness is promptly influenced and may be destroyed by drugs, alcohol, opiates, and the like (as in intoxication and anæsthetization). Modify the synapse and consciousness is changed. Vary synaptic resistance and one modifies, and may even reverse, behavior.

From this somewhat technical explanation, three things regarding the action of a human nervous system will be apparent. First, the simplest type of action, such as the knee-jerk, is a predictable, unchangeable, mechanical process, that is accomplished by the lower centres, such as the spinal cord, without the interposition of consciousness. Second, consciousness and the various centres represented by the brain, have been evolved to give a greater flexibility to one's responses; to enable the sensing of a wider horizon, and to adjust the organism more closely and more accurately to this more complex environment. Finally, all nervous action is controlled and modified only through synaptic action, and does not depend upon the nerves as such. If the synapses are single or simple as in primitive sensori-motor arcs, behavior is then simple and relatively predictable. If the synapses are numerous and sensitive as in those great sensori-motor arcs that include the brain, then behavior becomes relatively unpredictable and complex, depending not merely upon the character of the stimulus, but upon the condition of the synapses : whether they be in normal health, and how previous experiences (impulses) have left them disposed.

All this is physiology; in lowest terms this is the mechanism of nerve action. Now what of psychology? One is presented for the first time with a glass of beer. If no habits for or against beer-drinking have been previously formed, one drinks for the first time. The result is perhaps unpleasant : the beer tastes "queer," or "bitter," or "nauseating." This result will tend to raise the resistance at that synapse which controls the extending of the arm, and in general the acquiescent synapses of the brain ; upon a second presentation, the beer may be rejected, and so on, until habits of abstinence have become fixed. Or social restraint may in like manner prevent a repetition of the drinking. If one considers it immoral, unwise, or as opposed to the preferences of one's friends, these social reasons may sufficiently raise the resistance in given nerve channels so that the first beer-drinking will prove to be the last. In short, pleasant sensations — the cool draught on a hot day, the exhilaration, the gay companionship, — all tend to lower one chain of synapses, while unpleasant effects — displeasing taste, loss of social caste, pangs of conscience, — all tend to make another set of synapses become the point of least resistance. When these two tendencies balance each other, as often happens, little things will throw the victory to one side or the other. On the other hand, when one is an habitual drinker, or an habitual abstainer, resistance is so preponderatingly less in one nervous channel that there is no question of the result. The older the habit, the more predictable is behavior.

If there be no contrary habit to combat, habit formation is relatively easy; the only difficult feat being to perform the act the first time. Nervous systems are so constituted that, like garments, it is easier for them to stay in the same fold, than to take on new wrinkles, do new things. But so soon as a new thing becomes desirable, then, unless the first trial prove unpleasant, a habit may be established readily enough upon half a dozen trials. For instance, if I persuade you to try grape-fruit for the first time, the persuasion is necessary only because the experience is new: you have never tried grape-fruit before. But if upon taste it proves delectable, you find it agrees with your liver, and your doctor adds his recommendation, — if, in short, all the results of the first trial are favorable, thereafter you eat it without hesitancy, and the habit is already formed. Formation of habits of this sort offers no problem save that of initiation. There is an inertia to be overcome in making the first trial. This is the reason that venders and purveyors of foods, toilet articles, and general household minutiæ are so generous with the "sample package." If you can be but once persuaded to overcome your natural hesitancy to attempt the novel, their battle is largely won, and thereafter you "fall into the habit" of consuming their particular breakfast food, or cosmetic, as though it were indeed "the best thing on the market."

The difficulty lies in habit reformation. It is not only a question of breaking down a novel synapse, but there is now the greater question as to how that old path worn deep by many yieldings shall be dammed. The formation of a new channel is useless just so long as the old path still offers weak resistance. The new path must be formed, but the old path must be blocked, and this is indeed a yeoman's task. To form habits of slow eating, of poise, or of pure-mindedness, — to take three illustrations, — means just this: how can I break my habits of fast eating, of intemperance, of evil-mindedness? And the problem is great precisely in terms of the fixity of the bad habit. Old age is notoriously hard to reform. A matured nervous system is a bundle of habits, a closed corporation. Its battles are memories only; victory or defeat now lies permanently assured with one side or the other. Only some great mental or moral cataclysm can disturb the synapses that control the behavior of such a nervous system. Its demeanor has become predictable. The problem of habit reformation here is maximally great. Youth, on the contrary, is "golden" because habits are not yet hard and fast, and undesirable paths may still be blocked. This is the meaning of "opportunity," that habits may be established, and yet under favorable conditions be broken up, and newer, more worthy habits be substituted for them. Psychology as it comes to understand nerve laws is telling us how this can be done.

In the first place, to bring about this result, all possible brain paths must conspire to facilitate action in this one path. The nervous system must be prepared to work as a unit. Psychologically this means that there must be a lively sense of the undesirableness of the present habit. In some way, one must be convinced of the inadvisability or evil of continuing in his present course of action. Content never breeds reform, and no habit will be improved so long as its results are favorable. When it comes to be perceived as bad for the health, for social or business interests, as giving pain to one's friends, or as contrary to the moral standards and principles that one professes, only then is the soil fit for

the new seed.   Such realization is the first goal of education.
With newer ideals comes the desire for better things.   Divine
discontent is the prerequisite for reformation.   Even this
primary task will be no sinecure, for half-hearted action will
never succeed.

Secondly, if the old path is to be closed, new paths must
be provided to drain off the energy in suitable ways.   This
energy cannot be simply dammed up or thrown out of the
system, but must be given a legitimate outlet.   Some new
habit, that is, must be initiated to replace the old.   The old
stimulants, whether from the environment or from appetite
within, will always solicit, and one can neither avoid nor
exclude them.   One who tries to give up drinking will still
have saloons to pass.   The sight of each saloon, aided and
abetted by cravings from within, releases energy and sends
it to the centres as formerly.   These impulses must be
sublimated, that is, the energy they represent must be transformed into serviceable acts, lest, like loose energy of any
sort, it wreck the machinery.   It is the idle hands that the
devil proverbially provides with work.   To busy oneself with
other things *to do*, is better than merely clenching the teeth.

Next, since nerve paths vary greatly, and the nervous
system is subject to moments of great depletion, fatigue,
and ill-health, care should be taken that the initial effort
comes at the most favorable time.   The chief strain will
come at first, and therefore this must be at the "psychological moment" and the "psychological place"; a time
when all favorably predisposing conditions are present.
These secondary factors are of great importance.   The lure
of the saloon to the man, or of the cadet to the woman,
comes with peculiar force at the end of the day, when fatigue
sets in, resistances are hard to establish, and are easily
broken down.   Many a synapse battle has been won or lost
by the lay of the land.   Even artificial aids, such as choosing

the first day of the year, a birthday, or the signing of a pledge, or telling one's friends of the new resolution, help to set the stage with properties conducive to success.

Moreover, we, as human beings, have the power to image to ourselves the results of acts in advance of their actual performance. Synapses may be modified, that is, not alone by the results of previous action, but by the images of such action. Not only the memory of a past calamity may raise the resistance in an old synapse and thus prevent a repetition of the behavior that caused it, but one may image possible results to himself, and thereby avoid pitfalls in the first place. In short, the knowledge of consequent penalty, clearly held in mind, acts mightily in favor of the desirable synapse. So the chief aim of all true penal institutions and jail sentences is not so much to punish the offender, but rather to deter the would-be criminal. For the philosopher, to see the goal may be sufficient incentive to lead to right action, but for the average man morality must be dramatized, and the consequences of evil be sharply contrasted with the beneficent results of rectitude. The arousal of fears of bodily consequences is the very best deterrent that can be presented to youth as a plea for morality.

Now therefore, when all possible favorable conditions have been fulfilled, and the psychological moment arrives, the new impulse must be sent over its novel path "full-blown," the new activities strongly initiated, and the old paths closed forever. The old nerve path must be blocked once for all. Tapering off, the allowing of partial lapses, is a mischievous method. If the flood once breaks down the new dike across the old synapse, succeeding waves of impulse will be so much the harder to check. No dam was ever mended by the pouring in of sand. To make an exception, with the reservation that to-morrow or next week control of the synapses will be surer and victory easier, is to invite final defeat.

G

And last, though by no means of least importance, it should be borne in mind that human nervous systems are in process of constant metabolism : tissues are breaking down while new ones take their places; night or day, week in, week out, change is incessant. Because a synapse does not yield to-day is no guarantee that it will not yield to-morrow. Fatigue may catch one unawares, and the dam that appears so firm may, in a moment of passion or excitement, be sud denly loosed; the old channels may once more claim their own. Beware, then, of idle moments when the mind is filled with casual thoughts and vigilance is relaxed. One cannot afford to think about the old habit even censoriously, for to think of not doing a thing, is after all to think about that thing, and the mere negative will, under some sudden stimulus, lose its restraining force. There is a well-known story of a physician, who, to test his hysterical patient, left her the extraordinary instructions : "Do not put beans in your nose." Certainly this idea had never entered her mind until that moment. But the more she brooded upon the prohibited act the more fascinating it became. Finally the suggestion worked, the negative instructions were over-powered or forgotten, and the physician, on his return, found his patient in fact doing that very thing : putting beans in her nose !

We know that consciousness is motor, that the things of which we think are bound to get into action unless prevented by some other action. If you close your eyes and simply think of the window at your right or the door upon your left, you will find that your eyes have turned with your thoughts, unconsciously. Any idea whatsoever held contin-uously and unchecked before the mind is as fatally bound to get into action, as is water, unrestrained, to seek its level. The reason why at this moment I do not commit the atro-cious crime of which I may be thinking, is solely because other more powerful thoughts are restraining me. This is the psychology of all action. All acts are the direct result of ideas that, for the moment at least, are free and unchecked by contrary ideas. The safe rule is then in one's leisure moments to avoid thinking of the old habit at all, in any terms. Let bygones be bygones, and fill the mind with the new habit, with fresh ideas.

Primarily the possession of a good physique, of a healthy nervous system, depends upon birth: the character of the stock from which one comes. This fixes the capacity, a limit that one can never exceed. With this material, good or bad, one must work. This is heredity.

The character of the stimuli which surround one and solicit one's attention every hour, constitutes environment. In formative years of youth this environment, to a peculiar degree, makes a difference. Many a man knows well enough that he avoids evil only by avoiding its environment. Fewer, perhaps, realize that the finding of a new and more wholesome environment is part of the method of cure for undesirable habits.

But beyond heredity, and beyond environment, are those factors that determine motives: the things that prod us to capacity effort, that set us against the current of mere circumstance. These things are ideas, the stuff and substance of our knowledge, the results of the educative process. To realize the foolishness of evil, to understand the method of its avoidance, and to know how to substitute for its indulgence a vigorous habit of healthful activity is, for all robust natures, already to will, and to achieve, good behavior.

THE ODYSSEY OF THE SOCKEYE SALMON [1]

BY WILLIAM CHARLES SCULLY

I

THE fishing industry of British Columbia is of enormous importance. The aggregate value of the fish captured each year is over $14,000,000. Toward this the salmon — so-called — contributes about two-thirds, and of the five species of fish classed locally as salmon, that known as the "sockeye" is most numerous and economically the most valuable. However, it is not now proposed to deal either with the economic or the strictly scientific aspects of the sockeye, but rather to describe some of the known features of its remarkable life. These are of quite extraordinary interest.[2]

In a technical sense the five species of fish known as salmon on the Pacific Coast are not salmon at all — although more or less closely related to the *Salmo* genus. All five belong to the genus *Oncorhyncus*, the sockeye being known as *O. nerka*. The derivation of the term "sockeye" is obscure; Dr. Jordan suggests that it may be derived from the word "sukie," by which this fish was known to a tribe of Indians which in old days inhabited parts of the southern section of what is now British Columbia. The sockeye is the smallest but one of the five species, its adult weight being about six pounds and its length averaging some twenty-four inches. It is lithe and graceful in form. While in the sea the back

[1] Reprinted from "The Atlantic Monthly" for August, 1916, by special permission of the editors.

[2] What is here set forth is based upon official reports of the careful and searching investigations as to the life-history of the sockeye, made by such men as Dr. C. H. Gilbert of Stanford University and Mr. J. P. Babcock, Assistant Commissioner of Fisheries for British Columbia, and upon such observations as the writer has been enabled to make. — THE AUTHOR.

and upper portions of its sides are of dark, metallic blue; it is silvery-white beneath. When the fish enter the fresh water the colors dim; later the back becomes suffused with a reddish hue. Throughout the journey to the spawning-ground the sockeye never breaks its fast. And this journey (up the Yukon, for instance) may involve a swim for some fifteen hundred miles against a swift and turbulent current, the temperature of which is but little above freezing-point. The range of the sockeye is from Northern Alaska to the Columbia River.

The beginnings of this creature's life are well known. From the embryonic stage to the end of approximately the first year of its existence as a free-swimming "fingerling" in one of those crystal-clear lakes with which the northwestern part of America is so richly dappled, the nature and habits of the sockeye have been carefully observed and studied. But in late spring or early summer the young fish disappear into "the unplumbed, salt, estranging sea" — and of their life therein for upwards of two and a half years, there is literally no record. No sockeye between the fingerling and the adult stages has ever been captured. In early summer, just before the run inland, adult sockeye have been taken in purse-nets on the Swiftsure Bank, just outside the Strait of Juan de Fuca. Fragments of their meat, mixed with those of other fish, have been found in the stomachs of sea-lions killed farther north at the same season. The netted speci mens revealed that the sockeye feeds upon a small crustacean and upon a form of *Ammodytes*, or sea-lance. But no sock-eye has ever been known to take a bait.

The average four-years' life of this fish falls, therefore, into three periods, two of which are known and one unknown. This rule has exceptions. A few individuals, almost ex-clusively males, mature in three years and come in with the adult run. These are the so-called grilse. A few others remain for two years in the lake before migrating to the ocean. In the case of the Fraser River sockeye a curious fact has been observed — every fourth year an enormous run takes place. The last occurred in 1913. No such phenomenon has been observed in respect of the other spawning areas.

II

The approximate year having been spent in a fresh-water lake, the frail atom of a fish has grown to a length of from two to three inches. Some time between March and June, instinct prompts it to start on the perilous journey to the sea. This journey may take only a few uneventful days; on the other hand, it may involve traveling a thousand miles to some misty fjord where a brown spate, flung by melted snow from the Rocky Mountains, clashes with a brimming tide at the full of the moon. The little creature — so soft of texture, with its large, soft, apprehensive eye — has to run the gauntlet of numerous enemies. It is flung down foaming, vertical cascades; it is swept into shouting rapids combed by fang-like rocks. At the stream's mouth it is met by new dangers; fresh and menacing problems are found at every turn. There is the sudden transition from fresh to salt water, involving chemical, dynamic, and respiratory changes. There are fierce enemies, openly ravaging, and stealthy murderers with ingenious lures and devices in operation, lurking in every nook where shelter might be sought. Yet it miraculously adapts itself and survives, — to disappear from human ken in the mystery of the illimitable sea, — until it reappears, adult, some three-and-thirty months later.

It is about midsummer — although the time varies slightly according to locality and individual season — when the sea gives up these mysterious denizens, the adult sockeye, which entered it as fingerlings three seasons previously. From far and near the schools crowd in and assemble before those lone and misty gateways through which the Pacific rollers smoke and thunder. The southeast limit of Vancouver Island is approximately four hundred miles from Prince Rupert, at the mouth of the Skeena River; but the intervening coast is much broken and indented — probably more so than that of any other with the exception of Norway. It is said that if the coast-line of every island, promontory, and indentation on the British Columbian coast were to be followed, a journey of twenty-seven thousand miles would be involved. This is irrespective of the immense and convoluted expanse of the Alaskan coast, which also lies within the sockeye range. Practically every indentation on the coast north of the Columbia has its stream, and — here lies the greatest marvel — every stream suitable for spawning appears to have its separate frequenting pack. It has, in fact, been practically determined that the sockeye will spawn only where it has been spawned.

After having digested their last meal — for at this period the stomach of the sockeye is invariably found to be empty — the fish leave the salt water and, entering the gates through which they emerged, make for their respective spawning-grounds. These lie on the shallow margins of lakes or, preferably, on the margins of streams by which the lakes are fed. Enemies of many kinds beset the sockeye's course. North of smoky Quatsino Sound the predatory legions of sea-lions and hair-seals lie waiting for their easy harvest. Of the former there are believed to be over 11,000 within the compass of a small triangle north of Vancouver Island. A full-grown sea-lion weighs upwards of a ton. The havoc wrought by these creatures among the sockeye and other fish may thus be imagined.

The European fishermen with varied scientific devices

crowd the areas where the salmon assemble from the sea. It is computed that in the area including Georgia and Juan de Fuca Straits and Puget Sound, 33,000,000 salmon were taken from the sea in the 1913 season. All along the river-banks the Indians stand with their scoop-nets, lifting out fish at the rate of hundreds a day. Below each rocky bar over which the fish have to leap, the wearied wayfarers lie resting — gaining strength for the effort. If the obstacle to be surmounted should be one of those cascades whose course is over sharp rocks standing in foaming, swirling ed-dies through which contending currents are flung, a large number of fish may be injured, and in the pool below are assembled a sorry company of the halt and the maimed — many with their sides cruelly gashed. Every now and then one notes a gleam of silver on the surface — and a dead fish floats away downstream. Perhaps one of the gorged fish-eagles may swoop down and seize the carcass; oftener it will be swept unregarded away.

The number of salmon crowding into a stream when the run is heavy is almost incredible; occasionally they lie so densely packed that it seems almost as though one could walk from bank to bank on the mass. In the big Fraser run of 1913 many millions of fish were sacrificed owing to a landslide at Hell's Gate, near Yale. This narrowed the channel and increased the speed of the current to such an extent that the fish could not surmount it. They lingered, exhausted, for days below the rapid; then they floated down-stream, died, and were borne as carrion toward the sea. Below Hell's Gate are good spawning-grounds, to be reached via the Harrison, Lilloet, and Pitt tributaries; but rather than spawn at any other spot than that where they them-selves had been spawned, the fish forewent the great purpose of their lives.

The evidence in favor of the view that the sockeye will

spawn only at their birthplace is overwhelming. Anderson and Nahmint lakes in Vancouver Island lie less than two miles apart. The vent-streams from both run to Barkley Sound. Both lakes are fed from the same snow- and rain-fall; both lie embowered in cedar, hemlock, and pine; on both the same sky looks down between mountains of similar geology. Yet Dr. Gilbert will distinguish between a sockeye taken in Anderson Lake and one taken in Nah-mint. It may be by the shape or size of the scale, the form of a fin, the angle of the jaw, or, if the specimen be a female, by the size of the ovum. But the distinctive peculiarity will be there, and will be found constant in every specimen examined. It is quite possible that with a little further knowledge, it will be practicable to determine, not only the lake in which a given fish has spent the first year of its life, but the tributary streamlet on the gravel of which the ovum that gave it life was spawned.

That this habit will in course of time give rise to different races, and eventually to different species, is a fair inference. That the process is now going on is clear from the circum-stance that already racial strains are arising. For instance, a sockeye of very large size has been found at Yes Bay in Southern Alaska. A number of eggs of this variety have been laid in a lake down in Vancouver Island and another in the State of Washington. All this involves an astound-ing proposition, but one which, on the evidence, we can-not avoid accepting.

To what may we attribute this inevitable determination of the sockeye to return for the purpose of spawning — and then incontinently dying — at the spot where it was spawned? Is it to a blind, compelling instinct void of conscious thought, such as characterizes so many of the marvelous operations of the honey bee; or is it a passionate love on the part of the fish for its birthplace — an overwhelming desire to revisit and end its life in the beautiful spot where life and light first dawned upon it? For all the spots where the salmon spawn are beautiful. Is it perchance what Schopenhauer, in connection with higher animals, termed "the genius of the genus" working through the mind of each individual, urging it to forge the link of continuance between the generations in a perfect circle, ending where it began — spending the strength it amassed amid the rich pastures of the ocean in striving for a goal which has been an ever-present dream?

The evidence is, one may think, in favor of an intellectual rather than an instinctive process. Place twenty bees in an uncorked bottle of clear glass, and set the bottle on its side with the closed end in sunlight and the open end in shadow. The bees will die of exhaustion after vain struggles to penetrate the glass, but they will never attempt to escape through the open vent. Their instinct is based on a long racial experience that light indicates an opening, and their intellect is incapable of leaving the rut thus formed. But if a salmon-run be obstructed, the fish will diligently and intelligently seek in every possible direction for a passage. Moreover, they will at once make use of a fish-ladder or other arrangement placed for their convenience. If, owing to heavy rain, a river becomes swollen, and a fall, passable at ordinary times, becomes impassable, the sockeye will wait patiently in the pool below until the spate has gone by, and then resume the interrupted journey. Among bees, so far as can be observed, individual preferences are unknown; the individual is nothing; the dominant note of the bee's life is a passionate devotion to the commonwealth, manifested upon rigidly fixed lines. But the salmon have individual preferences; male and female mate together, and in their mating they exhibit jealousy and other characteristics which link them with the higher animals — and even with human beings.

It must, one thinks, be a fixed idea — a memory-visualization which guides them. Do these creatures, throughout the course of their perhaps worldwide wanderings during nearly three mystery-shrouded years, dream of the little submerged cairn of purple gravel over which the crystal water lapped and murmured — that cairn among the interstices of which they found safe refuge from watchful, ravening foes, from the greedy trout and their own hungry kin of a previous generation? Do they dream of the sombre, stately cedars growing from the edge of the stream; of the rugged pines festooned with sage-green *Usnea* moss; of the lace-like fronds of the hemlock and the swaying fingers of the maple? These trees stand, dreaming, between the sky and the murmuring water. Do the tired wanderers long for those fleeting glimpses of the folded hills, — perchance backed by sunlit, snowy peaks, — glimpses had when they sprang, playing, into the air at sunrise? Does the lure perhaps lie in the miraculous clearness of the peaceful water — a clearness so startling that its realization comes as a shock to the observer? One cannot tell what it is, but the lure is there; the magnet that draws the doomed creatures from the most distant and secret places of the sea, over stunning obstacles, by a memory strand so strong that only death can break it. And the most significant circumstance is that these salmon forego the purposed culmination of their tragic life — the fulfillment of the love-instinct and the consequent continuance of the species — when they fail to reach the shrine desired for its consummation.

At length, all difficulties surmounted, the goal is reached; perhaps one in ten, one in fifty, of those who as fingerlings ventured to the sea three seasons previously, may have escaped their legion of foes and surmounted the obstacles of their difficult path. The wanderers have returned to their native lake — to the placid sky-mirror in its frame of sombre green hills, or stark, snow-encumbered mountains, which they have never forgotten. But the perils are not at an end. In the central waters of the lake, in the larger pools of its tributary streams, safety is to be found, but spawning has to be effected on the margins — in water but a few inches deep — and close to these margins watchful enemies lie ambushed. If the lake lie near the ocean, the fish arrive in fair condition; they even appear to experience something of the joy of life; one may watch them leaping from the deeper pools of the tributary streams; occasionally from the lake itself. But if the latter lie very far inland, the effects of weariness and the long fast become apparent; the fish take on a gaunt and haggard look. In the male the upper jaw undergoes a marked change: that portion immediately behind the snout becomes depressed, the forward portion curves almost into a hook. This gives the fish a most sinister expression.

After a few days' rest the process of spawning begins, and, under the veritable shadow of the wing of Death, — in a furnace, as it were, of terror and pain, — the link joining past with future generations is forged; the perfect circle is completed.

III

The sockeye have now almost reached the final stage of their long travail. The supreme and most fatal sacrifice has yet to come — the immolation of a generation upon the cold and thankless altar of the Future. But there intervenes a period of rest, — of cessation from persecution, — a few score hours of luxurious, almost effortless gliding to and fro beneath the placid surface of the liquid mirror into which the inconstant sky glances as it is borne past by the circling earth. Beneath this surface the water is literally as limpid as the untroubled atmosphere which lies so lightly upon it. Midsummer is now gliding imperceptibly into the fall. The days are long and dreamful; the winds are hushed; the sky is unmarred, its blue unflecked save by occasional drifts of fleecy vapor — immaculate flocks born of snow which has melted on distant peaks, straying over the rare, pellucid pastures of the upper atmosphere. The shrieking tempest and the blinding snowfall have been — and will again be — in some distant and incredible future.

The days are sultry, and the nights are mild. The water is warm and delicious; nevertheless, it is fatally charged with the germs of a terrible disease, — with the spores of the *Saprolegnia*, that foul fungoid which will inevitably attack and destroy the debilitated fish when they have reached their final stage of exhaustion after the strenuous spawning effort. But in the meantime, in those lakes around which the shallow spawning ledges lie, there is little to suggest danger or death. It is true that the fish-eagles, having followed the run from the sea, perch expectantly upon the tall, gaunt stumps — those sinister reminders of long-past forest fires which, like skeletons at the feast, are seldom out of sight even in the most luxuriant of the forests of Northwestern America. Behind the inevitable rampart of dead logs — usually invisible owing to dense undergrowth — lurk bears, grizzly or black according to locality. These wait sulkily for the final holocaust. They sleep most of the time, their dreams, no doubt, being full of gustatory reminiscence and anticipation. Their taloned paws are pressed against their temporarily depleted paunches; it is not likely they will be disturbed, for their lairs have been cunningly chosen. Many of them have followed the pack from the coast, gorging luxuriously at each obstruction, going empty when the course was clear. But their final and most Gargantuan feast is now nearly at hand. The restless coyotes slink in and out of the thickets, hollow-flanked and impatient.

But in the meantime the fish are out of danger and at peace. There are exceptions to this rule. If the run be a great one there is considerable competition for the available gravel-beds; consequently the sockeye set to work preëmpting spawning-sites immediately upon arrival. At night the drumming of the ruffed grouse may fill a steep gorge with miniature thunder. Occasionally the long-drawn howl of a timber-wolf or the gulping snarl of a panther, as it tears at the throat of a slain deer, makes weird the night. But such sounds are rare; the North American forest is usually as silent as the grave.

However, under the surface of the lake is peace, utter and profound; and, for the moment, safety. Dawn sends its spell across the dreaming forest, dappling its darkness with softly-paling shades. As the light grows, each tall fellowship of firs stands forth in sombre relief. The nearer comes the sun, the darker grows the forest. The surface of the lake is like glass — except where broken here and there by a leaping trout. A piercing ray of light thrills like an arrow through the trees cresting the eastern horizon. Then the timid dawn flies westward, and morning, triumphant, reigns. The slow hours trail on to noon — to afternoon — in sultry procession, until evening essays to reproduce the rapture of daybreak, but fails for lack of mystery.

And what of the sockeye during those halcyon hours? One does not know; yet one may reasonably believe they enjoy a measure of content — even of happiness. May it not be that during this interval they seek their affinities — those mates in conjunction with whom the final and fatal mystery of their love's consummation may be fulfilled? That they do select their mates is certain; it is also certain, as will be shown, that the process of selection is marred by disharmonies and cruelties very similar to those which so often disfigure the sex-relations of human beings.

But may we not at least infer the sockeye's enjoyment of the sense of having triumphed over enormous difficulties and escaped frightful dangers — their realization of the desirous dream which was ever present during their long, eventful wanderings? Here is the region where they first swam freely — breathing and, by the same operation, feeding upon those microscopic organisms with which stepmother Nature had filled the limpid waters for their first nourishment. Here, by the constant discipline of escape from the Steelhead trout and their own aberrant kin who decided to spend a second, or even a third, year in the lake, they had braced and schooled themselves for tremendous achievements. Here Nature, in the guise of " the genius of the genus," had broken the cells of the germ-plasm with which their tiny brains were charged, and revealed to them — by the process we name instinctive — the tremendous purpose of their mysterious existence.

Nature has strange and often unthought-of methods of adjusting balances. May it not be that the happiness, the bliss realized by these creatures as they lie wrapped in the mild waters of their natal lake is deep and searching enough to compensate for all they have endured? May it not be that if only one in a hundred — one in a thousand — realizes it, the hundredth or thousandth chance of realization may be sufficient recompense? " Many are called, but few are chosen," was said by the Christ of men and the Kingdom of Heaven; and the God of Israel was justified in that terrible saying. May not the same be true of fishes — their travail in the Great Waters and their short interval of blissful peace in the Delectable Lakes? But who shall dare to justify the majestic, terrible, and blood-stained steps of that awful entity we term Nature?

The final act, the spawning, begins. The female sockeye selects a gravelly spot, usually near the margin of some tributary stream — a spot over which water, to the depth of some three or four inches, flows. Her chosen mate follows and watches her actions with anxious attention. The fish have now markedly changed their color: the clean metallic blue has given place to a hectic flush of red. The female lies sideways on the gravel, with her head upstream. Then she bends her body and immediately again straightens it with a quivering jerk. This displaces the gravel over an area about equal in extent to the palm of one's hand, and causes a slight hollow. The displaced gravel is pushed downstream and thus forms a hillock below the hollow. The fish then rubs her abdomen sideways and with a quivering motion on the lower edge of the hollow and close to the upper base of the hillock, emitting the ova as she does so. During the operation the hillock grows by accretion of the disturbed pebbles. The male fish is at hand; he expresses the milt in the same manner in which the female expresses the eggs. The milt has to reach the eggs within two minutes and twenty seconds of their emission; otherwise fertilization does not take place.

The eggs are carried by the milt-laden stream into the interstices of the hillock. The fish resulting from those eggs which remain exposed die within a few days after they have been hatched. Even if they escape the host of greedy enemies lying in wait for them, they become infected fatally in the region of the umbilical sac by the *Saprolegnia* fungus. It is still unexplained why the fry hatched out among the stones of the hillock are not attacked. Possibly the spores of the *Saprolegnia* cannot live in darkness; possibly some antidote-parasite exists which is ineffective in light. Herein lies an interesting subject for investigation.

The expression of the ova as well as that of the milt is a purely mechanical operation, for the sockeye has no muscular apparatus to assist in the process of voiding. It is solely through the bending of the body, the quivering jerk, and the rubbing on the pebbles that the expression is effected. The female normally contains some five thousand eggs. About four days are consumed in the work of expressing. By that time the abdomen of the fish is usually raw and void of scales in the vicinity of the vent.

Herein is manifested one of Nature's energy-saving devices. If the sockeye were furnished with the usual expressing apparatus, it would not have to jerk and struggle; thus the hillock would not be formed, and some roundabout way of eluding the *Saprolegnia* spores and other enemies would have to be devised. So Nature withheld from a highly specialized creature an organ proper to its rank in the zoölogical scale — forcing it to descend from the heights of specialization and perform a lowly, rudimentary action. It is almost as though the commander-in-chief of an army were set to the work of digging trenches.

If the run be a moderate or a small one, each female sockeye insists upon having a considerable space free around her spawning hillock, and will energetically attack any other female venturing into her vicinity. But if the run be large and space be consequently limited, other fish may spawn within a few feet and no objection be made. Should another female attempt to appropriate a preëmpted spot, a fierce combat would result.

Sockeye both male and female — unattached, unconventional beings not bound by the accepted ethical rules: piscatorial home-wreckers, in fact — are apt to disturb the harmony of the spawning grounds. Some female fish, whose symmetry is comparatively unmarred owing to a succession of lucky escapes, and who consequently has most of her strength in reserve, may glide in and try to appropriate the hillock on the erection of which some matron-fish has expended almost her last available energy. A combat

H

will inevitably ensue; contrary to all ethical canons, victory will most likely go to the intruder. The male fish will
not interfere. His tail fanning just enough to counteract
the pull of the current, he will impartially watch the contest. If his old companion be driven forth to a lonely death,
he will impartially mate with the newcomer. Again, one
may observe mateless males of comparatively superior
physique moving about over the spawning grounds, evidently
on the lookout for mated males whose physique is inferior.
When one of the latter is found, a combat — which may
exhibit great savagery — will follow. In such cases the female regards the situation with tranquil unconcern. Should
the male originally in possession be vanquished, he will
accept the inevitable and glide tranquilly to his death —
let us hope a euthanasia — in the profound calm of the
adjacent waters, while his wife accepts the companionship
of the victor with equanimity.

The foregoing represents ideal spawning conditions,
which, however, do not as a rule exist. When the pack arrives, the carnivora of the forest-covered ranges surrounding the lake crowd in to take their toll of the hapless sockeye.
The great grizzly bear lumbers over the gravel-beds, and, displaying unsuspected quickness with his murderously taloned
paws, flicks the wearied and preoccupied fish high and dry
into the undergrowth. After he has gorged his fill, the grizzly
will lay up treasure (that will soon smell to heaven) for the
coming weeks. Twenty to thirty fish he will collect into a
heap; over these he will pile logs and rocks so large and
heavy that, even remembering the strength of his thews,
one wonders at his ability to move them through the dense
jungle. The black bear gorges too, but apparently accumu-
lates no store. Nevertheless he becomes fetid, blear-eyed,
unhealthy generally, and filthy in his habits. Sometimes
his dulled fur falls off in patches until his once silky coat

suggests that of a mangy dog. The coyote, too, gorges to a point of scandalous obesity. Every creature capable of sustaining its life upon flesh crowds in to take toll of the hapless salmon.

Spawning over, the spent and exhausted creatures now mere living corpses, — distorted, emaciated, and disfigured, — cleave their slow and painful way back to the deep waters of the lake. The results of the *Saprolegnia* infection now develop: foul festoons — the bearers of spores to infect the next generation of sockeye — hang from lips, eye-rims, gill-shields, and fins. The pairs which have spawned together as a rule maintain their companionship, each pair seeming to shun the society of others. Their movements become slower, stiffer. This existence may be prolonged for a fortnight; it usually continues for a week. Then comes death. For a brief period, the poor, disfigured carcasses float at the surface; then they sink to the bottom, where the soft tissues undergo swift disintegration.

The hatching-period of the sockeye egg varies according to the temperature of the water. The governing principle has been ingeniously worked out and determined by Mr. Wallach, of the United States Fisheries Department. It is as follows. Take freezing point, 32° Fahrenheit, as the basis. Then take the mean temperature of the water on each day, starting with the day on which the egg was expressed, and deduct 32 from it. As soon as the remainders reach a total of 990, the egg will have hatched.

To make the thing quite clear the following table is given. Assume that on the day of spawning and the four subsequent days, the respective mean temperatures read as follows: 52, 55, 53, 60, 54.

$$1\text{st day, } 52 - 32 = 20$$
$$2\text{nd day, } 55 - 32 = 23$$

$$3\text{rd day, } 53 - 32 = 21$$
$$4\text{th day, } 60 - 32 = 28$$
$$5\text{th day, } 54 - 32 = 22$$

and so on. When the footing of the third column reaches 990, the egg will have hatched. The little fish soon becomes a free swimmer, but some eight weeks pass before the um bilical sac is fully absorbed. Then the minute, semitrans parent creature, helpless, except for the instinct that prompts it toward concealment from ever-vigilant enemies, starts on its independent career.

And what of that atom of faintly clouded jelly — its brain? Did any other physical substance ever bear such a tremendous load? Pictured or written therein is the vast and varied experience of the whole sockeye race, prob- ably dating from a period before Vancouver Island emerged from the ocean, when the highest peaks of the Rocky Moun- tains were wave-washed islands (there is evidence to be de duced from certain habits of the sockeye that this is the case). In that receptacle must be stored records of millions of pre cedents — clues for guidance through a life-embracing laby- rinth of dangers and difficulties. It contains the tragedy and the triumph of the sockeye race. One's mind reels before the abyss.

THE CORONATION OF CHARLES THE GREAT[1]

Charles the Great in 800 A.D. was already the most powerful ruler of Eu- rope. The coronation here described added nothing definite to his terri- tories, but made him nominally successor to the ancient Roman emperors.

[1] The six accounts are reprinted from Duncalf and Krey's "Parallel Source Problems" by special permission of the editors and of the publishers, Messrs. Harper & Brothers. Copyright, 1912, by Harper & Brothers.

The traditional awe with which the northern barbarians had viewed the one, undivided world empire of Rome lasted centuries after the collapse of her power, and could still be felt toward the Frankish king who — by however empty a claim — now became titular heir to the Cæsars. For this reason the coronation was a historic event. It conferred on Charlemagne no new lands, but gave him great prestige and a firmer hold on the popular imagination. The preceding pope, Hadrian I, had been disinclined to bestow on any king the emperorship or "imperium." However, Pope Leo III, successor to Hadrian in 795, was driven by the attacks of his enemies to seek help from Charles, who in the following year journeyed to Rome, and was crowned emperor ("imperator") in the manner here set forth.

Of the six following accounts, the first four were certainly, and the fifth was probably, the work of Charles's contemporaries. The sixth was written nearly a century after the coronation that it describes. The "Annales Laurissenses," though named from the abbey of Lorsch, were probably composed by prominent men connected with Charles's court, closely in touch with political life and the most reliable sources of information. The "Annales Laurishamenses," also named from the abbey of Lorsch, may or may not have been written there. Their style and matter indicate that they were the work of intelligent and well informed men. The "Vita Karoli" (Life of Charles) is a biography by Einhard, who was intimate with the emperor and one of the foremost historians and scholars of his time. Theophanis, the author of the "Chronographia," was a prominent Greek writer, living in the Eastern, or Byzantine Empire. He was thus in the position of an intelligent foreigner, discussing a contemporary event at a distance. The "Vita Leonis III" (Life of Leo III) is from the "Liber Pontificalis" or ". Book of The Popes," and describes the coronation from the point of view of the Church, which might not always agree with that of the lay historian. "De Gestis Karoli" (Concerning the Deeds of Charles), by the Monk of St. Gall, is of uncertain authorship and was written between 884 and 887. It contains many mythical tales about Charlemagne, some of which were local and confined to the region of Germany around St. Gall.

The Annales Laurissenses (the Annals of Lorsch)

800 And in the beginning of the month of August, when he [Charles] reached Mainz, he decided to journey into Italy. When he reached Ravenna with his army he made preparations for an expedition against the Beneventians.   After a delay of seven days Charles started for Rome, having ordered his son Pepin to ravage the lands of the Beneventians with the army.   As he approached Rome, Pope Leo, accompanied by Romans, met him at Nomentum, which is at the twelfth milestone from the city.   After greeting him with the greatest humility the pope dined with him at this town.   The pope then returned to the city, and on the following day he stationed himself on the steps of the basilica of the blessed apostle Peter, with the standard of the Roman city, and crowds of pilgrims and citizens arranged and disposed in suitable places to shout praises to those coming.   Leo himself with the clergy and bishops received Charles when he dismounted from his horse and ascended the steps.   When an oration had been delivered, while all were chanting psalms, the king was led into the basilica of the blessed apostle Peter.   This happened on the eighth day before the Calends of December (November 24).

Seven days later the king began to busy himself with the important affairs that had brought him and all his men to the city of Rome, and thenceforth daily he was occupied with these matters.   The first and most difficult of these tasks was the investigation of the crimes of which the holy pontiff had been accused.   As no one wished to be sponsor for the pope's guilt, Leo ascended to the altar of the church of the apostle Peter in the presence of all the people, with the Evangel in his hand, and by oath, in the name of the Holy Trinity, purged himself of the charges which had been made against him.

On the same day Zachary returned from the East with two monks, whom the Patriarch of Jerusalem had sent back with him.[1]   One of them was from the Mount of Olives

[1] In 799 Charles was visited by a monk from the Patriarch of Jerusalem, who brought blessings and relics from the Holy Sepulcher.   On Christmas

and the other from St. Saba. As a blessing they brought the keys of the Holy Sepulchre and of Mount Calvary, also the keys of the city and of the Mount (Zion) and a banner. The king received them graciously, and kept them with him many days, sending them away in April with gifts. He celebrated the birthday of the Lord at Rome. And the number of the years changed into

801.[1]

On the most sacred birthday of the Lord, while the king was at mass, and just as he was rising from prayer before the grave of St. Peter, Pope Leo placed the crown on his head, and all the people shouted "Charles Augustus, crowned great and peace-giving *Imperator* of the Romans, life and victory!" After this praise he was saluted by the apostle [2] according to the custom of the ancient emperors.[3] The title *Patrician* was dropped, and he was called *Imperator* and *Augustus*. After a few days he ordered the men who had deposed the pontiff the preceding year to be brought before him. They were tried according to the Roman law for the crime of treason, and were condemned to death. The pope interceded for them, and life and the integrity of their bodies was granted to them. Some of them were

day of the same year Charles sent back a priest, Zachary, with gifts for the Holy Sepulchre, and other sacred spots around Jerusalem. On his return one year later Zachary found Charles at Rome.

[1] The year did not always begin on January 1st in the Middle Ages. In the present case Christmas day was regarded as the first day of the year, hence, according to most of the writers, the coronation occurred on the first day of the year 801.

[2] The pope.

[3] At the accession of a new emperor to the throne at Constantinople, an election was first necessary. This election was made by the senate, with the army and the people participating. The coronation proper was a religious ceremony in which the patriarch of Constantinople crowned the new emperor. Compare this custom with that followed in 800.

sent into exile as a punishment for their most serious
crime. . . .

2

The Annales Laurishamenses [1] (*the Annals of Lorsch*)

And in the summer he [Charles] called together his lords
and nobles at the city of Mainz. When he had assured
himself that peace reigned throughout all his dominions
800 he called to mind the injury that the Romans had inflicted
on Pope Leo, and setting his face toward Rome, he journeyed thither. When he had arrived there he summoned
a great council of bishops and abbots, also priests, deacons,
counts, and other Christian people. Those who wished to
condemn the apostle himself were brought before this as-
sembly. When the king had made investigation he was
convinced that they did not want to condemn the pope with
justice, but through spite. It was therefore clear to the
most pious prince, Charles, and to all the bishops and holy
fathers present, that, if the pope wished and should ask it,
he ought to purify himself by his own will, voluntarily, and
not by the judgment of the council; and this was done.
When he had taken the oath, the holy bishops and all the
clergy, Prince Charles and the devote Christian people
began the hymn, *Te Deum laudamus, te Dominum con-
fitemur*. When this was entirely finished, the king and all
the faithful people with him gave thanks to God, who had
preserved the apostle Leo sound in body and mind. And
he passed the winter in Rome.

Inasmuch as the title of *Imperator* had ceased among the
Greeks at this time and the *imperium* was in the hands of
a woman,[2] it was evident to the apostle Leo and all the
800 holy fathers who had taken part in the council, as well as

[1] *Laurissenses* and *Laurishamenses* are merely different ways of spelling
the Latin name for Lorsch.
Empress Irene, queen of Byzantium.

to all the Christian people, that Charles, king of the Franks, ought to be called *Imperator*. For he held the city of Rome, where the Cæsars had always resided, and he also ruled Italy, Gaul, and Germany likewise. Because God Almighty had placed all these countries in his power it seemed just to them that, with God favoring it and all the Christian people demanding it, he should have the title itself. King Charles was not willing to refuse this demand, but with all humility, and obedient to the Lord and the petition of the clergy and all the Christian people, on the very day of the nativity of our Lord Jesus Christ he was consecrated by the lord pope Leo, and received the title of *Imperator*. Then, first of all he restored peace and concord to the Holy Roman Church, and he celebrated Easter at Rome. When summer approached he directed his journey to Ravenna, giving justice and restoring order. He then returned to his palace in France. . . .

3

The Vita Karoli (the Life of Charles) by Einhard

Although he [Charles] regarded Rome highly, during all the forty-seven years of his reign he went to the city only four times to pay his vows and to offer his prayers.

This was not the only reason for his last visit, however. Indeed, the Romans had greatly injured Pope Leo. They tore out his eyes and cut off his tongue, and thus he was forced to ask protection from the king. So he went to Rome to improve the condition of the Church, which was greatly disturbed, and remained there the entire winter. At this time he received the titles of *Imperator* and *Augustus*, which he was so opposed to at first that he said he would never have entered the church on that day, although it was a very important festival of the Church, if he had known the intention of the pope. Nevertheless, having accepted the title, he endured with great patience the jealousy that it caused, for the Roman emperors were very indignant. He overcame their pride by magnanimity, in which he doubtless excelled them, and by sending frequent embassies to them, and by calling them brothers in his letters. . . .

4

The Chronographia (Annals) of Theophanis

In the same year [801] partisans of the Roman pope, Hadrian, of blessed memory, started a riot against Pope Leo and injured his eyesight. The men who were selected to put out his eyes were moved by pity and spared him, so that he was not completely blinded. Leo immediately fled to Charles, king of the Franks. The king took vengeance on the enemies of the pope and restored him to his seat. Thus at this time Rome fell into the hands of the Franks and continued thus. Leo repaid Charles by anointing him from head to foot with oil in the church of the blessed apostle, and, having saluted him with the title of *Imperator*, he crowned him. He also clothed him with the imperial robes and insignia. This happened on the 25th day of the month of December, in the ninth indiction.[1] . . .

5

Vita Leonis III. (Life of Leo III.) 'from the Liber Pontificalis

. . A few days after [the arrival of Leo at Rome], the faithful *missi*,[2] who had returned with the pope to Rome in

---

[1] The indiction was originally a period of fifteen years, at the close of which the Roman government revived its tax assessments. Later it was used to reckon time. The first indiction was that of 312 A.D. The ninth indiction means the ninth year of one of these fifteen-year periods, and not the ninth period. According to the Greek calendar, the year began on September 1st, so that Charles was crowned in the year 801, which would make it the ninth year of that indictional period.

[2] The *missi* were officials of the Carolingian kings, of which the famous

obedience to the pontifical desires — namely, Hildebald and Arno, both most reverend archbishops; Cunibert, Bernhard, Otto, and Jesse, most reverend and holy bishops; also Flaccus, bishop-elect; and Helingot, Rothgar, and Germar, famous counts. They were entertained at the table of the lord pope Leo, and were examining those malicious offenders for more than a week to discover what evidence they might have against the pope. Neither Pascal nor Campulus[1] had any evidence that they could report, and neither did their accomplices say anything against him. So the aforementioned *missi* of the great king seized the culprits and sent them into France.

After a time the great king joined them at the basilica of the blessed apostle Peter, and was received with great honor. He called a council of the archbishops, the bishops, the abbots, and all the French nobles, as well as the prominent Romans in the same church. The great king as well as the most blessed pontiff were seated, likewise they made the most holy archbishops and abbots seat themselves, but all the other priests and the French and Roman nobles remained standing. He summoned this council to investigate all the charges that had been made against the sanctity of the pontiff. When all the archbishops, the bishops, and the abbots heard this they said: "We do not dare to judge the apostolic see, which is the head of all the churches of God, for we are all judged by it and its vicar. Furthermore, it should be judged by no one, according to what was the ancient custom. Whatever the chief pontiff proposes we will obey canonically." The venerable chief said: "I follow the footsteps of the

---

missi dominici were a special type. The men whose names are given were prominent men in the service of Charles, who were sent on a special mission to look after his interests at Rome.

[1] Pascal and Campulus were the leaders of the conspiracy and attack that was made on Pope Leo in 799.

pontiffs who were my predecessors. I am ready to purify myself of such false charges as have been basely made against me."

On a later day in the same church of the blessed apostle Peter, when all were present — namely, archbishops, bishops, abbots, all the Franks, who were in the service of the great king, and all the Romans, the venerable pontiff, grasping the four Gospels of Christ, mounted to the altar and with a clear voice took the oath : "Inasmuch as I have no know ledge of these false crimes, which the Romans, who have persecuted me, have basely charged me with, I say that I do not need to have such knowledge." When this was done litanies were chanted, and all the archbishops, bishops, ab- bots, and all the clergy gave praise to God and to the Virgin Mary, the mother of God, to the blessed apostle Peter, chief of the apostles, and to all the saints of God.

On the natal day of our Lord Jesus Christ all were again gathered together in the same basilica of the blessed apostle Peter, and there the venerable, holy pontiff with his own hands crowned Charles the Great with a crown of great value. Then all the faithful Romans, when they realized how great protection and care the Holy Roman Church and its vicar would have because of this act which had the favor of God and the blessed Peter, the key-bearer of the kingdom of heaven, unanimously shouted with loud voices, "Charles, most pious *Augustus*, crowned great, peace-giving *Im- perator* by God, life and victory !" This was shouted three times, and many saints were invoked before the grave of the blessed apostle Peter, and thus by all he was made *Imperator* of the Romans. There the most holy bishop and pontiff anointed Charles with the sacred oil, also his most excellent son [Charles] as king, on the birthday of our Lord Jesus Christ.

After the celebration of the mass the most serene lord

Imperator presented a silver table weighing . . . pounds with its legs. Likewise, at the grave of the apostle of God, the *Imperator* and his son, the king, and his daughters presented various vases to accompany this table, all of pure gold, weighing . . . pounds, also a gold crown set with large gems, to be hung over the altar, and two swords weighing fifty-eight pounds, and a large vessel of gold, set with gems, . . [the list of gifts continues].

Afterward those iniquitous malefactors — namely, Pascal and Campulus — and their associates were brought into the presence of the most pious lord *Imperator*, with all the noble Franks and Romans standing about. All were indignant about the misdeeds of these men. Campulus turned to Pascal and said, "It was an evil day when I saw your face, for you are to blame for my being in this trouble." And so, each condemning the other, they themselves proved their own guilt. When the lord *Imperator* realized how cruel and iniquitous they were he sent them into France.

6

De Gestis Caroli Magni (The Deeds of Charles the Great), by the Monk of St. Gall

Although other mortals may be deceived by the works of the devil and his satellites, it is fitting to meditate on the words of the Lord when He commended the brave confession of Saint Peter, saying, "Because you are Peter, I will build my church upon this rock, and the gates of hell shall not prevail against it," for even in these evil and troubled days the Church has remained firm and unshaken.

Because jealous people are always consumed by envy it was generally customary among the Romans to show hostility and even to fight against the great popes who were elevated to the apostolic seat. Thus it happened that certain of the Romans who were blinded by envy accused Leo, of holy memory, whom we have referred to above, of terrible crimes. Moreover, they attacked him with the intention of blinding him, but, checked and restrained by the divine will, they failed to tear out his eyes, although they did cut them across the middle with knives. Secretly the pope had the news of this sent by his servants to Michael, emperor at Constantinople, who withheld all aid, saying, "The pope has a kingdom of his own, higher than mine, and must revenge himself on his own enemies." Then the holy pope, following the divine will, summoned to Rome the unconquerable Charles who was in reality ruler of many peoples, in order that he might gloriously obtain the titles of *Imperator, Cæsar*, and *Augustus* by apostolic authority.

Charles, who was always engaged in campaigns and military affairs, although he was ignorant of the cause of the summons, without delay came with all his warriors and fighting men : the lord of the world came to the capital of the world. And when that most depraved people heard of his unexpected arrival, just as sparrows hide themselves from the sight of their master so the Romans hid in various hiding-places. But they were not able to escape the energy and sagacity of Charles under heaven, and so they were captured and led into the basilica of St. Peter in chains. There the undefiled Father Leo took the Evangel and, holding it over his head before Charles and his men, with his persecutors present, took the following oath, "On the great judgment day may I enjoy the fulfilment of the promises of the Gospel, as I am innocent of the charges that have been made against me." Then the terrible Charles said to his men, "Take care that none of them escape." All were seized and condemned either to different kinds of death or to perpetual exile.

As Charles remained in the city for several days to give his army a necessary rest the chief of the apostolic see summoned all who would come from the surrounding country to Rome. In the presence of all these people and the invincible counts of the most glorious Charles, who did not suspect anything, the pope pronounced him *Imperator* and Defender of the Roman Church. Since he was not able to refuse the title, for he believed that he had received it by divine favor, nevertheless he did not receive it with joy, because he believed that the Greeks, fired by greater jealousy, would lay plots against the kingdom of the Franks, or at least be more careful to make all necessary preparations to prevent Charles from suddenly coming to subjugate their empire, for there was a rumor that he intended to do this. For on a former occasion when the legate of the Byzantine king visited him, and had told him that his master wished to be a faithful friend, and that if they were only not separated from each other by so great a distance, that he would treat Charles as a son and relieve his poverty, Charles, who was not able to restrain his burning spirit, burst forth, "Oh! If that pool were not between us, we could either divide or hold together in common the wealth of the East."

Indeed, the Giver and Restorer of health showed his belief in the innocence of the blessed Leo, for even after that cruel wound had been received He made his eyes brighter than they were before, except that a most beautiful scar remained as a sign of virtue to decorate his eyelids, very like a fine thread in the white snow. . . .

ACCOUNTS OF THE NAVAL BATTLE OF JUTLAND[1]

I

The first German Admiralty report of the battle was issued on Thursday, June 1, and reads as follows·

[1] Reprinted from "The Current History Magazine" of "The New York Times" (July, August, and September numbers for 1916) by special permission of the editors.

Berlin, June 1, 1916.

During an enterprise directed to the northward our high sea fleet on May 31 encountered the main part of the English fighting fleet, which was considerably superior to our forces.

During the afternoon, between Skagerrak and Horn Riff, a heavy engagement developed, which was successful to us, and which continued during the whole night.

In this engagement, so far as known up to the present, there were destroyed by us the large battleship *Warspite*, the battle cruisers *Queen Mary* and *Indefatigable*, two armored cruisers, apparently of the Achilles type; one small cruiser, the new flagships of destroyer squadrons, the *Turbulent*, *Nestor*, and *Alcaster*, a large number of torpedo-boat destroyers, and one submarine.

By observation, which was free and clear of objects, it was stated that a large number of English battleships suffered damage from our ships and the attacks of our torpedo-boat flotilla during the day engagement and throughout the night. Among others, the large battleship *Marlborough* was hit by a torpedo. This was confirmed by prisoners.

Several of our ships rescued parts of the crews of the sunken English ships, among them being two and the only survivors of the *Indefatigable*.

On our side the small cruiser *Wiesbaden*, by hostile gun fire during the day engagement, and his Majesty's ship *Pommern*, during the night, as the result of a torpedo, were sunk.

The fate of his Majesty's ship *Frauenlob*, which is missing, and of some torpedo boats, which have not returned yet, is unknown.

The High Sea Fleet returned to-day (Thursday) into our port.

The first report of the British Admiralty was issued a day later, and is as follows:

London, June 2, 1916.

On the afternoon of Wednesday, the 31st of May, a naval engagement took place off the coast of Jutland.

The British ships on which the brunt of the fighting fell were the battle cruiser fleet and some cruisers and light cruisers, supported by four fast battleships. Among these the losses were heavy.

The German battle fleet, aided by low visibility, avoided a prolonged action with our main forces. As soon as these appeared on the scene the enemy returned to port, though not before receiving severe damage from our battleships.

The battle cruisers *Queen Mary*, *Indefatigable*, and *Invincible*, and the cruisers *Defense* and *Black Prince* were sunk.

The *Warrior* was disabled, and after being towed for some time had to be abandoned by her crew.

It is also known that the destroyers *Tipperary*, *Turbulent*, *Fortune*, *Sparrowhawk*, and *Ardent* were lost, and six others are not yet accounted for.

No British battleships or light cruisers were sunk.

The enemy's losses were serious. At least one battle cruiser was destroyed and one was severely damaged. One battleship is reported to have been sunk by our destroyers.

During the night attack two light cruisers were disabled and probably sunk.

The exact number of enemy destroyers disposed of during the action cannot be ascertained with any certainty, but must have been large.

Later this further statement was published:

Since the foregoing communication was issued a further report has been received from the Commander in Chief of the Grand Fleet stating that it has now been ascertained that our total losses in destroyers amount to eight boats in all.

The Commander in Chief also reports that it is now possible to form a closer estimate of the losses and the damage sustained by the enemy fleet.

One dreadnought battleship of the Kaiser class was blown up in an attack by British destroyers, and another dreadnought battleship of the Kaiser class is believed to have been sunk by gunfire. Of three German battle cruisers, two of which, it is believed, were the *Derfflinger* and the *Lützow*, one was blown up, another was heavily engaged by our battle fleet and was seen to be disabled and stopping, and the third was observed to be seriously damaged.

One German light cruiser and six German destroyers were sunk, and at least two more German light cruisers were seen to be disabled. Further repeated hits were observed on three other German battleships that were engaged.

Finally, a German submarine was rammed and sunk.

The Chief of the German Admiralty Staff issued this secondary statement on June 3:

In order to prevent fabulous reports, it is again stated that in the battle off Skagerrak on May 31 the German high sea forces were in battle with the entire modern English fleet.

To the already published statements it must be added that, according to the official British report, the battle cruiser *Invincible* and the armored cruiser *Warrior* were also destroyed.

We were obliged to blow up the small cruiser *Elbing*, which, on the night of May 31–June 1, owing to a collision with other German war vessels, was heavily damaged, and it was impossible to take her to port. The crew was rescued by torpedo boats, with the exception of the commander, two other officers, and eighteen men, who remained aboard in order to blow up the vessel. According to Dutch reports they were later brought to Ymuiden on a tug and landed there.

The British Admiralty's next statement, dated June 4, impugns the truth of the German report in these terms:

The Grand Fleet came in touch with the German High Seas Fleet at 3 : 30 on the afternoon of May 31. The leading ships of the two fleets carried on a vigorous fight, in which the battle cruisers, fast battleships, and subsidiary craft all took an active part.

The losses were severe on both sides, but when the main body of the British fleet came into contact with the German High Seas Fleet, a very brief period sufficed to compel the latter, who had been severely punished, to seek refuge in their protected waters. This manœuvre was rendered possible by low visibility and mist, and, although the Grand Fleet were now and then able to get in momentary contact with their opponents, no continuous action was possible. They continued the pursuit until the light had wholly failed, while the British destroyers were able to make a successful attack upon the enemy during the night.

Meanwhile, Admiral Sir John Jellicoe, having driven the enemy into port, returned to the main scene of the action and scoured the sea in search of disabled vessels. By noon the next day, June 1, it became evident that there was nothing more to be done. He returned, therefore, to his bases, 400 miles away, refueled his fleet, and in the evening of June 2 was again ready to put to sea. . . .

There seems to be the strongest ground for supposing that included in the German losses are two battleships, two dreadnought battle cruisers of the most powerful type, two of the latest light cruisers, the *Wiesbaden* and *Elbing;* a light cruiser of the Rostock type, the light cruiser *Frauenlob*, nine destroyers, and a submarine.

To this was added the following on June 6:

An official statement given out in Berlin to-day, signed "Fleet Command," claims the British lost the *Warspite, Princess Royal, Birmingham,* and

Acasta in the action of May 31. This is claimed on the evidence of British sailors picked up by German ships.

This is false. The complete list of British losses is as published.

The German Admiralty, in an official statement issued on June 2, stated that, among other casualties, a British submarine was sunk in the course of the battle during the afternoon and night of May 31.

All British submarines at sea on that date have now returned. It must, therefore, be assumed, if any importance is to be attached to the German official statement, that the submarine sunk was an enemy submarine. This vessel should be added to the list of German losses stated in the British Admiralty communiqué of June 4.

An official German statement admitting the loss of the *Lützow* and *Rostock* was issued June 8. The losses of the British are again said to have been heavier than admitted by them. The official writer continues

It is asserted, for instance, that the German fleet left the battlefield and that the English fleet remained master of the battlefield. With regard to this it is stated that by repeated, effective attacks of our torpedo-boat flotillas during the battle on the evening of May 31 the English main fleet was forced to turn around, and it never again came within sight of our forces. In spite of its superior speed and reinforcement by an English squadron of twelve vessels, which came up from the southern North Sea, it never attempted to come again into touch with our forces to continue the battle or attempt in conjunction with the above-mentioned squadron to bring about the desired destruction of the German fleet.

The English assertion that the English fleet in vain attempted to reach the fleeing German fleet in order to defeat it before reaching its home points of support is contradicted by the alleged official English statement that Admiral Jellicoe, with his Grand Fleet, already had reached the basin of Scalpa Flow, in the Orkneys, 300 miles from the battlefield, on June 1.

Numerous German torpedo-boat flotillas sent out after the day battle for a night attack toward the north, and beyond the theatre of the day battle, did not find the English main fleet in spite of a keen search. Moreover, our torpedo boats had an opportunity of rescuing a great number of English survivors of the various sunken vessels.

As further proof of the fact, contested by the English, of the participation of their entire battle fleet in the battle of May 31, it is pointed out that the British Admiralty report too announced that the *Marlborough* had been disabled. Furthermore, one of our submarines on June 1 sighted another of the Iron Duke class heavily damaged steering toward the English coast. Both mentioned vessels belonged to the English main fleet.

In order to belittle the great German success the English press also traces the loss of numerous English vessels largely to the effect of German mines, submarines, and airships. Regarding this, it is especially pointed out that neither mines, which, by the way, would have been just as dangerous to our own fleet as to that of the enemy, nor submarines were employed by our High Seas Fleet. German airships were used exclusively for reconnoissance on June 1.

The German victory was gained by able leadership and by the effect of our artillery and torpedo weapons

The British indicate that the *Pommern*, which we reported lost, is not the ship of the line of 13,000 tons from the year 1905, but a modern dreadnought of the same name. We state that the total loss of the German high sea forces during the battle of May 31-June 1, and the following time are: One battle cruiser, one ship of the line of older construction, four small cruisers, and five torpedo boats. Of these losses, the *Pommern*, launched in 1905; the *Wiesbaden, Elbing, Frauenlob,* and five torpedo boats already have been reported in official statements. For military reasons, we refrained until now from making public the losses of the vessels *Lützow* and *Rostock*.

In view of the wrong interpretation of this measure, and, moreover, in order to frustrate English legends about gigantic losses on our side, these reasons must no longer be regarded. Both ships were lost on the way to the harbor, to be repaired after attempts to keep the badly damaged vessels afloat had failed. The crews of both, including all the severely wounded, are safe.

While the German list of losses is herewith closed, there are positive indications at hand that the actual British losses were materially higher than admitted. It has been established by us on the basis of our own observations and of what has been made public, as well as from statements of British prisoners, that, in addition to the *Warspite,* the *Princess Royal* and *Birmingham* were destroyed. According to reliable reports, the dreadnought *Marlborough* also sank before reaching harbor. . . .

CHIEF OF THE ADMIRALTY STAFF.

To Jellicoe's assertion that Germany's losses were as great as those of Britain the Admiralty at Berlin retorted on June 15 with the following definite figures:

Against this we point out the comparison of losses officially published on the 7th, showing a total loss in tonnage of German war vessels of 60,720, against the British loss of 117,150, where only those English vessels and destroyers were taken into account whose losses until now have been officially admitted on the English side.

According to statements of English prisoners, further vessels were sunk, among them the dreadnought *Warspite*.

No other German vessels were lost than those made public. They are the *Lützow, Pommern, Wiesbaden, Frauenlob, Elbing, Rostock*, and five torpedo boats. This shows that the human losses to the English in the battle were considerably greater than the German.

While from the English side the officer losses announced were 343 dead or missing and 51 wounded, our losses in officers, engineers, sanitary officers, paymasters, ensigns, and petty officers, are 172 dead or missing and 41 wounded.

The total losses among the English crews as far as published by the Admiralty are 6,104 dead or missing, 513 wounded. On the German side the losses are 2,414 dead or missing, 449 wounded.

During and after the battle our vessels rescued 177 English, while up to now no German prisoners from this battle are known to be in English hands. The names of the English prisoners will be communicated to the British Government in the usual manner.

An informal British account of the battle of Jutland in detail which appeared in "The Glasgow Herald" and which evidently has official authority behind it, runs as follows:

First Phase, 3 : 30 P.M., May 31. — Beatty's battle cruisers, consisting of the *Lion, Princess Royal, Queen Mary, Tiger, Inflexible, Indomitable, Invincible, Indefatigable,* and *New Zealand,* were on a southeasterly course, followed at about two miles distance by the four Queen Elizabeths.

Enemy light cruisers were sighted, and shortly afterward the head of the German battle cruiser squadron, consisting of the new cruiser *Hindenburg,* the *Seydlitz, Derfflinger, Lützow, Moltke,* and possibly the *Salamis.*

Beatty at once began firing at a range of about 20,000 yards, (twelve miles,) which shortened to 16,000 yards (nine miles) as the fleets closed. The Germans could see the British distinctly outlined against the light yellow sky.

The Germans, covered by a haze, could be very indistinctly made out by our gunners.

The Queen Elizabeths opened fire on one after another as they came within range. The German battle cruisers turned to port and drew away to about 20,000 yards.

Second Phase, 4:40 P.M. — A destroyer screen then appeared beyond the German battle cruisers. The whole German High Seas Fleet could be seen approaching on the northeastern horizon in three divisions, coming to the support of their battle cruisers.

The German battle cruisers now turned right round 16 points and took station in front of the battleships of the high fleet.

Beatty with his battle cruisers and supporting battleships, therefore, had before him the whole of the German battle fleet, and Jellicoe was still some distance away.

The opposing fleets were now moving parallel to one another in opposite directions, and but for a master manœuvre on the part of Beatty the British advance ships would have been cut off from Jellicoe's grand fleet. In order to avoid this and at the same time prepare the way so that Jellicoe might envelop his adversary, Beatty immediately also turned right around 16 points, so as to bring his ships parallel to the German battle cruisers and facing in the same direction.

As soon as he was around he increased to full speed to get ahead of the Germans and take up a tactical position in advance of their line. He was able to do this owing to the superior speed of our battle cruisers.

Just before the turning point was reached, the *Indefatigable* sank, and the *Queen Mary* and the *Invincible* also were lost at the turning point, where, of course, the High Seas Fleet concentrated their fire.

A little earlier, as the German battle cruisers were turning, the Queen Elizabeths had in similar manner concentrated their fire on the turning point and destroyed a new German battle cruiser, believed to be the *Hindenburg*.

Beatty had now got around and headed away with the loss of three ships, racing parallel to the German battle cruisers. The Queen Elizabeths followed behind, engaging the main High Seas Fleet.

Third Phase, 5 P.M. — The Queen Elizabeths now turned short to port 16 points in order to follow Beatty. The *Warspite* jammed her steering gear, failed to get around, and drew the fire of six of the enemy, who closed in upon her.

I am not surprised that the Germans claim her as a loss, since on paper she ought to have been lost, but as a matter of fact, though repeatedly straddled by shell fire with the water boiling up all around her, she was not seriously hit, and was able to sink one of her opponents. Her Captain recovered control of the vessel, brought her around, and followed her consorts.

In the meantime the *Barham*, *Valiant*, and *Malaya* turned short so as to avoid the danger spot where the *Queen Mary* and the *Invincible* had been lost, and for an hour until Jellicoe arrived fought a delaying action against the High Seas Fleet.

The *Warspite* joined them at about 5:15 o'clock, and all four ships were so successfully manœuvred in order to upset the spotting corrections of their opponents that no hits of a seriously disabling character were suffered. They had the speed over their opponents by fully four knots, and were able to draw away from part of the long line of German battleships, which almost filled up the horizon.

At this time the Queen Elizabeths were steadily firing at the flashes of German guns at a range which varied between 12,000 and 15,000 yards, especially against those ships which were nearest them. The Germans were enveloped in a mist, and only smoke and flashes were visible.

By 5 : 45 half of the High Seas Fleet had been left out of range, and the Queen Elizabeths were steaming fast to join hands with Jellicoe.

I must now return to Beatty's battle cruisers. They had succeeded in outflanking the German battle cruisers, which were, therefore, obliged to turn a full right angle to starboard to avoid being headed.

Heavy fighting was renewed between the opposing battle cruiser squadrons, during which the *Derfflinger* was sunk; but toward 6 o'clock the German fire slackened very considerably, showing that Beatty's battle cruisers and the Queen Elizabeths had inflicted serious damage on their immediate opponents.

Fourth Phase, 6 P.M. — The Grand Fleet was now in sight, and, coming up fast in three directions, the Queen Elizabeths altered their course four points to the starboard and drew in toward the enemy to allow Jellicoe room to deploy into line.

The Grand Fleet was perfectly manœuvred, and the very difficult operation of deploying between the battle cruisers and the Queen Elizabeths was perfectly timed.

Jellicoe came up, fell in behind Beatty's cruisers, and, followed by the damaged but still serviceable Queen Elizabeths, steamed right across the head of the German fleet.

The first of the ships to come into action were the *Revenue* and the *Royal Oak* with their fifteen-inch guns, and the *Agincourt*, which fired from her seven turrets with the speed almost of a Maxim gun.

The whole British fleet had now become concentrated. They had been perfectly manœuvred, so as to "cross the T" of the High Seas Fleet, and, indeed, only decent light was necessary to complete their work of destroying the Germans in detail. The light did improve for a few minutes, and the conditions were favorable to the British fleet, which was now in line approximately north and south across the head of the Germans.

During the few minutes of good light Jellicoe smashed up the first three German ships, but the mist came down, visibility suddenly failed, and the defeated High Seas Fleet was able to draw off in ragged divisions.

Fifth Phase, Night. — The Germans were followed by the British, who still had them enveloped between Jellicoe on the west, Beatty on the north, and Evan Thomas with his three Queen Elizabeths on the south. The *Warspite* had been sent back to her base.

During the night our torpedo boat destroyers heavily attacked the German ships, and, although they lost seriously themselves, succeeded in sinking two of the enemy.

Co-ordination of the units of the fleet was practically impossible to keep up, and the Germans discovered by the rays of their searchlights the three Queen Elizabeths, not more than 4,000 yards away. Unfortunately they were then able to escape between the battleships and Jellicoe, since we were not able to fire, as our own destroyers were in the way.

So ended the Jutland battle, which was fought as had been planned and very nearly a great success. It was spoiled by the unfavorable weather conditions, especially at the critical moment, when the whole British fleet was concentrated and engaged in crushing the head of the German line.

It was an action on our part of big guns, except of course for the destroyer work, since at a very early stage our big ships ceased to feel any anxiety from the German destroyers. The German small craft were rounded up by their British opponents and soon ceased to count as an organized body

A semi-official account of the battle of the Skagerrak, issued in Berlin on June 5, gives a very different version of certain

aspects of the fight, especially of the number of vessels engaged on both sides:

The German High Seas Fleet had pushed out into the North Sea in the hope of engaging portions of the English fleet, which had recently been repeatedly reported off the Norwegian south coast.   At 3 : 15 o'clock in the afternoon, some seventy miles off the Skagerrak, some small cruisers of the Calliope class were sighted.   Our cruisers at once pursued the enemy, which fled northward at highest speed.

At 5 : 20 o'clock our cruisers sighted two enemy columns to the west, consisting of six battle cruisers and a great number of small cruisers.   The enemy passed toward the south, and our ships, approaching to nineteen kilometers, opened very effective fire' on south-southeastern courses. During the battle two English battle cruisers and one destroyer were sunk.

After half an hour's fighting heavy enemy reinforcements, later observed to be five vessels of the Queen Elizabeth class, were sighted to the north.   Soon afterward the German main force entered the fight, and the enemy at once turned north.

The British commander, driving his ships at full speed, attempted to evade our extremely effective fire by taking an echelon formation.   Our fleet followed at top speed the movements of the enemy.   In the course of this period of the fighting one cruiser of the Achilles or Shannon class and two destroyers were sunk, while a number of other vessels suffered heavy damage.

The battle against superior forces lasted until darkness fell.   Besides numerous light detachments, at least twenty-five British battleships, six battle cruisers, and four armored cruisers engaged sixteen German battleships, five battle cruisers, six older ships of the line, and no armored cruisers.

After dark our flotillas opened a night attack.   During

this attack several cruiser and torpedo boat engagements occurred, resulting in the destruction of one battle cruiser, one cruiser of the Achilles class, probably two small cruisers, and at least ten destroyers. Six of the latter, including the new destroyer leaders, the *Turbulent* and the *Tipperary*, were destroyed by the leading vessels of our High Seas Fleet.

The British squadron of older battleships, which hurried up from the south, did not arrive until Thursday morning, after the conclusion of the battle, and returned without taking any part in the fighting or coming within sight of our main force.

II

ADMIRAL JELLICOE'S OFFICIAL REPORT OF THE BATTLE OF JUTLAND

Vice Admiral Sir John Jellicoe's official report of the North Sea naval battle, which the British call the battle of Jutland and the Germans the battle of the Skagerrak, was made public on July 6. Even here the full list of ships and commanders is " withheld from publication for the present, in accordance with the usual practice." Following is the full text of all the vital portions of the document

The ships of the Grand Fleet, in pursuance of the general policy of periodical sweeps through the North Sea, had left their base on the previous day in accordance with instructions issued by me. In the early afternoon of Wednesday, May 31, the first and second battle cruiser squadrons, the first, second, and third light cruiser squadrons, and destroyers from the first, ninth, tenth, and thirteenth flotillas, supported by the fifth battle squadron, were, in accordance with my directions, scouting to the southward of the battle fleet, which was accompanied by the third battle cruiser squadron, the first and second cruiser squadrons, the fourth light cruiser squadron, and the fourth, eleventh, and twelfth flotillas.

The junction of the battle fleet with the scouting force after the enemy had been sighted was delayed owing to the southerly course steered by our advanced force during the first hour after commencing their action with the enemy battle cruisers. This, of course, was unavoidable, as had our battle cruisers not followed the enemy to the southward the main fleets would never have been in contact.

The battle cruiser fleet, gallantly led by Vice Admiral Beatty, and admirably supported by the ships of the fifth battle squadron under Rear Admiral Evan-Thomas, fought the action under, at times, disadvantageous conditions, especially in regard to light, in a manner that was in keeping with the best traditions of the service.

Admiral Jellicoe estimates the German losses at two battleships of the dreadnought type, one of the Deutschland type, which was seen to sink; the battle cruiser *Lützow*, admitted by the Germans, one battle cruiser of the dreadnought type, one battle cruiser seen to be so severely damaged that its return was extremely doubtful; five light cruisers, seen to sink — one of them possibly a battleship; six destroyers seen to sink, three destroyers so damaged that it was doubtful if they would be able to reach port, and a submarine sunk. In concluding Admiral Jellicoe says:

The conditions of low visibility under which the day action took place and the approach of darkness enhanced the difficulty of giving an accurate report of the damage inflicted or the names of the ships sunk by our forces. But after a most careful examination of the evidence of all the officers who testified to seeing enemy vessels actually sink, and personal interviews with a large number of these officers, I am of the opinion that the list shown in the inclosure gives the minimum numbers, though it is possible it is not accurate as regards the particular class of vessel, especially those which were sunk during the night attack. In addition to the vessels sunk, it is unquestionable that many other ships were very seriously damaged by gunfire and torpedo attack.

The hardest fighting fell to the battle cruiser fleet, says Admiral Jellicoe, the units of which were less heavily armored than their opponents, and he expresses high appreciation of the handling of all the vessels and commends Admirals Burney, Jerram, Sturdee, Evan-Thomas, Duff, and Leveson, and continues:

Vice Admiral Sir David Beatty once again showed his fine qualities of gallant leadership, firm determination, and correct strategic fighting. He appreciated situations at once on sighting the first enemy's lighter forces, then his battle cruisers, finally his battleships. I can fully sympathize with his feelings when the evening mist and fading light robbed the fleet of that complete victory for which he had manœuvred, for which the vessels in company with him had striven so hard. The services rendered by him, not only on this but on two previous occasions, have been of the very greatest value.

Vice Admiral Beatty's report to Admiral Jellicoe particularly mentions the work of the *Engadine*, Commander Robinson, which towed the *Warrior* seventy-five miles during the night of May 31, and continues

It is impossible to give a definite statement of the losses inflicted on the enemy. Visibility was for the most part low and fluctuating. Caution forbade me to close the range too much with my inferior force. A review of all the reports leads me to conclude that the enemy's losses were considerably greater than those we sustained in spite of their superiority, and included battleships, battle cruisers, light cruisers, and destroyers. This is eloquent testimony to the very high standard of gunnery and torpedo efficiency of his Majesty's ships. The control and drill remained undisturbed throughout, in many cases, despite the heavy damage to material and personnel.

Our superiority over the enemy in this respect was very marked, their efficiency becoming rapidly reduced under punishment, while ours was maintained throughout. As was to be expected, the behavior of the ships' companies under the terrible conditions of a modern sea battle was magnificent without exception. The strain on their morale was a severe test of discipline and training. The officers and men were imbued with one thought a desire to defeat the enemy.

Extracts from Vice Admiral Beatty's report give the course of events before the battle fleet came on the scene of action. At 2:20 o'clock in the afternoon the *Galatea* reported the presence of enemy vessels. At 2:35 o'clock considerable smoke was sighted to the eastward. This made it clear that the enemy was to the northward and eastward, and that it would be impossible for him to round

Horn Reef without being brought to action. The course of the British ships consequently was altered to the eastward, and subsequently northeastward.

The enemy was sighted at 3 : 31 o'clock. His force consisted of five battle cruisers. Vice Admiral Beatty's first and third light cruiser squadrons, without awaiting orders, spread eastward, forming a screen in advance of the battle cruiser squadron under Admiral Evan-Thomas, consisting of four battleships of the Queen Elizabeth class. The light cruisers engaged the enemy; and the cruiser squadron came up at high speed, taking station ahead of the battle cruisers. At 3 : 30 o'clock Vice Admiral Beatty increased the speed to 25 knots and formed the line of battle, the second battle cruiser squadron forming astern of the first, with two destroyer flotillas ahead.

Vice Admiral Beatty then turned east-southeast slightly, converging on the enemy now at a range of 23,000 yards. The fifth battle cruiser squadron was then bearing north-northwest 10,000 yards distant. The visibility was good. Continuing his report, Vice Admiral Beatty said :

The sun was behind us. The wind was southeast. Being between the enemy and his base, our situation was both tactically and strategically good.

Both forces opened fire simultaneously at 3 : 48 at a range of 18,500 yards. The course was altered southward, the enemy steering parallel, distant 18,000 to 14,500 yards. The fifth battle squadron opened fire at a range of 20,000 yards at 4 : 08. The enemy fire then seemed to slacken. Although the presence of destroyers caused inconvenience on account of smoke, they preserved the battleships from submarine attack.

Two submarines being sighted, and a flotilla of ten destroyers being ordered to attack the enemy with torpedoes, they moved out at 4 : 15 o'clock simultaneously with the approach of German destroyers. The attack was carried out gallantly with great determination. Before arriving at a favorable position to fire torpedoes they intercepted an enemy force consisting of one light cruiser and fifteen destroyers. A fierce engagement at close quarters ensued, and the enemy was forced to retire on their battleships, having two destroyers sunk and their torpedo attack frustrated. Our destroyers sustained no loss, but the attack on the enemy cruisers was rendered less effective.

The *Nestor*, *Nomad*, and *Mineator*, under Commander Edward Bingham, pressed the attack on the battle cruisers and fired two torpedoes. Being subjected to a heavy fire at 3,000 yards, the *Nomad* was badly hit and remained between the lines. The *Nestor* also was badly hit, but was afloat when last seen. The *Petard*, *Nerissa*, *Turbulent*, and *Termagant* also are praised.

These destroyer attacks were indicative of the spirit pervading the navy and worthy of its highest traditions.

From 4:15 to 4:43 o'clock the conflict between the battle cruiser squadrons was fierce, and the resolute British fire began to tell. The rapidity and accuracy of the Germans' fire depreciated considerably. The third German ship was seen to be afire. The German battle fleet was reported ahead, and the destroyers were recalled.

Vice Admiral Beatty altered his course to the northward to lead the Germans toward the British battle fleet. The second light cruiser squadron closed to 13,000 yards of the German battle fleet and came under heavy but ineffective fire. The fifth battle squadron engaged the German battle cruisers with all guns, and about 5 o'clock came under the fire of the leading ships of the German battle fleet.

The weather became unfavorable, Vice Admiral Beatty's ships being silhouetted against a clear horizon to the Germans, whose ships were mostly obscured by mist.

Between 5 and 6 o'clock the action continued at 14,000 yards on a northerly course, the German ships receiving very severe punishment, one battle cruiser quitting the line considerably damaged. At 5:35 o'clock the Germans were gradually hauling eastward and receiving severe punishment at the head of the line, probably acting on information from their light cruisers which were engaged with the third battle cruiser squadron or from Zeppelins which possibly were present.

At 5:56 o'clock the leading ships of the British battle fleet were sighted bearing north, distant five miles. Vice Admiral Beatty thereon proceeded east at the greatest speed, bringing the range to 12,000 yards. Only three German battle cruisers were then visible, followed by battle-ships of the König type.

Vice Admiral Jellicoe then takes up the story of the battle fleet. Informed that the Germans were sighted, the fleet proceeded at full speed on a southeast by south course during two hours before arriving on the scene of the battle. The steaming qualities of the older ships were severely tested. When the battle fleet was meeting the battle cruisers and the fifth battle squadron, great care was necessary to insure that the British ships were not mistaken for the German war-ships.

Vice Admiral Beatty reported the position of the German battle fleet at 6:15 o'clock. Vice Admiral Jellicoe then formed the line of battle, Vice Admiral Beatty meantime having formed the battle cruisers ahead of the battle fleet; and the fleets became engaged. During the deployment the *Defense* and *Warrior* were seen passing between the British and German fleets under heavy fire. The *Defense* disappeared; and the *Warrior* passed to the rear, disabled.

Vice Admiral Jellicoe considers it probable that Sir Robert K. Arbuthnot, the Rear Admiral who was lost on board the *Defense*, was not aware, during the engagement with the German light cruisers, of the approach of their heavy ships, owing to the mist, until he found himself in close proximity to the main German fleet. Before he could withdraw, his ships were caught under a heavy fire and disabled. When the *Black Prince* of the same squadron was sunk is not known, but a wireless signal was received from her between 8 and 9 o'clock.

Owing principally to the mist, it was possible to see only

a few ships at a time. Toward the close of the battle only four or five were visible, and never more than eight to twelve.

The third battle cruiser squadron, under Rear Admiral Horace Alexander Hood, was in advance of the battle fleet and ordered to reinforce Vice Admiral Beatty. While en route the *Chester*, Captain Lawson, engaged three or four German light cruisers for twenty minutes. Despite many casualties, her steaming qualities were unimpaired.

Describing the work of the third squadron, Vice Admiral Beatty said Rear Admiral Hood brought it into action ahead of the *Lion* "in the most inspiring manner, worthy of his great naval ancestors." Vice Admiral Hood, at 6:25 P.M., was only 8,000 yards from the leading German ship, and the British vessels poured a hot fire into her and caused her to turn away. Vice Admiral Beatty, continuing, reports:

By 6:50 o'clock the battle cruisers were clear of our leading battle squadron, and I ordered the third battle cruiser squadron to prolong the line astern, and reduced the speed to eighteen knots. The visibility at this time was very indifferent, not more than four miles, and the enemy ships were temporarily lost sight of after 6 P.M. Although the visibility became reduced, it undoubtedly was more favorable to us than to the enemy. At intervals their ships showed up clearly, enabling us to punish them very severely and to establish a definite superiority over them. It was clear that the enemy suffered considerable damage, battle cruisers and battleships alike. The head of their line was crumpled up, leaving their battleships as a target for the majority of our battle cruisers. Before leaving, the fifth battle squadron was also engaging battleships.

The report of Rear Admiral Evan-Thomas shows excellent results were obtained. It can safely be said that his magnificent squadron wrought great execution.

The action between the battle fleets lasted, intermittently, from 6:17 to 8:20 o'clock at ranges between 9,000 and 12,000 yards. The Germans constantly turned away and opened the range under the cover of destroyer attacks and smoke screens as the effect of the British fire was felt; and

K

alterations of the course from southeast by east to west in an endeavor to close up brought the British battle fleet, which commenced action in an advantageous position on the Germans' bow, to a quarterly bearing from the German battle line, but placed Vice Admiral Jellicoe between the Germans and their bases.

Vice Admiral Jellicoe says: "During the somewhat brief periods that the ships of the High Sea Fleet were visible through the mist, a heavy and effective fire kept up by the battleships and battle cruisers of the Grand Fleet caused me much satisfaction. The enemy vessels were seen to be constantly hit, some being observed to haul out of the line. At least one sank. The enemy's return fire at this period was not effective, and the damage caused to our ships was insignificant."

Vice Admiral Beatty's report covering this period says the German ships he was engaging showed signs of punishment. The visibility improved at sunset at 7:17, when he re-engaged, and destroyers at the head of the German line emitted volumes of gray smoke, covering their capital ships as with a pall, under cover of which they turned away and disappeared. At 7:45 the light cruiser squadrons, sweeping westward, located two German battleships and cruisers. At 8:20 Vice Admiral Beatty heavily engaged them at 10,000 yards. The leading ship, being repeatedly hit by the *Lion*, turned away in flames with a heavy list. The *Princess Royal* set fire to a three-funneled battleship. The *New Zealand* and *Indomitable* reported that the ship they engaged left the line heeling over and afire. At 8:40 the battle cruisers felt a heavy shock as if struck by a mine or torpedo. This was assumed to be a vessel blowing up.

Vice Admiral Beatty reported that he did not consider it desirable or proper to engage the German battle fleet during the dark hours, as the strategical position made it appear certain he could locate them at daylight under most favorable circumstances.

Vice Admiral Jellicoe reports that, as anticipated, the Germans appeared to have relied much upon torpedo attacks, which were favored by low visibility and by the fact that the British were in the position of a following or chasing fleet. Of the large number of torpedoes apparently fired only one took effect, and this was upon the *Marlborough*, which was able to continue in action. The efforts of the Germans to keep out of effective gun range were aided, he says, by weather ideal for that purpose. The Germans made two separate destroyer attacks. The first battle squadron at 11,000 yards administered severe punishment to battleships, battle cruisers, and light cruisers. The fire of the *Marlborough* was particularly effective and rapid. She commenced by firing seven salvos at a ship of the Kaiser class, and then engaged a cruiser and next a battleship. The *Marlborough* was hit by a torpedo at 6:54 P.M., and took a considerable list to starboard, but reopened fire at 7:03 at a cruiser. At 7:12 she fired fourteen rapid salvos at a cruiser of the König class, hitting her frequently until she left the line.

During the action the range decreased to 5,000 yards. The first battle squadron received more of the enemy's fire than the remainder of the fleet, excepting the fifth squadron. The *Colossus* was hit, but not seriously.

The fourth squadron, led by the flagship *Iron Duke*, engaged a squadron consisting of the König and Kaiser classes with battle cruisers and light cruisers. The British fire was effective, although a mist rendered range-taking difficult. The *Iron Duke* fired on a battleship of the König class at 12,000 yards. The hitting commenced at the second salvo, and only ceased when the target turned away. Other ships of the squadron fired principally at German ships as they appeared out of the mist, and several of the German vessels were hit.

The second squadron under Admiral Jerram engaged vessels of the Kaiser or König classes and also a battle cruiser, which apparently was severely damaged. A squadron under the command of Rear Admiral Heath, with the cruiser *Duke of Edinburgh*, acted as a connecting link between the battle fleet and the battle cruiser fleet, but did not get into action.

The German vessels were entirely out of the fight at 9 o'clock, says the report. The threat of destroyer attacks during the rapidly approaching darkness made it necessary to dispose of the fleet with a view to its safety, while providing for a renewal of action at daylight. Vice Admiral Jellicoe manœuvred the fleet so as to remain between the Germans and their bases, placing flotillas of destroyers where they could protect the fleet and attack the heavy German ships.

The British heavy ships were not attacked during the night, but three British destroyer flotillas delivered a series of gallant and successful attacks, causing heavy losses. The fourth flotilla, under Captain Wintour, suffered severe losses, including the *Tipperary*. The twelfth flotilla, under Captain Stirling, attacked a squadron of six large vessels of the Kaiser class, taking it by surprise and firing many torpedoes. The second, third, and fourth ships in the line were hit, and the third blew up. The destroyers were under a heavy fire of German light cruisers. Only the *Onslaught* received material injuries. The *Castor* sank a German destroyer at point-blank range.

The thirteenth flotilla, under Captain Farie, was stationed astern of the battle fleet. A large vessel crossed in the rear of the flotilla after midnight at high speed. Turning on her searchlights, she fired heavily on the *Petard* and the *Turbu-*

lent, and the latter was disabled. The *Champion* was engaged for a few minutes with four German destroyers, while the *Moresby* fired a torpedo at a ship of the Deutschland class and felt an explosion.

Concluding his account of the battle, Vice Admiral Jellicoe wrote:

At daylight on the first of June the battle fleet, being southward of Horn Reef, turned northward in search of the enemy vessels and for the purpose of collecting our own cruisers and torpedo boat destroyers. The visibility early on the first of June was three to four miles less than on May 31; and the torpedo boat destroyers, being out of visual touch, did not rejoin the fleet until 9 A.M. The British fleet remained in the proximity of the battlefield and near the line of approach to the German ports until 11 A.M., in spite of the disadvantage of long distances from fleet bases and the danger incurred in waters adjacent to the enemy's coasts from submarines and torpedo craft.

The enemy, however, made no sign, and I was reluctantly compelled to the conclusion that the High Sea Fleet had returned into port. Subsequent events proved this assumption to have been correct. Our position must have been known to the enemy, as at 4 A.M. the fleet engaged a Zeppelin about five minutes, during which time she had ample opportunity to note and subsequently report the position and course of the British fleet.

The waters from the latitude of Horn Reef to the scene of action were thoroughly searched, and some survivors from the destroyers *Ardent, Fortune,* and *Tipperary* were picked up. The *Sparrow Hawk,* which had been in collision, was no longer seaworthy and was sunk after the crew was taken off. A large amount of wreckage was seen, but no enemy ships; and at 1:15, it being evident that the German fleet had succeeded in returning to port, our course was shaped for our bases, which were reached without further incident on Friday, June 2.

The cruiser squadron was detached to search for the *Warrior,* which had been abandoned while in tow of the *Engadine* on the way to the base, owing to bad weather setting in and the vessel becoming unseaworthy. No trace of her was discovered, and subsequent search by the light cruiser squadron having failed to locate her, it was evident she had foundered.

The fleet was fueled, replenished its ammunition, and at 9:30 P.M., on June 2, was reported ready for further action.

Two estimates of the total tonnage lost by the Germans in the Jutland battle have been made by British officials.

The more conservative one, who included in his list only vessels "seen to sink" and based his estimate on the theory that the battleships sunk were of the oldest dreadnought type, gives the German tonnage lost as 109,220, as com pared with a British loss in tonnage of 112,350. He concludes that the Germans lost two battleships of the dreadnought type of 18,900 tons each, one of the Deutschland type of 13,200 tons, the battle cruiser *Lützow* of 28,000 tons, five cruisers of the Rostock type, making a total of 24,500 tons for this type; six destroyers, aggregating 4,920 tons, and one submarine of 800 tons.

The more liberal estimate places the German loss at 117,220 tons, as follows:

One dreadnought of the Kronprinz type, 25,480 tons; one of the Heligoland type, 22,440 tons; battleship *Pommern*, 13,000 tons; battle cruiser *Lützow*, 28,000 tons; five Rostocks, aggregating 24,500 tons; destroyers aggregating 4,000 tons, and a submarine of 800 tons.

III

FROM THE BATTLE OF JUTLAND ANALYZED

BY ADMIRAL SIR CYPRIAN BRIDGE

British Naval Veteran and Expert

Interesting evidence of the decisive character of the victory is shown by the fact that during the month of June the British vessels which had been shut up in the Baltic since the beginning of the war have been returning day after day to British ports. This shows that the Germans have less control than ever of the seas.

FROM NAVAL LOSSES OF BRITAIN AND GERMANY

BY ARCHIBALD HURD

Naval Expert of The London Telegraph

It is now known that the battle cruiser *Seydlitz* was run ashore to save her from sinking; she is practically a wreck, and useless for months, if not forever, but has been got into port. It is asserted by travelers who have returned to Amsterdam that the battle cruiser *Derfflinger* sank "on being towed into Wilhelmshaven," and it is reported from Copenhagen that the *Pommern* was not the battleship which was torpedoed in the Baltic by a British submarine in July last, but a new battle cruiser which, after that battleship had disappeared, was named, for territorial reasons, after the German State, thus perpetuating its association with the navy. The story of the sinking of the dreadnought battleship *Ostfriesland* awaits confirmation.

GERMAN ADMIRALTY'S OFFICIAL REPORT OF BATTLE OF THE SKAGERRAK

The German Admiralty issued a report June 29 on the battle of the Skagerrak. In consequence of the mail blockade, the full official document has not reached this country, but the abstract printed below, which was officially furnished for transmission by wire, is comprehensive.

The High Sea Fleet, consisting of three battleship squadrons, five battle cruisers, and a large number of small cruisers, with several destroyer flotillas, was cruising in the Skagerrak on May 31 for the purpose, as on earlier occasions, of offering battle to the British fleet. The vanguard of small cruisers at 4 : 30 o'clock in the afternoon (German time) suddenly encountered ninety miles west of Hanstholm, (a cape on the northwest coast of Jutland,) a group of eight of the newest cruisers of the Calliope class and fifteen or twenty of the most modern destroyers.

While the German light forces and the first cruiser squadron under Vice Admiral Hipper were following the British, who were retiring northwestward, the German battle cruisers sighted to the westward Vice Admiral Beatty's battle cruiser squadron of six ships, including four of the Lion type and two of the Indefatigable type.   Beatty's squadron developed a battle line on a southeasterly course, and Vice Admiral Hipper formed his line ahead of the same general course and approached for a running fight.   He opened fire at 5:49 o'clock in the afternoon with heavy artillery at a range of 13,000 meters against the superior enemy.   The weather was clear and light, and the sea was light with a northwest wind.

After about a quarter of an hour a violent explosion occurred on the last cruiser of the Indefatigable type.   It was caused by a heavy shell, and destroyed the vessel.

About 6:20 o'clock in the afternoon five warships of the Queen Elizabeth type came from the west and joined the British battle cruiser line, powerfully reinforcing with their fifteen-inch guns the five British battle cruisers remaining after 6:20 o'clock.   To equalize this superiority Vice Admiral Hipper ordered the destroyers to attack the enemy. The British destroyers and small cruisers interposed, and a bitter engagement at close range ensued, in the course of which a light cruiser participated.

The Germans lost two torpedo boats, the crews of which were rescued by sister ships under a heavy fire.   Two British destroyers were sunk by artillery, and two others — the *Nestor* and *Nomad* — remained on the scene in a crippled condition.   These later were destroyed by the main fleet after German torpedo boats had rescued all the survivors.

While this engagement was in progress a mighty explosion, caused by a big shell, broke the *Queen Mary*, the third ship in line, asunder at 6:30 o'clock.

Soon thereafter the German main battleship fleet was sighted to the southward, steering north. The hostile fast squadrons thereupon turned northward, closing the first part of the fight, which lasted about an hour.

The British retired at high speed before the German fleet, which followed closely. The German battle cruisers continued the artillery combat with increasing intensity, particularly with the division of the vessels of the Queen Elizabeth type, and in this the leading German battleship division participated intermittently. The hostile ships showed a desire to run in a flat curve ahead of the point of our line and to cross it.

At 7:45 o'clock in the evening British small cruisers and destroyers launched an attack against our battle cruisers, who avoided the torpedoes by manœuvring, while the British battle cruisers retired from the engagement, in which they did not participate further, as far as can be established. Shortly thereafter a German reconnoitring group, which was parrying the destroyer attack, received an attack from the northeast. The cruiser *Wiesbaden* was soon put out of action in this attack. The German torpedo flotillas immediately attacked the heavy ships.

Appearing shadow-like from the haze bank to the northeast was made out a long line of at least twenty-five battleships, which at first sought a junction with the British battle cruisers and those of the Queen Elizabeth type on a northwesterly to westerly course and then turned on an easterly to a southeasterly course.

With the advent of the British main fleet, whose centre consisted of three squadrons of eight battleships each, with a fast division of three battle cruisers of the Invincible type on the northern end, and three of the newest vessels of the Royal Sovereign class, armed with fifteen-inch guns, at the southern end, there began about 8 o'clock in the evening the third section of the engagement, embracing the combat between the main fleets.

Vice Admiral Scheer determined to attack the British main fleet, which, he now recognized, was completely assembled and about doubly superior. The German battleship squadrons, headed by battle cruisers, steered first toward the extensive haze bank to the northeast, where the crippled cruiser *Wiesbaden* was still receiving a heavy fire. Around the *Wiesbaden* stubborn individual fights under quickly changing conditions now occurred.

The light enemy forces, supported by an armored cruiser squadron of five ships of the Minatour, Achilles, and Duke of Edinburgh classes coming from the northeast, were encountered and apparently surprised on account of the decreasing visibility by our battle cruisers and leading battleship division. The squadron came under a violent and heavy fire, by which the small cruisers *Défense* and *Black Prince* were sunk. The cruiser *Warrior* regained its own line a wreck and later sank. Another small cruiser was damaged severely.

Two destroyers already had fallen victims to the attack of German torpedo boats against the leading British battleships, and a small cruiser and two destroyers were damaged. The German battle cruisers and leading battleship division had in these engagements come under increased fire of the enemy's battleship squadron, which, shortly after eight o'clock, could be made out in the haze turning to the northeastward and finally to the east. Germans observed, amid the artillery combat and shelling of great intensity, signs of the effect of good shooting between 8 : 20 and 8 : 30 o'clock particularly. Several officers on German ships observed that a battleship of the Queen Elizabeth class blew up under conditions similar to that of the *Queen Mary*. The *Invincible* sank after being hit severely. A ship of the Iron Duke class had earlier received a torpedo hit, and one of the Queen Elizabeth class was running around in a circle, its steering apparatus apparently having been hit.

The *Lützow* was hit by at least fifteen heavy shells and was unable to maintain its place in line. Vice Admiral Hipper, therefore, transshipped to the *Moltke* on a torpedo boat and under a heavy fire. The *Derfflinger* meantime took the lead temporarily. Parts of the German torpedo flotilla attacked the enemy's main fleet and heard detonations. In the action the Germans lost a torpedo boat. An enemy destroyer was seen in a sinking condition, having been hit by a torpedo.

After the first violent onslaught into the mass of the superior enemy the opponents lost sight of each other in the smoke by powder clouds. After a short cessation in the artillery combat Vice Admiral Scheer ordered a new attack by all the available forces.

German battle cruisers, which with several light cruisers and torpedo boats again headed the line, encountered the enemy soon after 9 o'clock and renewed the heavy fire, which was answered by them from the mist, and then by the leading division of the main fleet. Armored cruisers now flung themselves in a reckless onset at extreme speed against the enemy line in order to cover the attack of torpedo boats. They approached the enemy line, although covered with shot from 6,000 meters distance. Several German torpedo flotillas dashed forward to attack, delivered torpedoes, and returned, despite the most severe counterfire, with the loss of only one boat. The bitter artillery fight was again interrupted, after this second violent onslaught, by the smoke from guns and funnels.

Several torpedo flotillas, which were ordered to attack somewhat later, found, after penetrating the smoke cloud, that the enemy fleet was no longer before them ; nor, when the fleet commander again brought the German squadrons upon the southerly and southwesterly course, where the enemy was last seen, could our opponents be found. Only once more — shortly before 10 : 30 o'clock — did the battle flare up. For a short time in the late twilight German battle cruisers sighted four enemy capital ships to seaward and opened fire immediately. As the two German battle-ship squadrons attacked, the enemy turned and vanished in the darkness. Older German light cruisers of the fourth reconnoissance group also were engaged with the older enemy armored cruisers in a short fight. This ended the day battle.

The German divisions, which, after losing sight of the enemy, began a night cruise in a southerly direction, were attacked until dawn by enemy light force in rapid succession.

The attacks were favored by the general strategic situation and the particularly dark night.

The cruiser *Frauenlob* was injured severely during the engagement of the fourth reconnoissance group with a superior cruiser force, and was lost from sight.

One armored cruiser of the Cressy class suddenly appeared close to a German battleship and was shot into fire after forty seconds, and sank in four minutes.

The *Florent*, (?) *Destroyer* 60, (the names were hard to decipher in the darkness and therefore were uncertainly established,) and four destroyers — 3, 78, 06, and 27 — were destroyed by our fire. One destroyer was cut in two by the ram of a German battleship. Seven destroyers, including the G-30, were hit and severely damaged. These, including the *Tipperary* and *Turbulent*, which, after saving survivors, were left behind in a sinking condition, drifted past our line, some of them burning at the bow or stern.

The tracks of countless torpedoes were sighted by the German ships, but only the *Pommern* (a battleship) fell an immediate victim to a torpedo. The cruiser *Rostock* was hit, but remained afloat. The cruiser *Elbing* was damaged by a German battleship during an unavoidable manœuvre. After vain endeavors to keep the ship afloat the *Elbing* was blown up, but only after her crew had em barked on torpedo boats. A post torpedo boat was struck by a mine laid by the enemy

[The report closes with a summary of the German losses as already published.]

GERMAN OFFICIAL ACCOUNT, BASED ON STATEMENTS OF BRITISH PRISONERS

A supplementary narrative of the battle of the Skagerrak, in the form of a telegram based on statements of 177 British prisoners, was transmitted officially on June 20 by the German Admiralty. The text is as follows.

The British forces participating in the battle were the reconnoitring forces under Vice Admiral Beatty and the main body of the British Navy under Admiral Jellicoe. The reconnoitring forces comprised six battle cruisers — the flagship *Lion*, the *Queen Mary*, the *Princess Royal*, and the *Tiger* as the first division, and the *Indefatigable* and the flagship *New Zealand* as the second division. The first division was complete, but *H. M. S. Australia* of the second division was absent for secret reasons. Besides these ships, there were under Beatty's command five swift battleships of the Queen Elizabeth type and a large number of small modern cruisers, the names of thirteen of which were verified by each of the prisoners. There were also two destroyer flotillas, comprising about forty destroyers, among which were the most modern types.

The main body of the fleet engaged in the battle was composed of three battleship squadrons of from six to eight dreadnoughts each, one special squadron of three of the most modern battleships of the Royal Sovereign type, one division formed by the battle cruisers *Invincible, Indomitable,* and *Inflexible,* a squadron of armored cruisers comprising six ships, and at least ten small cruisers and four flotillas of from eighty to one hundred destroyers.

When Beatty sighted the German reconnoitring forces to the east he formed a middle line with his six battle cruisers and turned southeast. The ships of the Queen Elizabeth type also turned southeast and attempted to join the battle cruisers. Between 5 and 6 o'clock in the afternoon the Germans opened fire at a distance of about eighteen kilometers, [approximately eleven miles.] Shortly after 6 o'clock a huge explosion occurred on board the *Queen Mary,* midships, on the port side. Two other explosions followed, and the forward part of the ship sank rapidly. At the fourth and most severe explosion the entire ship sank. This was the work of from only five to ten minutes.

Scarcely had the *Indefatigable* arrived on the scene of the accident when she was also shaken by an explosion. The ship capsized and sank so quickly that of the fourteen men who were in the fighting top only two were rescued. These two are apparently the only survivors of the *Indefatigable's* crew of about 1,000. After the sinking of these two ships Admiral Beatty signaled to the Thirteenth British flotilla to attack the German battle cruisers. The order was understood only by the nearest destroyers and was regarded by several of the prisoners as a desperate resort. In this attack the most modern British destroyers, the *Nestor* and the *Nomad*, were sunk. Their crews were later rescued from rafts and lifeboats by German torpedo boats.

In the meanwhile, the ships of the Queen Elizabeth type approached. The distance between the British ships and the German cruisers had diminished to ten kilometers, [approximately six miles.] The British battle cruisers steamed northward at high speed and were soon out of range. The Queen Elizabeth type ships continued battle, turning northward in order to "cut off the enemy," as ordered by Beatty. Soon one of the Queen Elizabeth type ships left the British line with a heavy list. The prisoners state expressly that it was the *Warspite*. The wireless sent by the *Turbulent* that the *Warspite* was sunk was intercepted by about eight British destroyers.

The rescued prisoners disagree as to the time of Admiral Jellicoe's arrival with the main body of the fleet. Prisoners from Jellicoe's fleet state that they were steaming southward in several columns when they received Beatty's first wireless transmitted by the small cruiser *Galatea*. Thereupon Jellicoe gave the order to continue southward at top speed. The prisoners saw only the flames from Beatty's artillery when Jellicoe turned north and formed a line toward the northwest and west. The battle cruisers of the main body, the *Invincible*, the *Indomitable*, and the *Inflexible*, were ahead with the armored cruisers. At this time the British battleship *Marlborough* was hit by a torpedo which is said to have been fired by a submarine. If so, the submarine must have been British, since there were no German submarines in the battle.

A British armored cruiser attacked a large isolated German ship which steered slowly southward. At the same time the British main body opened fire. When the armored cruisers returned to the main body, the *Défense* was missing. By this time the *Warrior* had large holes midships just above the waterline. Shortly after the British main body entered the battle a German shot set fire to the *Invincible*, an explosion followed, and the ship sank. The Germans shot at long range and annihilated the destroyer *Acasta*, standing near the head of the line. The reports of other prisoners about the movements of the British main body until dark conflict. The point on which they agree is that at dark the British Navy steered northward in columns. The destroyer *Tipperary* asked permission to turn southward alone to attack the Germans. Permission was granted, but she encountered the German flotilla and was defeated and sunk. The survivors were rescued by the Germans. Beatty's thirteenth flotilla had failed to join the battle cruisers and turned southward at dark. It encountered several large ships which it mistook for British. The Germans opened fire and destroyed the *Turbulent*. All the officers and a part of the crew were lost. The survivors were rescued by German torpedo boats.

Almost all the British prisoners expressed dissatisfaction at the fact that the British made no effort to rescue them although almost all the best British ships participated in the battle. The survivors of the *Queen Mary* and of the *Indefatigable* had been in the water for almost four hours before they were rescued by the Germans. They had already given up all hope, for nothing had been seen of the British ships for hours.

VIVID STORY OF AN EYEWITNESS

BY A BRITISH NAVAL OFFICER

We, the fast battleships, were, as has already been stated, astern of the battle cruisers and had opened fire between ten and twenty minutes of their first shots. Now we all of us got going hard, the battle cruisers and ourselves against the German battle cruisers and the German High Sea Fleet, which had now put in an appearance. So, in spite of the stories of the Germans, they were most undoubtedly considerably superior to the British force present, and remained so until the arrival of the Grand Fleet some hours later, and yet, in spite of this overwhelming superiority, they only succeeded at this stage of the battle in sinking two of our big ships at a huge cost to themselves, because there can be little doubt that up to then they got as good as they gave and a bit more.

The firing now became very general indeed, and the continued roar and shriek of our own guns, coupled with one's work, left little opportunity to think about outside matters. The only predominant thing I, in common with others, remember was the rapid bang, bang, bang of our smaller secondary armament, as we thought; but during a lull we discovered that this was the German shell bursting on the water all round the ship with so loud an explosion that it could be heard right deep down in the heart of the ship. We were at this time receiving a very heavy fire indeed, our own battle cruisers having become disengaged for twenty minutes to half an hour, so that the fire of the whole German fleet was concentrated on us. However, we stuck it, and gave back a good deal, I fancy.

Especially unpleasant, though, was a period of half an hour during which we were unable to see the enemy, while they could see us most clearly. Thus we were unable to fire a shot and had to rest content with steaming through a tornado of shell fire without loosing off a gun, which was somewhat trying. However, about 6:30 the sun silhouetted up the Germans and completely turned the tables as far as light was concerned, and for a period of some twenty minutes we gave them a most terrific dressing down, which we trust they will remember. Then down came the mist again, and we had to close them right down to four miles in the attempt to see the enemy, and four miles is, of course, about as near as one likes to get to the foe, as torpedoes then come into play.

It was at this stage that, owing to some temporary defect, the *Warspite's* helm jammed, and she went straight at the enemy into a hell of fire. She looked a most wonderful sight, every gun firing for all it was worth in reply. Luckily she got under control quickly and returned to the line, and it was this incident that gave rise to the German legend that she had been sunk.

The action continued with unabated fury until the arrival of the Grand Fleet somewhere about 7. It was just before this that the *Invincible* had met her fate, as also the *Défense* and *Black Prince* — the two latter, apparently, in a gallant attempt to save the *Warrior*, which was successful in so far that the crew of the *Warrior* were saved, although the ship had eventually to be abandoned.

The arrival of the Grand Fleet relieved the tension upon us somewhat, and the battle cruiser force went on ahead, while we dropped back, content to let the Grand Fleet finish off the work, but the Germans were not "having any," as they say in America, and almost immediately turned to run, pursued by our fleet. We were, of course, considerably superior now, but it was little use. For about half an hour the Grand Fleet and ourselves were firing, during which time it is pretty certain that we inflicted very material damage on the enemy, but after that the failing light and the very evident desire of the enemy to get away from such unpleasant company rendered it impossible to turn an undoubted success into a certain and decisive victory, for by that the navy means annihilation.

And at last, about 9, we discontinued the action, but continued to follow them. Right through the darkness there were constant destroyer attacks, and the sky was lighted up the whole night by the flashes of the guns and by fires caused among the enemy by our shells. It was in fact a very awe-inspiring sight.

As is known, the enemy succeeded in attacking the *Marlborough*, but fruitlessly, as she returned to port, and is no doubt once more at sea.

We continued to cruise about all night and the next day, offering battle to the enemy, but they were scuttling back to security, and we saw nothing of them, and so finally returned home.

IV

TWO EXPLANATIONS OF THE BATTLE OF JUTLAND

A Berlin dispatch in the Hamburger Fremdenblatt, evidently with official sanction, offers the following diagrammatic explanation of the great naval engagement of May 31 in the North Sea. The numbers in the text refer to the arrows representing the tactical moves of the opposing fleets.

I. — THE GERMAN VIEW

In its official report of June 5 the German Admiralty Staff has described in brief outlines the victorious course of the naval battle at the Skagerrak. This account is confirmed in all details upon the basis of the more precise information which has since been received. The accompanying sketches illustrate in four periods the chief individual phases of the battle, while the accompanying map shows plainly the strategic importance of the German victory for the war position in the North Sea.

On May 31, at 4:35 P.M., our cruisers (I, 1), proceeding ahead of the High Seas Fleet, sighted, seventy nautical miles

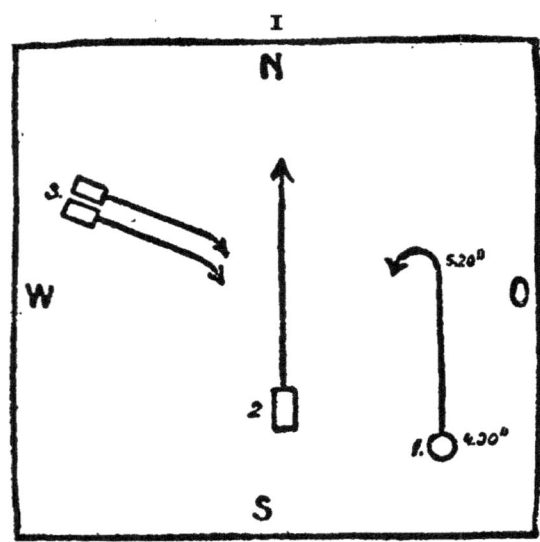

to southwest of the Skagerrak, four small English cruisers of the Calliope class (2), which ran at highest speed northward, pursued by our cruisers.

At 5:30 our pursuing cruisers sight to the westward two further enemy columns (3), consisting of six battle cruisers, a considerable number of small cruisers and destroyers. Our cruisers take a course toward the new opponent — this becoming a course toward the south.

Our cruisers (II, 1) (compare also sketch 1) have advanced to thirteen · kilometers from the English battle cruisers and destroyers, which meanwhile have moved southward (2), and open fire on southerly to southeasterly courses. In the course of this fight two English battle cruisers and a de-

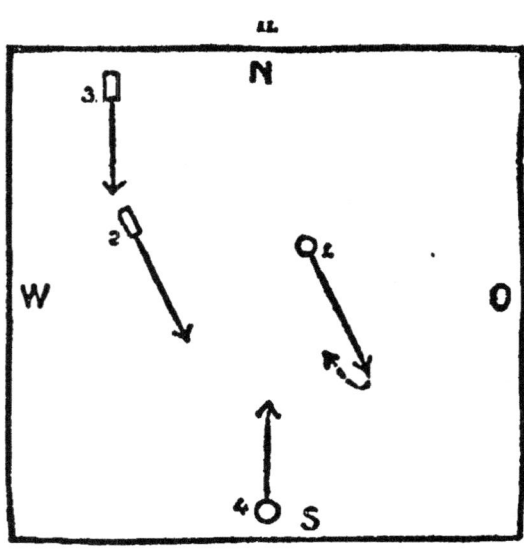

stroyer were sunk. After half an hour's fighting powerful new enemy forces come in sight from the north of the enemy; they prove to be five ships of the Queen Elizabeth class (3). At the same time the main German force (4) approaches from the south and intervenes in the fight. Our cruisers place themselves ahead of their own main force.

The five big ships of the Queen Elizabeth class (compare sketch II) have attached themselves to the enemy cruisers. The whole combined German fleet (III, 1) is now steering north-ward, and in face of its attack the enemy (2) immediately turns away to the north, and attempts at the highest speed to escape from our ex-tremely effective fire, and at the same time, with an easterly course, and employing its speed, which is

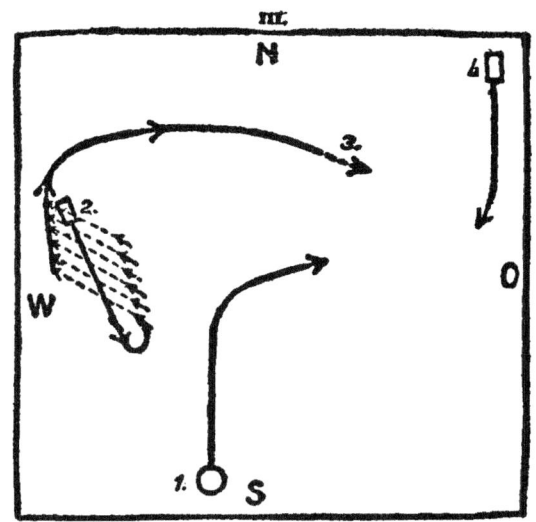

superior to that of our fleet as a whole, to pass (3) the head of our line, while the German battleship squadron in the rear of the line cannot yet get into action with the enemy. Our fleet, the cruisers still leading, follows the movement of the enemy at highest speed. An English cruiser of the Achilles class and two destroyers are sunk. This period of the battle lasts some two and a half hours.

Meanwhile, there approaches from the north, presumably coming from Norwegian waters, the English main force, consisting of more than twenty battleships (4).

The climax of the battle is reached. Toward 10 o'clock

all the German ships (IV, 1) are together facing the whole English fleet. At a distance of some fifteen nautical miles the battle now pursues its course eastward. While the English cruiser fleet (2) continues its attempts to catch up the head of our line, Admiral Jellicoe is striving to put himself with his large battleships (3) like the cross of a T in front of the head of our line. As the head of our line thus comes for a time under fire from both sides, Admiral Scheer throws the

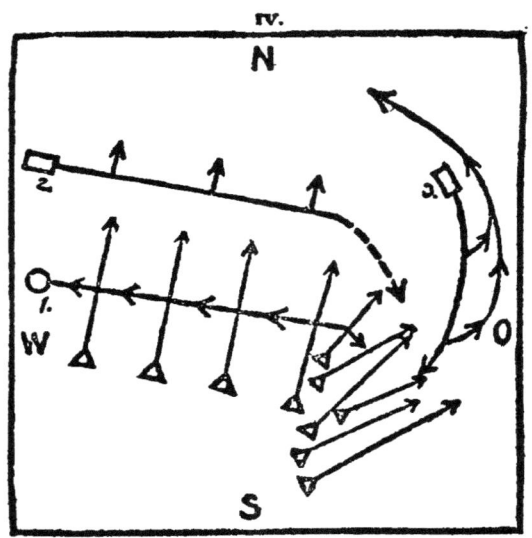

German line round on to a westerly course, and at the same time our torpedo boat flotillas (marked with triangles in the sketch) are ordered to attack the enemy, and they do so three times in succession with splendid vigor and visible success. A number of the large English battleships suffer severe damage, and one sinks before our eyes. By these attacks the English main fleet is driven away to the east, whence it will afterward have taken a northwesterly course homeward. The German fleet ceases its violent cannonade at 11 : 30, as the English had already stopped firing, and after nightfall there was nothing but the flash of their salvos to give us a target. As the enemy cannot be found again the main battle is broken off.

During the night numerous cruiser fights and torpedo boat attacks develop against individual enemy ships, which either had gone astray or had been ordered to worry us and to cover the retreat of the English. In these actions an enemy battle cruiser, a cruiser of the Achilles or Shannon class, several small enemy cruisers, and at least ten destroyers are sunk — six of them by the *Westfalen* alone.

A squadron of English battleships came up from the south, but not until June 1, after the battle was over, and it turned away without coming into action or even coming in sight of the main German force. It was observed by one of our Zeppelins, which, as is well known, owing to the foggy weather on the previous day, could not make reconnoissances until June 1.

II. — THE BRITISH VIEW

A British naval authority, writing with official sanction for The London Daily News, interprets Admiral Jellicoe's report in a very different diagram and commentary:

Seen in its broadest aspect, the battle of Jutland stands out as a case of a tactical division of the fleet, which had the effect of bringing an unwilling enemy to battle. Such a method of forcing an action is drastic and necessarily attended with risk, but for great ends great risks must be taken.

In the present case there was only an appearance of division. The battle fleet was to the north and the battle cruiser fleet to the south, but they formed in fact one fleet under a single command acting in combination. They were actually carrying out, as they had been in the habit of doing periodically, a combined sweep of the North Sea; and Admiral Beatty's fleet was in effect the observation or advanced squadron. The measure of the risk, should he have the fortune to find the enemy at sea, was the length of the period which must necessarily elapse before the Commander in Chief would be able to join the battle. It was a risk that would be measured mainly by the skill with which Admiral Beatty could entice the enemy northward, without being overwhelmed by superior force.

In the light of this outstanding feature the action will be judged, and the handling of the battle cruiser fleet and the splendid group of four battleships that was attached to it appraised.

When Admiral Beatty got contact with the German battle cruisers they were proceeding northward; and, being inferior to his force, they turned to the southward. The inference was they were either trying to escape or bent on leading him

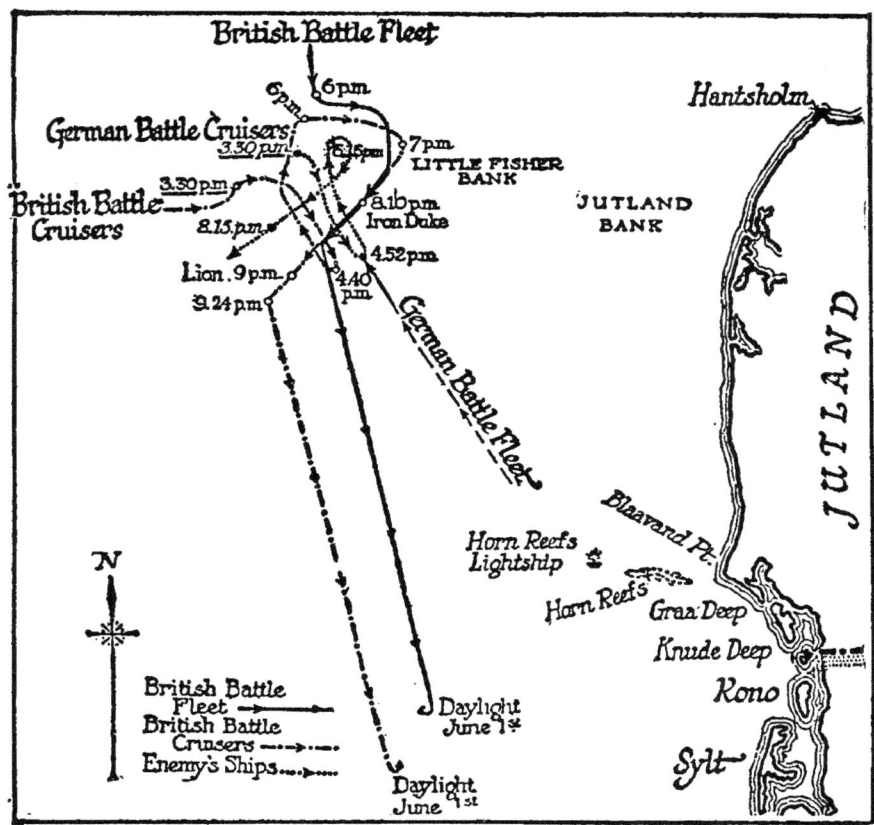

This chart must be taken as diagrammatic only, and as a general indication of the course of the battle from the time when the opposing battle cruisers sighted each other (3:30) until, owing to the growing darkness and the dispersal of the enemy's forces, it became impossible to continue the action as an organized whole. Sir David Beatty's successful manœuvre in doubling the head of the enemy's line, and, reinforced by the battle fleet, establishing himself between the Germans and the Danish coast, is graphically shown. The enemy was compelled not only to make a complete turn, but to cross his original course almost at right angles after circling, and when the battle proper came to an end soon after 8:30 the bulk of the German fleet was heading southwest into the open sea with the British fleet between it and its bases.

It is amusing to recall that the most "authentic" German plan of this stage of the battle shows one arrow stretching from Denmark toward the Orkneys to indicate the line of the British retreat, and another from Heligoland, pointing north, to represent the Germans in chase. For comparative purposes it may be pointed out that the distance from Heligoland to Blaavand Point is ninety-three miles. The official tracks of the British fleet end at daylight on June 1, but it will be observed from Sir John Jellicoe's report that it was not until 1:15 P.M. that "course was shaped for our bases."

into danger. . . . Admiral Beatty engaged and continued to engage as closely as he could till he found the enemy's battle fleet coming north. Then he turned, but he did not break off the action. The enemy was in overwhelming force, but it was his duty to cling to them as long as his teeth would hold. . He did not flinch, but continued the fight to the northward, and signaled the four Queen Elizabeths to turn sixteen points.

Now was the hour of greatest risk, but he was well disposed for concentrating on the van of the enemy's line, and the Commander in Chief was hurrying down at full speed. For an hour and a half the unequal battle raged as Admiral Beatty and Admiral Evan-Thomas led the enemy on, before Admiral Hood could appear with his battle cruiser squadron. The action was then at its hottest, but Admiral Hood, without a moment's hesitation, and in a manner that excited the high admiration of all who were privileged to witness it, placed his ships in line ahead of Admiral Beatty's squadron. . . .

With his fine manœuvre the risk was in a measure reduced, but there still remained the more delicate work of the Grand Fleet effecting its junction and entering the ill-defined action. With the exact position of the enemy's fleet shrouded in smoke and in the gathering mist, the danger of interference was very great, and before the Commander in Chief lay a task as difficult as any Admiral could be called upon to perform. To the last moment he kept his fleet in steaming order, so as to preserve up till the end the utmost freedom of deployment, but by what precise manœuvres the deployment was carried out must for obvious reasons be left in a mist as deep as that which was hiding all that was most important for him to know. Suffice it to say that the junction was effected with consummate judgment and dexterity. So nicely was it timed that the deployment was barely completed when, at 6:15 P.M., the first battle squadron came into action with the enemy, who had by that time turned to the eastward and was already attempting to avoid action.

Thus the fine combination had succeeded, and the unwilling enemy had been brought to action against the concentrated British fleet. They had fallen into the midst of the net which had been drawn about them, but in the plan of the sweep there was inherent the inevitable limitation that the time left for completing the business could but barely suffice. There were hardly three hours of daylight left, and, as darkness approached, the action must be broken off unless a needless chance were to be given to the enemy for redressing his battle inferiority. Still our battle fleet was between the enemy and his base, and there would have been little hope of his escaping a decisive defeat but for the mist that robbed those who had prepared for the chance, and those who had seized it with so much skill and boldness, of the harvest they deserved.

GROUP TWO

(TO ACCOMPANY CHAPTER II)

A DEFENCE OF PENNY DREADFULS [1]

By G. K. CHESTERTON

ONE of the strangest examples of the degree to which ordinary life is undervalued is the example of popular literature, the vast mass of which we contentedly describe as vulgar. The boy's novelette may be ignorant in a literary

[1] Reprinted by special permission of the author.

sense, which is only like saying that a modern novel is ignorant in the chemical sense, or the economic sense, or the astronomical sense; but it is not vulgar intrinsically — it is the actual centre of a million flaming imaginations.

In former centuries the educated class ignored the ruck of vulgar literature. They ignored, and therefore did not, properly speaking, despise it. Simple ignorance and indifference does not inflate the character with pride. A man does not walk down the street giving a haughty twirl to his moustaches at the thought of his superiority to some variety of deep-sea fishes. The old scholars left the whole underworld of popular compositions in a similar darkness.

To-day, however, we have reversed this principle. We do despise vulgar compositions, and we do not ignore them. We are in some danger of becoming petty in our study of pettiness; there is a terrible Circean law in the background that if the soul stoops too ostentatiously to examine anything it never gets up again. There is no class of vulgar publications about which there is, to my mind, more utterly ridiculous exaggeration and misconception than the current boys' literature of the lowest stratum. This class of composition has presumably always existed, and must exist. It has no more claim to be good literature than the daily conversation of its readers to be fine oratory, or the lodging-houses and tenements they inhabit to be sublime architecture. But people must have conversation, they must have houses, and they must have stories. The simple need for some kind of ideal world in which fictitious persons play an unhampered part is infinitely deeper and older than the rules of good art, and much more important. Every one of us in childhood has constructed such an invisible *dramatis personæ*, but it never occurred to our nurses to correct the composition by careful comparison with Balzac. In the East the professional story-teller goes from village to village with a small carpet; and I wish sincerely that any one had the moral courage to spread that carpet and sit on it in Ludgate Circus. But it is not probable that all the tales of the carpet-bearer are little gems of original artistic workmanship. Literature and fiction are two entirely different things. Literature is a luxury; fiction is a necessity. A work of art can hardly be too short, for its climax is its merit. A story can never be too long, for its conclusion is merely to be deplored, like the last halfpenny or the last pipelight. And so, while the increase of the artistic conscience tends in more ambitious works to brevity and impressionism, voluminous industry still marks the producer of the true romantic trash. There was no end to the ballads of Robin Hood; there is no end to the volumes about Dick Deadshot and the Avenging Nine. These two heroes are deliberately conceived as immortal.

But instead of basing all discussion of the problem upon the common-sense recognition of this fact — that the youth of the lower orders always has had and always must have formless and endless romantic reading of some kind, and then going on to make provision for its wholesomeness — we begin, generally speaking, by fantastic abuse of this reading as a whole and indignant surprise that the errand-boys under discussion do not read "The Egoist" and "The Master Builder." It is the custom, particularly among magistrates, to attribute half the crimes of the Metropolis to cheap novelettes. If some grimy urchin runs away with an apple, the magistrate shrewdly points out that the child's knowledge that apples appease hunger is traceable to some curious literary researches. The boys themselves, when penitent, frequently accuse the novelettes with great bitterness, which is only to be expected from young people possessed of no little native humour. If I had forged a will, and could obtain sympathy by tracing the incident to the influence of Mr. George Moore's novels, I should find the greatest entertainment in the diversion. At any rate, it is firmly fixed in the minds of most people that gutter-boys, unlike everybody else in the community, find their principal motives for conduct in printed books.

Now it is quite clear that this objection, the objection brought by magistrates, has nothing to do with literary merit. Bad story writing is not a crime. Mr. Hall Caine walks the streets openly, and cannot be put in prison for an anticlimax. The objection rests upon the theory that the tone of the mass of boys' novelettes is criminal and degraded, appealing to low cupidity and low cruelty. This is the magisterial theory, and this is rubbish.

So far as I have seen them, in connection with the dirtiest book-stalls in the poorest districts, the facts are simply these : The whole bewildering mass of vulgar juvenile literature is concerned with adventures, rambling, disconnected, and endless. It does not express any passion of any sort, for there is no human character of any sort. It runs eternally in certain grooves of local and historical type : the medieval knight, the eighteenth-century duellist, and the modern cowboy recur with the same stiff simplicity as the conventional human figures in an Oriental pattern. I can quite as easily imagine a human being kindling wild appetites by the contemplation of his Turkey carpet as by such dehumanised and naked narrative as this.

Among these stories there are a certain number which deal sympathetically with the adventures of robbers, outlaws, and pirates, which present in a dignified and romantic light thieves and murderers like Dick Turpin and Claude Duval. That is to say, they do precisely the same thing as Scott's "Ivanhoe," Scott's "Rob Roy," Scott's "Lady of the Lake," Byron's "Corsair," Wordsworth's "Rob Roy's Grave," Stevenson's "Macaire," Mr. Max Pemberton's "Iron Pirate," and a thousand more works distributed systematically as prizes and Christmas presents. Nobody imagines that an admiration of Locksley in "Ivanhoe," will lead a boy to shoot Japanese arrows at the deer in Richmond Park; no one thinks that the incautious opening of Wordsworth at the poem on Rob Roy will set him up for life as a blackmailer. In the case of our own class, we recognise that this wild life is contemplated with pleasure by the young, not because it is like their own life, but because it is different from it. It might at least cross our minds that, for whatever other reason the errand-boy reads "The Red Revenge," it really is not because he is dripping with the gore of his own friends and relatives.

In this matter, as in all such matters, we lose our bearings entirely by speaking of the "lower classes" when we mean humanity minus ourselves. This trivial romantic literature is not especially plebeian: it is simply human. The philanthropist can never forget classes and callings. He says, with a modest swagger, "I have invited twenty-five factory hands to tea." If he said, "I have invited twenty-five chartered accountants to tea," every one would see the humor of so simple a classification. But this is what we have done with this lumberland of foolish writing: we have probed, as if it were some monstrous new disease, what is, in fact, nothing but the foolish and valiant heart of man. Ordinary men will always be sentimentalists: for a sentimentalist is simply a man who has feelings and does not trouble to invent a new way of expressing them. These common and current publications have nothing essentially evil about them. They express the sanguine and heroic truisms on which civilisation is built; for it is clear that unless civilisation is built on truisms, it is not built at all. Clearly, there could be no safety for a society in which the remark by the Chief Justice that murder was wrong was regarded as an original and dazzling epigram.

If the authors and publishers of "Dick Deadshot," and such remarkable works, were suddenly to make a raid upon the educated class, were to take down the names of every man, however distinguished, who was caught at a University Extension Lecture, were to confiscate all our novels and warn us all to correct our lives, we should be seriously annoyed. Yet they have far more right to do so than we; for they, with all their idiotcy, are normal and we are abnormal. It is the modern literature of the educated, not of the uneducated, which is avowedly and aggressively criminal. Books recommending profligacy and pessimism, at which the high-souled errand-boy would shudder, lie upon all our drawing-room tables. If the dirtiest old owner of the dirtiest old bookstall in Whitechapel dared to display works really recommending polygamy or suicide, his stock would be seized by the police. These things are our luxuries. And with a hypocrisy so ludicrous as to be almost unparalleled in history, we rate the gutter-boys for their immorality at the very time that we are discussing (with equivocal German professors) whether morality is valid at all. At the very instant that we curse the Penny Dreadful for encouraging thefts upon property, we canvass the proposition that all property is theft. At the very instant we accuse it (quite unjustly) of lubricity and indecency, we are cheerfully reading philosophies which glory in lubricity and indecency. At the very instant that we charge it with encouraging the young to destroy life, we are placidly discussing whether life is worth preserving.

But it is we who are the morbid exceptions; it is we who are the criminal class. This should be our great comfort. The vast mass of humanity, with their vast mass of idle books and idle words, have never doubted and never will doubt that courage is splendid, that fidelity is noble, that distressed ladies should be rescued, and vanquished enemies spared. There are a large number of cultivated persons who doubt these maxims of daily life, just as there are a large number of persons who believe they are the Prince of Wales; and I am told that both classes of people are entertaining conversationalists. But the average man or boy writes daily in these great gaudy diaries of his soul, which we call Penny Dreadfuls, a plainer and better gospel than any of those iridescent ethical paradoxes that the fashionable change as often as their bonnets. It may be a very limited aim in morality to shoot a "many-faced and fickle traitor," but at least it is a better aim than to be a many-faced and fickle traitor, which is a simple summary of a good many modern systems from Mr. d'Annunzio's downwards. So long as the coarse and thin texture of mere current popular romance is not touched by a paltry culture it will never be vitally immoral. It is always on the side of life. The poor — the slaves who really stoop under the burden of life — have often been mad, scatter-brained, and cruel, but never hopeless. That is a class privilege, like cigars. Their drivelling literature will always be a "blood and thunder" literature, as simple as the thunder of heaven and the blood of men.

THE CASE OF THE FORGOTTEN MAN [1]

By William Graham Sumner

There is a beautiful notion afloat in our literature and in the minds of our people that men are born to certain "natural rights." If that were true, there would be something on earth which was got for nothing, and this world would not be the place it is at all. The fact is, that there is

---

[1] Reprinted by special permission of the Yale University Press.

M

no right whatever inherited by man which has not an equivalent and corresponding duty by the side of it.   The rights,
advantages, capital, knowledge, and all other goods which
we inherit from past generations have been won by the struggles and sufferings of past generations; and the fact that the
race lives, though men die, and that the race can by heredity
accumulate within some cycle its victories over nature, is
one of the facts which make civilization possible.   The
struggles of the race as a whole produce the possessions of
the race as a whole.   Something for nothing is not to be
found on earth.

If there were such things as natural rights, the question
would arise, Against whom are they good?   Who has the
corresponding obligation to satisfy these rights?   There
can be no rights against nature, except to get out of her
whatever we can, which is only the fact of the struggle for
existence stated over again.   The common assertion is that
the rights are good against society; that is, that society is
bound to obtain and secure them for the persons interested.
Society, however, is only the persons interested plus some
other persons; and as the persons interested have by the
hypothesis failed to win the rights, we come to this, that
natural rights are the claims which certain persons have
by prerogative against some other persons.   Such is the
actual interpretation in practice of natural rights — claims
which some people have by prerogative on other people.

This theory is a very far-reaching one, and of course it is
adequate to furnish a foundation for a whole social philos
ophy.   In its widest extension it comes to mean that if
any man finds himself uncomfortable in this world it must
be somebody else's fault, and that somebody is bound to come
and make him comfortable.   Now the people who are most
uncomfortable in this world — for if we should tell all our
troubles it would not be found to be a very comfortable world

for anybody — are those who have neglected their duties, and consequently have failed to get their rights. The people who can be called upon to serve the uncomfortable must be those who have done their duty, as the world goes, tolerably well. Consequently the doctrine which we are discussing turns out to be in practice only a scheme for making injustice prevail in human society by reversing the distribution of rewards and punishments between those who have done their duty and those who have not.

We are constantly preached at by our public teachers as if respectable people were to blame because some people are not respectable — as if the man who has done his duty in his own sphere was responsible in some way for another man who has not done his duty in his sphere. There are relations of employer and employee which need to be regulated by compromise and treaty. There are sanitary precautions which need to be taken in factories and houses. There are precautions against fire which are necessary. There is care needed that children be not employed too young, and that they have an education. There is care needed that banks, insurance companies, and railroads be well managed, and that officers do not abuse their trusts. There is a duty in each case on the interested parties to defend their own interest. The penalty of neglect is suffering. The system of providing for these things by boards and inspectors throws the cost of it, not on the interested parties, but on the tax-payers. Some of them, no doubt, are the interested parties, and they may consider that they are exercising the proper care by paying taxes to support an inspector. If so, they only get their fair deserts when the railroad inspector finds out that a bridge is not safe after it is broken down, or when the bank examiner comes in to find out why a bank failed after the cashier has stolen all the funds. The real victim is the Forgotten Man again —

the man who has watched his own investments, made his own machinery safe, attended to his own plumbing, and educated his own children, and who, just when he wants to enjoy the fruits of his care, is told that it is his duty to go and take care of some of his negligent neighbors, or, if he does not go, to pay an inspector to go.   No doubt it is often his interest to go or to send, rather than to have the matter neglected, on account of his own connection with the thing neglected and his own secondary peril; but the point now is, that if preaching and philosophizing can do any good in the premises, it is all wrong to preach to the Forgotten Man that it is his duty to go and remedy other people's neglect. It is not his duty.   It is a harsh and unjust burden which is laid upon him, and it is only the more unjust because no one thinks of him when laying the burden so that it falls on . him.   The exhortations ought to be expended on the negligent — that they take care of themselves.

It is an especially vicious extension of the false doctrine above mentioned that criminals have some sort of a right against or claim on society.   Many reformatory plans are based on a doctrine of this kind when they are urged upon the public conscience.   A criminal is a man who, instead of working with and for the society, has turned against it and become destructive and injurious.   His punishment means that society rules him out of its membership and separates him from its association, by execution or imprisonment, according to the gravity of his offense.   He has no claims against society at all.   What shall be done with him is a question of expediency to be settled in view of the interests of society — that is, of the non-criminals.   The French writers of the school of '48 used to represent the badness of the bad men as the fault of "society."   As the object of this statement was to show that the badness of the bad men was not the fault of the bad men, and as society contains only good men and bad men, it followed that the badness of the bad men was the fault of the good men. On that theory of course the good men owed a great deal to the bad men who were in prison and at the galleys on their account. If we do not admit that theory, it behooves us to remember that any claim which we allow to the criminal against the "state" is only so much burden laid upon those who have never cost the State anything for discipline or correction. The punishments of society are just, like those of God and nature — they are warnings to the wrong-doer to reform himself.

When public offices are to be filled numerous candidates at once appear. Some are urged on the ground that they are poor, or cannot earn a living, or want support while getting an education, or have female relatives dependent on them, or are in poor health, or belong in a particular district, or are related to certain persons, or have done meritorious service in some other line of work than that which they apply to do. The abuses of the public service are to be condemned on account of the harm to the public interest, but there is an incidental injustice of the same general character with that which we are discussing. If an office is granted by favoritism or for any personal reason to A, it cannot be given to B. If an office is filled by a person who is unfit for it, he always keeps out somebody somewhere who is fit for it; that is, the social injustice has a victim in an unknown person — the Forgotten Man — and he is some person who has no political influence, and who has known no way in which to secure the chances of life except to deserve them. He is passed by for the noisy, pushing, importunate, and incompetent.

I have said elsewhere, disparagingly, something about the popular rage against combined capital, corporations, corners, selling futures, etc. The popular rage is not without reason, but it is sadly misdirected, and the real things which deserve attack are thriving all the time. The greatest social evil with which we have to contend is jobbery. Whatever there is in legislative charters, watering stocks, and so on which is objectionable comes under the head of jobbery. Jobbery is any scheme which aims to gain, not by the legitimate fruits of industry and enterprise, but by extorting from somebody a part of his product under guise of some pretended industrial undertaking. Of course it is only a modification when the undertaking in question has some legitimate character, but the occasion is used to graft upon it devices for obtaining what has not been earned. Jobbery is the vice of plutocracy, and it is the especial form under which plutocracy corrupts a democratic and republican form of government. The United States is deeply afflicted with it, and the problem of civil liberty here is to conquer it. It affects everything which we really need to have done to such an extent that we have to do without public objects which we need through fear of jobbery. Our public buildings are jobs — not always, but often. They are not needed, or are costly beyond all necessity or even decent luxury. Internal improvements are jobs. They are not made because they are needed to meet needs which have been experienced. They are made to serve private ends, often incidentally the political interests of the persons who vote the appropriations. Pensions have become jobs. In England pensions used to be given to aristocrats, because aristocrats had political influence, in order to corrupt them. Here pensions are given to the great democratic mass, because they have political power, to corrupt them. Instead of going out where there is plenty of land and making a farm there, some people go down under the Mississippi River to make a farm, and then they want to tax all the people in the United States to make dikes to keep the river off their farms. The California gold-miners have washed out gold and have washed the dirt down into the rivers and on the farms below. They want the Federal Government to clean out the rivers now and restore the farms. The silver-miners found their product declining in value and they got the Federal Government to go into the market and buy what the public did not want, in order to sustain, as they hoped, the price of silver. The Federal Government is called upon to buy or hire unsalable ships, to build canals which will not pay, to furnish capital for all sorts of experiments, and to provide capital for enterprises of which private individuals will win the profits. All this is called "developing our resources," but it is, in truth, the great plan of all living on each other.

The greatest job of all is a protective tariff. It includes the biggest log-rolling and the widest corruption of economic and political ideas. It was said that there would be a rebellion if the taxes were not taken off whisky and tobacco, which taxes were paid into the public Treasury. Just then the importations of Sumatra tobacco became important enough to affect the market. The Connecticut tobacco-growers at once called for an import duty on tobacco which would keep up the price of their product. So it appears that if the tax on tobacco is paid to the Federal Treasury there will be a rebellion, but if it is paid to the Connecticut tobacco-raisers there will be no rebellion at all. The farmers have long paid tribute to the manufacturers; now the manufacturing and other laborers are to pay tribute to the farmers. The system is made more comprehensive and complete and we are all living on each other more than ever.

Now the plan of plundering each other produces nothing. It only wastes. All the material over which the protected interests wrangle and grab must be got from somebody outside of their circle. The talk is all about the American laborer and American industry, but in every case in which there is not an actual production of wealth by industry there are two laborers and two industries to be considered — the one who gets and the one who gives. Every protected industry has to plead, as the major premise of its argument, that any industry which does not pay *ought* to be carried on at the expense of the consumers of the product, and as its minor premise, that the industry in question does not pay; that is, that it cannot reproduce a capital equal in value to that which it consumes plus the current rate of profit. Hence every such industry must be a parasite on some other industry. What is the other industry? Who is the other man? This, the real question, is always overlooked.

In all jobbery the case is the same. There is a victim somewhere who is paying for it all. The doors of waste and extravagance stand open, and there seems to be a general agreement to squander and spend. It all belongs to somebody. There is somebody who had to contribute it and who will have to find more. Nothing is ever said about him. Attention is all absorbed by the clamorous interests, the importunate petitioners, the plausible schemers, the pitiless bores. Now, who is the victim? He is the Forgotten Man. If we go to find him, we shall find him hard at work tilling the soil to get out of it the fund for all the jobbery, the object of all the plunder, the cost of all the economic quackery, and the pay of all the politicians and statesmen who have sacrificed his interests to his enemies. We shall find him an honest, sober, industrious citizen, unknown outside his little circle, paying his debts and his taxes, supporting the church and the school, reading his party newspaper, and cheering for his pet politician.

We must not overlook the fact that the Forgotten Man, is not infrequently a woman. I have before me a newspaper which contains five letters from corset-stitchers who complain that they cannot earn more than seventy-five cents a day with a machine and that they have to provide the thread. The tax on the grade of thread used by them is prohibitory as to all importation, and it is the corset-stitchers who have to pay day by day out of their time and labor the total enhancement of price due to the tax. Women who earn their own living probably earn on an average seventy-five cents per day of ten hours. Twenty-four minutes' work ought to buy a spool of thread at the retail price, if the American work-woman were allowed to exchange her labor for thread on the best terms that the art and commerce of to-day would allow; but after she has done twenty-four minutes' work for the thread she is forced by the laws of her country to go back and work sixteen minutes longer to pay the tax — that is, to support the thread-mill. The thread-mill, therefore, is not an institution for getting thread for the American people, but for making thread harder to get than it would be if there were no such institution.

In justification, now, of an arrangement so monstrously unjust and out of place in a free country, it is said that the employes in the thread-mill get high wages and that, but for the tax, American laborers must come down to the low wages of foreign thread-makers. It is not true that American thread-makers get any more than the market rate of wages, and they would not get less if the tax were entirely removed, because the market rate of wages in the United States would be controlled then, as it is now, by the supply and demand of laborers under the natural advantages and opportunities of industry in this country. It makes a great impression on the imagination, however, to go to a manufacturing town and see great mills and a crowd of operatives; and such a sight is put forward, *under the special allegation that it would not exist but for a protective tax,* as a proof that protective taxes are wise. But if it be true that the thread-mill would not exist but for the tax, then how can we form a judgment as to whether the **protective** system is wise or not unless we call to mind all the seamstresses, washer-women, servants, factory-hands, saleswomen, teachers, and laborers' wives and daughters, scattered in the garrets and tenements of great cities and in cottages all over the country, who are paying the tax which keeps the mill going and pays the extra wages ? If the sewing-women, teachers, servants, and washer-women could once be collected over against the thread-mill, then some inferences could be drawn which would be worth something. Then some light might be thrown upon the obstinate fallacy of "creating an industry" and we might begin to understand the difference between wanting thread and wanting a thread-mill. Some nations spend capital on great palaces, others on standing armies, others on iron-clad ships of war. Those things are all glorious and strike the imagination with great force when they are seen, but no one doubts that they make life harder for the scattered insignificant peasants and laborers who have to pay for them all. They "support a great many people," they "make work," they "give employment to other industries." We Americans have no palaces, armies, or iron-clads, but we spend our earnings on protected industries. A big protected factory, if it really needs the protection for its support, is a heavier load for the Forgotten Men and Women than an iron-clad ship of war in time of peace.

It is plain that the Forgotten Man and the Forgotten Woman are the real productive strength of the country. The Forgotten Man works and votes — generally he prays — but his chief business in life is to pay. His name never gets into the newspapers except when he marries or dies. He is an obscure man. He may grumble sometimes to his wife, but he does not frequent the grocery, and he does not talk politics at the tavern. So he is forgotten. Yet who is there whom the statesman, economist, and social philosopher ought to think of before this man? If any student of social science comes to appreciate the case of the Forgotten Man, he will become an unflinching advocate of strict scientific thinking in sociology and a hard-hearted skeptic as regards any scheme of social amelioration. He will always want to know, Who and where is the Forgotten Man in this case, who will have to pay for it all?

The Forgotten Man is not a pauper. It belongs to his character to save something. Hence he is a capitalist, though never a great one. He is a "poor" man in the popular sense of the word, but not in a correct sense. In fact, one of the most constant and trustworthy signs that the Forgotten Man is in danger of a new assault is that "the poor man" is brought into the discussion. Since the Forgotten Man has some capital, anyone who cares for his interest will try to make capital secure by securing the inviolability of contracts, the stability of currency, and the firmness of credit. Anyone, therefore, who cares for the Forgotten Man will be sure to be considered a friend of the capitalist and an enemy of the poor man.

It is the Forgotten Man who is threatened by every extension of the paternal theory of government. It is he who must work and pay. When, therefore, the statesmen and social philosophers sit down to think what the state can do or ought to do, they really mean to decide what the Forgotten Man shall do. What the Forgotten Man wants, therefore, is a fuller realization of constitutional liberty. He is suffering from the fact that there are yet mixed in our institutions mediæval theories of protection, regulation, and authority, and modern theories of independence and individual liberty and responsibility. The consequence of this mixed state of things is that those who are clever enough to get into control use the paternal theory by which to measure their own rights — that is, they assume privileges — and they use the theory of liberty to measure their own duties; that is, when it comes to the duties, they want to be "let alone." The Forgotten Man never gets into control. He has to pay both ways. His rights are measured to him by the theory of liberty — that is, he has only such as he can conquer; his duties are measured to him on the paternal theory — that is, he must discharge all which are laid upon him, as is the fortune of parents. In a paternal relation there are always two parties, a father and a child; and when we use the paternal relation metaphorically, it is of the first importance to know who is to be father and who is to be child. The rôle of parent falls always to the Forgotten Man. What he wants, therefore, is that ambiguities in our institutions be cleared up and that liberty be more fully realized.

It behooves any economist or social philosopher, whatever be the grade of his orthodoxy, who proposes to enlarge the sphere of the "state," or to take any steps whatever having in view the welfare of any class whatever, to pursue the analysis of the social effects of his proposition until he finds that other group whose interests must be curtailed or whose energies must be placed under contribution by the course of action which he proposes, and he cannot maintain his proposition until he has demonstrated that it will be more advantageous, *both quantitatively and qualitatively*, to those who must bear the weight of it than complete non-interference by the state with the relations of the parties in question.

LIFE, ART AND AMERICA[1]

By Theodore Dreiser

I do not pretend to speak with any historic or sociologic knowledge of the sources of the American ethical, and therefore critical, point of view, though I suspect the origin, but I, personally, am at last convinced that, whatever its source or sense, it does not accord with the facts of life as I have noted or experienced them. To me, the average or somewhat standardized American is an odd, irregularly developed soul, wise and even froward in matters of mechanics, organizations, and anything that relates to technical skill in connection with material things, but absolutely devoid of any true spiritual insight, any correct knowledge of the history of literature or art, and confused by and mentally lost in or overcome by the multiplicity of the purely material and inarticulate details by which he finds himself surrounded. . . .

My concern is with the mental and critical standards of America as they exist to-day, and of England, from which they seem to be derived. The average American has such an odd, such a naïve conception of what the world is like, what it is that is taking place under his eyes and under the sun. If you should chance to consult a Methodist, a Baptist, a Presbyterian, a Lutheran, or any other current American sectarian, on this subject, you would find (which, after all, is a dull thing to point out at this day and date) that his conception of the things which he sees about him is bounded by what he was taught in his Sunday school or his church, or what he has stored up or gathered from the conventions of his native town. (His native town! Kind heaven!) And, although the world has stored up endless treasuries of

[1] Reprinted from "The Seven Arts" by special permission of the publishers and the author.

knowledge in regard to itself chemically, sociologically, historically, philosophically — still the millions and millions who tramp the streets and occupy the stores and fill the highways and byways, and the fields, and the tenements of the city, have no faintest knowledge of this, or of anything else that can be said to be intellectually "doing." They live in theories and isms, and under codes dictated by a church or a state or an order of society, which has no least regard for or relationship to their natural mental development. The darkest side of democracy, like that of autocracies, is that it permits the magnetic and the cunning and the unscrupulous among the powerful individuals, to sway vast masses of the mob, not so much to their own immediate destruction as to the curtailment of their natural privileges and the ideas which they should be allowed to entertain if they could think at all, and, incidentally, to the annoying and sometimes undoing of individuals who have the truest brain interests of the race at heart — Vide! Giordano Bruno! Jan Huss! Savonarola! Tom Paine! Walt Whitman! Edgar Allan Poe!

For, after all, as I have pointed out somewhere, the great business of life and mind is life. We are here, I take it, not merely to moon and vegetate, but to do a little thinking about this state in which we find ourselves. It is perfectly legitimate, all priests and theories and philosophies to the contrary notwithstanding, to go back, in so far as we may, to the primary sources of thought, i.e., the visible scene, the actions and thoughts of people, the movements of nature and its chemical and physical subtleties, in order to draw original and radical conclusions for ourselves. The great business of an individual, if he has any time after struggling for life and a reasonable amount of entertainment or sensory satiation, should be this very thing. A man, if he can, should question the things that he sees — not some things, but everything — stand, as it were, in the center of this whirling storm of contradiction which we know as life, and ask of it its source and its import. Else why a brain at all? If only one could induce a moderate number of individuals, out of all that pass this way and come no more, apparently, to pause and think about life and take an individual point of view, the freedom and the individuality and the interest of the world might, I fancy, be greatly enhanced. We com plain of the world as dull, at times. If it is so, lack of think ing by individuals is the reason. But to ask the poor, half-equipped mentality of the mass to think, to be individual — what an anachronism! You might as well ask of a rock to move, or a tree to fly.

Nevertheless, here in America, by reason of an idealistic constitution which is largely a work of art and not a work-able system, you see a nation dedicated to so-called intellectual and spiritual freedom, but actually devoted with an almost bee-like industry to the gathering and storing and articula-tion and organization and use of purely material things. In spite of all our base-drum announcement of our servitude to the intellectual ideals of the world, no nation has ever contributed less, philosophically or artistically or spiritually, to the actual development of the intellect and the spirit. I shall have more to say concerning this later on. We have invented many things, it is true, which have relieved man from the crushing weight of a too-grinding toil, and this perhaps may be the sole mission of America in the world and the universe, its destiny, its end. Personally, I think it is not a half bad thing to have done, and the submarine and the flying machine and the armored dreadnought, no less than the sewing machine and the cotton gin and the binder and the reaper and the cash register and the trolley car and the telephone, may, in the end, or perhaps already have, proved as significant in breaking the chains of physical and mental slavery of man as anything else.   I do not know.

One thing I do know is that America seems profoundly interested in these things, to the exclusion of anything else. It has no time, you might almost say, no taste, to stop and contemplate life in the large, from an artistic or a philosophic point of view. Yet, after all, when all the machinery for lessening man's burdens has been invented, and all the safeguards for his preservation completed and possibly shattered by forces too deep or superior for his cunning, may not a phrase, a line of poetry, or a single act of some half forgotten tragedy be all that is left of what we now see or dream of as materially perfect? For, after all, is it not a thought alone, of many famous and powerful things that have already gone, that alone endures — a thought conveyed by art as a medium?

But let me not become too remote or too fine-spun in my conception of the ultimate significance of art itself. The point which I wish to make here is just this: That in a land so devoted to the material, although dedicated by its constitution to the ideal, the condition of art and intellectual freedom is certainly anomalous. Your trade and your trust builder, most obviously dominant in America at this time, is of all people most indifferent to, or most unconscious of, the ultimate and pressing claims of mind and spirit as expressed by art. If you doubt this, you have only to look about you to see for what purposes, to what end, the increment of men of wealth and material power in America is devoted. We have something like twenty-five hundred colleges and schools and institutions of various kinds, largely furthered by the money of American men of wealth, and all devoted to the development of the mental equipment of man, yet all set against anything which is related to truly radical investigation, or thought, or action, or art.

As a matter of fact, in spite of the American constitution and the American oratorical address of all and sundry occasions, the average American school, college, university, institution, is very much against the development of the individual in the true sense of that word. What it really wants is not an individual, but an automatic copy of some altruistic and impossible ideal, which has been formulated here and in England, under the domination of Christianity. This is literally true. I defy you to read any college or university prospectus or address or plea, which concerns the purposes or the ideals of these institutions, and not agree with me. They are not after individuals, they are after types or schools of individuals, all to be very much alike, all to be like themselves. And what type? Listen. I know of an American college professor in one of our successful state universities who had this to say of the male graduates of his institution, after having watched the output for a number of years: "They are all right, quite satisfactory as machines for the production of material wealth or for the maintenance of certain forms of professional skill, now very useful to the world, but as for having ideas of their own, being creators or men with the normal impulses and passions of manhood, they do not fulfill the requisite in any respect. They are little more than types, machines, made in the image and likeness of their college. They do not think; they cannot think, because they are bound hard and fast by the iron band of convention. They are moral young beings, Christian beings, model beings, but they are not men in the creative sense, and by far the large majority will never do a single original thing until by chance or necessity the theories and the conventions imposed or generated by their training and their surroundings are broken, and they become free, independent, self thinking individuals."

I know of one woman's college, for instance, an American

N

institution of the very highest standing which, since its inception, has sent forth into life some thousands of graduates and post graduates, to battle life as they may for individual supremacy or sensory comfort. They are, or were, supposed to be individuals, capable of individual thought, procedure, invention, development, yet out of all of them, not one has ever even entered upon any creative or artistic labor of any kind. Not one. (Write me for the name of the college, if you wish.) There is not a chemist, a physiologist, a botanist, a biologist, an historian, a philosopher, an artist, of any kind or repute, among them, not one. No one of them has attained to even passing repute in these fields. They are secretaries to corporations, teachers, missionaries, college librarians, educators in any of the scores of pilfered meanings that may be attached to that much abused word. They are curators, directors, keepers. They are not individuals in the true sense of that word; they have not been taught to think, they are not free. They do not invent, lead, create. They only copy or take care of, yet they are graduates of this college and its theory, mostly ultra conventional or, worse yet, anæmic, and glad to wear its collar, to clank the chains of its ideas or ideals — automatons in a social scheme whose last and final detail was outlined to them in the classrooms of their alma mater. That, to me, is one phase, amusing enough, of intellectual freedom in America.

But the above is a mere detail in any chronicle or picture of the social or intellectual state of the United States. No country in the world, at least none that I know anything about, has such a peculiar, such a seemingly fierce determination, to make the Ten Commandments work. It would be amusing if it were not pitiful, their faith in these binding religious ideals. I, for one, have never been able to make up my mind whether this springs from the zealotry of the

Puritans who landed at Plymouth Rock, or whether it is indigenous to the soil (which I doubt when I think of the Indians who preceded the whites), or whether it is a product of the federal constitution, compounded by such idealists as Paine and Jefferson and Franklin, and the more or less religious and political dreamers of the pre-constitutional days. Certain it is that no profound moral idealism animated the French in Canada, the Dutch in New York, the Swedes in New Jersey, or the mixed French and English in the extreme south and New Orleans.

The first shipload of white women that was ever brought to America was sold, almost at so much a pound. They were landed at Jamestown. The basis of all the first large fortunes was laid, to speak plainly, in graft — the most outrageous concessions obtained abroad. The history of our relations with the American Indians is sufficient to lay any claim to financial or moral virtue or worth in the white men who settled this country. We debauched, then robbed, and murdered them. There is no other conclusion to be drawn from the facts covering that relationship as set down in any history worthy of the name. In regard to the development of our land, our canals, our railroads, and the vast organizations supplying our present day necessities, their history is a complex of perjury, robbery, false witness, extortion, and indeed every crime to which avarice, greed, and ambition are heir. If you do not believe this, examine at your leisure the various congressional and state legislative investigations which have been held on an average of every six months since the government was founded, and see for yourself. The cunning and unscrupulousness of American brains can be matched against any the world has ever known.

But an odd thing in connection with this financial and social criminality is that it has been consistently and regularly accompanied, outwardly at least, by a religious and a sex puritanism which would be scarcely believable if it were not true. I do not say that the robbers and thieves who did so much to build up our great commercial and social structures were in themselves inwardly or outwardly always religious or puritanically moral from the sex point of view, although in regard to the latter, they most frequently made a show of so being.   But I do say this, that the communities and the states and the nation in which they were committing their depredations have been individually and collectively, in so far as the written, printed, and acted word are concerned, and in pictures and music, militantly pure and religious during all the time that this has been going forward under their eyes, and, to a certain extent, with their political consent.   Why? I have a vague feeling that it is the American of Anglo-Saxon origin only who has been most vivid in his excitement over religion and morals where the written, printed, acted, or painted word was concerned, yet who, at the same time, and perhaps for this very reason, was failing or deliberately refusing to see, the contrast which his ordinary and very human actions presented to all this.   Was he a hypocrite?   Oh, well! — is he one?   I hate to think it, but he certainly acts the part exceedingly well.   Either he is that or a fool — take your choice.

Your American of Anglo-Saxon or any other origin is actually no better, spiritually or morally, than any other creature of this earth, be he Turk or Hindu or Chinese, except from a materially constructive or wealth-breeding point of view, but for some odd reason or another, he thinks he is. The only real difference is that, cast out or spewed out by conditions over which he had no control elsewhere, he chanced to fall into a land overflowing with milk and honey. Nature in America was, and still is, kind to the lorn foreigner seeking a means of subsistence, and he seems to have immediately attributed this to three things: First, his inherent capacity to dominate and control wealth; second, the especial favor of God to him; third, to his superior and moral state (due, of course, to his possession of wealth). These three things, uncorrected as yet by any great financial pressure, or any great natural or world catastrophe, have served to keep the American in his highly romantic state of self deception. He still thinks that he is a superior spiritual and moral being, infinitely better than the creatures of any other land, and nothing short of a financial cataclysm, which will come with the pressure of population on resources, will convince him that he is not. But that he will yet be convinced is a certainty. You need not fear. Leave it to nature.

One of the interesting phases of this puritanism or phariseeism is his attitude toward women and their morality and their purity. If ever a people has refined eroticism to a greater degree than the American, I am not aware of it. The good American, capable of the same gross financial crimes previously indicated, has been able to look upon most women, but more particularly those above him in the social scale, as considerably more than human — angelic, no less, and possessed of qualities the like of which are not to be found in any breathing being, man, woman, child, or animal. It matters not that his cities and towns, like those of any other nation, are rife with sex.

Only a sex-blunted nature or race such as the Anglo-Saxon could have built up any such asinine theory as this. The purity, the sanctity, the self-abnegation, the delicacy of women — how these qualities have been exaggerated and dinned into our ears, until at last the average scrubby non-reasoning male, quite capable of taking a girl off the street, is no more able to clearly visualize the creature before him than he is the central wilds of Africa which he has never seen. A princess, a goddess, a divine mother or creative principle, all the virtues, all the perfections, no vices, no weaknesses, no errors — some such hodge-podge as this has come to be the average Anglo-Saxon, or at least American, conception of the average American woman. I do not say that a portion of this illusion is not valuable — I think it is. But as it stands now, she is too good to be true: a paragon, a myth! Actually, she doesn't exist at all as he has been taught to imagine her. She is nothing more than a two-legged biped like the rest of us, but in consequence of this delusion sex itself, being a violation of this paragon, has become a crime. We enter upon the earth, it is true, in a none too artistic manner (conceived in iniquity and born in sin, is the biblical phrasing of it), but all this has long since been glozed over — ignored — and to obviate its brutality as much as possible, the male has been called upon to purify himself in thought and deed, to avoid all private speculation as to women and his relationship to them, and, much more than that, to avoid all public discussion, either by word of mouth or the printed page.

To think of women or to describe them as anything less than the paragon previously commented upon, has become, by this process, not only a sin — it is a shameful infraction of the moral code, no less. Women are too good, the sex relationship too vile a thing, to be mentioned or even thought of. We must move in a mirage of illusion. We must not know what we really do. We must trample fact under foot and give fancy, in the guise of our so-called better natures, free rein. How this must affect or stultify the artistic and creative faculties of the race itself must be plain. Yet that is exactly where we stand to-day, ethically and spiritually, in regard to sex and women, and that is what is the matter with American social life, letters, and art.

I do not pretend to say that this is not a workable and a satisfactory code in case any race or nation chooses to follow it, but I do say it is deadening to the artistic impulse, and I mean it. Imagine a puritan or a moralist attempting anything in art, which is nothing if not a true reflection of insight into life! Imagine! And contrast this moral or art narrowness with his commercial, or financial, or agricultural freedom and sense, and note the difference. In regard to all the latter, he is cool, skeptical, level-headed, understanding, natural — consequently well developed in those fields. In regard to this other, he is illusioned, theoretic, religious. In consequence, he has no power, except for an occasional individual who may rise in spite of these untoward conditions (to be frowned upon) to understand, much less picture, life as it really is. Artistically, intellectually, philosophically, we are weaklings; financially, and in all ways commercial we are very powerful. So one-sided has been our development that in this latter respect we are almost giants. Strange, almost fabulous creatures, have been developed here by this process, men so singularly devoid of a rounded human nature that they have become freaks in this one direction — that of money getting. I refer to Rockefeller, Gould, Sage, Vanderbilt the first, H. H. Rogers, Carnegie, Frick. Strong in all but this one capacity, the majority of our great men stand forth as true human rarities, the like of which has scarcely ever been seen before.

/ America could be described as the land of Bottom the Weaver. And by Bottom I mean the tradesman or manufacturer who by reason of his enthusiasm for the sale of paints or powder or threshing machines or coal, has accumulated wealth and, in consequence and by reason of the haphazard privileges of democracy, has strayed into a position of counsellor, or even dictator, not in regard to the things about which he might readily be supposed to know, but about the many things about which he would be much more likely

not to know: art, science, philosophy, morals, public policy
in general.   You recall him, of course, in "A Midsummer
Night's Dream," unconscious of his furry ears and also that
he does not know how to play the lion's part — that it is
more difficult than mere roaring.   Here he is now, in America,
enthroned as a lion, and in his way he is an epitome of the
Anglo-Saxon temperament.   All merchants, judges, lawyers,
priests, politicians — what a goodly company of Bottoms
they are.   Solidified, they are Bottom to the life.

Bottom is so wise in his own estimation.   He never once
suspects his furry ears or that he is not a perfect actor in the
rôle of the lion — or (if you will take it for what it is meant)
the arts.   He is just a dull weaver, really, made by this dream
of our constitution ("an exposition of sleep" come upon him)
into a roaring lion — in his own estimation.   No one must say
that Bottom is not: he will be driven out of the country —
deported or exiled.   No one must presume to practise the arts
save as Bottom understands them.   If you do, presto, there
is his henchman Comstock and all Comstockery to take you
into custody.   Men who have come here from foreign shores
(England excepted) have been amazed at Bottom's ears and
his presumption in passing upon what is a lion's part in
life.   Indeed he is the Anglo-Saxon temperament personified.
He is convinced that liberty was not made for Oberon or
Peaseblossom or Cobweb or Mustard, but for bishops and
executives and wholesale grocers and men who have become
vastly rich canning tomatoes or selling oil.   We must be
"marvelous furry about the face" and do things his way,
to be free.   The great desire of Bottom is for all of us to
have furry ears and long ones and to believe that he is the
greatest actor in the world.   He is bewildered by a world
that will not play Pyramus his way.   Quince, Snug, Flute,
Snout, and Starveling (all those who came over with him in
the *Mayflower*) agree that he is a great actor, but there are

others, and Bottom is convinced that these others are in error — trying to wreck that dream, the American Constitution, which brought this "exposition of sleep" upon him and made him into a lion — "marvelous furry about the face" and with great ears.

Alas, alas! for art in America. It has a hard, stubby row to hoe.

But my quarrel is not with America as a comfortable industrious atmosphere in which to move and have one's being, but largely because it is no more than that — because it tends to become a dull, conventionalized, routine, material world. We are drifting, unless most of the visible signs are deceiving, into the clutches of a commercial oligarchy whose mental standards outside of trade are so puerile as to be scarcely worth discussing. Contemplate, if you please, what has happened to one of the shibboleths or bulwarks of our sacred liberties and intellectual freedom, *i.e.*, the newspaper, under the dominance of trade. Look at it. I have not time here to stop and set forth *seriatim* all the charges that have been made, and in the main thoroughly substantiated, against the American newspaper. But consider for yourselves the newspapers which you know and read. How much, I ask you, if you are in trade, do the newspapers you know, know about trade? How much actual truth do they tell? How far could you follow their trade judgment or understanding? And if you are a member of any profession, how much reported professional knowledge or news, as presented by a newspaper, can you rely on? If a newspaper reported a professional man's judgment or dictum in regard to any important professional fact, how fully would you accept it without other corroborative testimony?

You are a play-goer: do you believe the newspaper dramatic critics? You are a student of literature: do you accept the mouthings of their literary critics or even look

to them for advice? You are an artist or a lover of art·
do you follow the newspapers for anything more than the
barest intelligence as to the whereabouts of anything artistic? I doubt it. And in regard to politics, finance, social
movements and social affairs, are they not actually the
darkest, the most misrepresentative, frequently the most
biased and malicious guides in the world of the printed
word? Take their mouthings concerning ethics and morals
alone and contrast them, if you please, with their private
policy or their financial connections — the forces by which
they are directed, editorially and otherwise. I am not
speaking of all newspapers, but never mind the exception.
It is always unimportant in mass conditions, anyhow.
Newspaper criticism, like newspaper leadership, has already
long since come to be looked upon by the informed and intelligent as little more than the mouthings or bellowings
of mercenaries or panderers to trade, or, worse still, rank
incompetents. The newspaper man, *per se*, either does not
know or cannot help himself. The newspaper publisher is
very glad of this and uses his half intelligence or inability
to further his own interests. Politicians, administrations,
department stores, large interests, and personalities of
various kinds, use or control or compel newspapers to do their
bidding. This is a severe indictment to make against the
press in general. Is it not literally true? Do you not, of
your own knowledge, know it to be so?

Take again the large, the almost dominant religious and
commercial organizations of America. What relationship,
if any, do they bear to a free mental development, a refined
taste, a subtle understanding, art or life in its poetic or tragic
moulds, its drift, its character? Would you personally look
to the Methodist, or the Presbyterian, or the Catholic, or the
Baptist church to further individualism, or freedom of
thought, or directness of mental action, or art in any form?

Do not they really ask of all their adherents that they lay aside this freedom in favor of the reported word or dictum of a fabled, a non-historic, an imaginary ruler, of the universe? Think of it. And they are among the powerful, constructive, and controlling elements in government — in this government, to be accurate — dedicated and presumably devoted to individual liberty, not only of so-called conscience, but of constructive thought and art.

And our large corporations, with their dominant and controlling captains of industry, so-called. What about their relationship to individuality, the freedom of the individual to think for himself — to grow along constructural lines? Take, for instance, the tobacco trust, the oil trust, the milk trust, the coal trust — in what way, do you suppose, do they help? Are they actively seeking a better code of ethics, a wider historic or philosophic perspective, a more delicate art perception for the individual, or are they definitely and permanently concerned with the customary bludgeoning tactics of trade, piling up fortunes out of which they are to be partially bled later by pseudo art collectors and swindling dealers in antiques and so-called historic art and literature? Of current life and its accomplishments, what do they actually know? Yet this is a democracy. Here, as in every other realm of the world, the individual is permitted, compelled, to seek his own material and mental salvation as best he may. The trouble with a democracy as opposed to an autocracy, with a line of titled idlers permitted the gift of leisure and art indulgence, is that there is no central force or group to foster art, to secure letters and art in their inalienable rights, to make of superior thought a noble and a sacred thing. I am not saying that democracy will not yet produce such a central force or group. I believe it can and will. I believe when the time arrives it may prove to be better than any form of hereditary autocracy. But I am talking about the mental, the social, the artistic condition of America as it is to-day.

To me it is a thing for laughter, if not for tears : one hundred million Americans, rich (a fair percentage of them, anyhow) beyond the dreams of avarice, and scarcely a sculptor, a poet, a singer, a novelist, an actor, a musician, worthy of the name. One hundred and forty years (almost two hundred, counting the Colonial days) of the most prosperous social conditions, a rich soil, incalculable deposits of gold, silver, and precious and useful metals and fuels of all kinds, a land amazing in its mountains, its streams, its valley prospects, its wealth-yielding powers, and now its tremendous cities and far-flung facilities for travel and trade, and yet contemplate it. Artists, poets, thinkers, where are they ? Run them over in your mind. Has it produced a single philosopher of the first rank — a Spencer, a Nietzsche, a Schopenhauer, a Kant ? Do I hear someone offering Emerson as an equivalent ? or James ? Has it produced a historian of the force of either Macaulay or Grote or Gibbon ? A novelist of the rank of Turgenev, de Maupassant, or Flaubert ? A scientist of the standing of Crookes or Roentgen or Pasteur ? A critic of the insight and force of Taine, Sainte-Beuve, or the de Goncourts ? A dramatist the equivalent of Ibsen, Chekhov, Shaw, Hauptmann, Brieux ? An actor, since Booth, of the force of Coquelin, Sonnenthal, Forbes-Robertson, or Sarah Bernhardt ? Since Whitman, one poet, Edgar Lee Masters. In painting, a Whistler, an Inness, a Sargent. Who else ? (And two of these shook the dust of our shores forever.) Inventors, yes. By the hundreds, one might almost say by the thousands. Some of them amazing enough, in all conscience, world figures, and enduring for all time. But of what relationship to art — the supreme freedom of the mind ? . . .

I am constantly astonished by the thousands of men, exceedingly capable in some mechanical or narrow technical sense, whose world or philosophic vision is that of a child. As a nation, we accept and believe naïvely in such impossible things. I am not thinking alone of the primary tenets of all religions, which are manifestly based on nothing at all, and which millions of Americans, along with the humbler classes of other countries, accept, but rather of those sterner truths which life itself teaches — the unreliability of human nature; the crass chance which strikes down and destroys our finest dreams; the fact that man in all his relations is neither good nor evil, but both.

The American, by some hocus pocus of atavism, has seemingly borrowed or retained from lower English middle-class puritans all their fol de rol notions about making human nature perfect by fiat or edict — the written word, as it were, which goes with all religions. So, although by reason of the coarsest and most brutal methods, we, as a nation, have built up one of the most interesting and domineering oligarchies in the world, we are still by no means aware of the fact.

All men, in the mind of the unthinking American, are still free and equal. They have in themselves certain inalienable rights; what they are, when you come to test them, no human being can discover. Your so-called rights disappear like water before a moving boat. They do not exist. Life here, as elsewhere, comes down to the brutal methods of nature itself. The rich strike the poor at every turn; the poor defend themselves and further their lives by all the tricks which stark necessity can conceive. No inalienable right keeps the average cost of living from rising steadily, while most of the salaries of our idealistic Americans are stationary. No inalienable right has ever yet prevented the strong from either tricking or browbeating the weak. And, although by degrees the average American everywhere is feeling more and more keenly the sharpening struggle for existence, yet his faith in his impossible ideals is as fresh as ever. God will save the good American, and seat him at His right hand on the Golden Throne.

On earth the good American is convinced that the narrower and more colorless his life here the greater his opportunity for a more glorious life hereafter. His pet theory is that man is made useful and successful and constructive — a perfect man, in short — by the kinds and numbers of things he is not permitted to do or think or say. A pale, narrow, utterly restrained life, according to his theory, is the perfect one. If one accepted St. James's version and kept utterly unspotted by the world, entirely out of contact with it, he would be the perfect American. Indeed, ever since the *Mayflower* landed, and the country began to grow westward, we have been convinced that we were destined to make the Ten Commandments, in all their arbitrary perfection, work. One might show readily enough that America attained its amazing position in life by reason of the fact that, along with boundless opportunities, the Ten Commandments did not and do not work, but what would be the use? With one hand the naïve American takes and executes with all the brutal insistence of nature itself; with the other he writes glowing platitudes concerning brotherly love, virtue, purity, truth, etc., etc.

A part of this right or left hand tendency, as the case might be, is seen in the constant desire of the American to reform something. No country in the world, not even England, the mother of fol de rol reforms, is so prolific in these frail ventures as this great country of ours. In turn we have had campaigns for the reform of the atheist, the drunkard, the lecher, the fallen woman, the buccaneer financier, the drug fiend, the dancer, the theatregoer, the reader of novels, the wearer of low-neck dresses, and surplus jewelry — in fact, every human taste and frivolity, wherever sporadically it has chanced to manifest itself with any interesting human force. Your reformer's idea is that any human being, to be a successful one, must be a pale spindling sprout, incapable of any vice or crime. And all the while the threshing sea of life is sounding in his ears. The thief, the lecher, the drunkard, the fallen woman, the greedy, the inordinately vain, as in all ages past, pass by his door, and are not the whit less numerous for the unending campaigns which have been launched to save them. In other words, human nature is human nature, but your American cannot be made to believe it.

He will not give up the illusion which was piled safely in the hold of the *Mayflower* when it set sail. He is going to reform man and the world willy nilly, and, while in his rampant idealism he is neglecting to build up a suitable army and navy wherewith to defend himself, he is busy propagating little cults whereby man is to be made less vigorous, more the useless anæmic thing that he has in mind.

Personally, my quarrel is with America's quarrel with original thought. It is so painful to me to see one after another of our alleged reformers tilting Don Quixote-like at the giant windmills of fact. We are to have no pictures which the puritan and the narrow, animated by an obsolete dogma, cannot approve of. We are to have no theatres, no motion pictures, no books, no public exhibitions of any kind, no speech even, which will in any way contravene his limited view of life. A few years ago it was the humble dealer in liquor whose life was anathematized, and whose property was descended upon with torches, axes, and bombs. Now comes prohibition. A little later, our cities growing and the sections devoted to the worship of Venus becoming more manifest, the Vice Crusader was bred, and we had the spectacle of whole areas of fallen women scattered to the four winds, and allowed to practise separately what they could not do collectively. Then came Mr. Comstock, vindictive, persistent, and with a nose and a taste for the profane and erotic, such as elsewhere has not been equaled since. Pictures, books, the theatre, the dance, the studio — all came under his watchful eye. During the twenty or thirty years in which he acted as a United States Postoffice Inspector, he was, because of his dull charging against things which he did not rightly understand, never out of the white light of publicity which he so greatly craved. One month it would be a novel by D'Annunzio; another, a set of works by Balzac or de Maupassant, found in the shade of some grovelly bookseller's shop; the humble photographer attempting a nude; the painter who allowed his reverence for Raphael to carry him too far; the poet who attempted a recrudescence of Don Juan in modern iambics, was immediately seized upon and hauled before an equally dull magistrate, there to be charged with his offense and to be fined accordingly. All this is being continued with emphasis.

Then came the day of the White Slave Chasers, and now no American city, and no backwoods Four Corners, however humble, is complete without a vice commission of some kind, or at least a local agent or representative, charged with the duty of keeping the art, the literature, the press, and the private lives of all those at hand up to that standard of perfection which only the dull can set for themselves.

Several years ago, when the white slave question was at its whitest heat, the problem of giving expression to its fundamental aspects was divided between raiding plays which attemped to show the character of the crime in too graphic a manner, and licensing those which appealed to the intelligence of those who were foremost in the crusade. Thus we had the spectacle of an uncensored, but nevertheless approved, ten-reel film ꜱ wing more details of the crime and better methods of securing white slaves, than any other production of the day, running undisturbed to packed houses all over the country, while two somewhat more dramatic, but far less effective distributors of information in the way of plays were successfully harried from city to city and finally withdrawn.

Shakespeare has been ordered from the schools in some of the states. A production of "Antony and Cleopatra" has been raided in Chicago. Japanese prints of a high art value, intended for the seclusion of a private collection, have been seized and the most valuable of them held to be destroyed. By turns, an artistic fountain to Heine in New York, loan exhibits of paintings in Denver, Kansas City, and elsewhere, scores of books by Stevenson, James Lane Allen, Frances H. Burnett, have been attacked, not only, as in the case of the latter, with the invisible weapons of the law, as might be expected, but, in regard to the former, with actual axes. A male dancer of repute and some artistic ability, has been raided publicly by the vice crusaders for his shameless exposure of his person! No play, no picture, no book, no public or private jubilation of any kind, is complete any more without its vice attack

This sort of interference with serious letters is, to me, the worst and most corrupting form of espionage which is conceivable to the human mind. It plumbs the depths of ignorance and intolerance; if not checked, it can and will dam initiative and inspiration at the source. Life, if it is anything at all, is a thing to be observed, studied, interpreted. We cannot know too much about it, because as yet we know nothing. It is our one great realm of discovery. The artist, if left to himself, may be safely trusted to observe, synchronize, and articulate human knowledge in the most palatable and delightful form. Human nature will seek and have what it needs, the vice crusaders to the contrary notwithstanding. There is no compulsion on any

o

one to read.   One must pay to do so.   What is more, one must have taste inherently to select, and a brain and a heart to understand.   With all these safeguards and a double score of capable critics in every land to praise or blame, what need really is there for a censor, or a dozen of them, each far less fitted than any of the working critics, to indulge his personal predilection and opposition, and to appeal to the courts if he is disagreed with?

Personally, I rise to protest.   I look on this interference with serious art and serious minds as an outrage.   I fear for the ultimate intelligence of America, which in all conscience, judged by world standards, is low enough.   In our youth and conceit we think ourselves wise.   Intelligent cosmopolitans actually know that our ignorance is appalling.   In the main we are unbelievably dull and wishy-washy.   Now appears a band of wasp-like censors to put the finishing touches on a literature and an art that has struggled all too feebly as it is.   Poe, Hawthorne, Whitman, and Thoreau, each in turn was the butt and jibe of unintelligent Americans, until by now we are well nigh the laughing stock of the world. Where is it to end?   When will we lay aside our swaddling clothes, enforced on us by ignorant, impossible puritans and their uneducated followers, and stand up, free thinking men and women?   Life is to be learned as much from books and art as from life itself — almost more so, in my judgment. Art is the stored honey of the human soul, gathered on wings of misery and travail.   Shall the dull and the self-seeking and the self-advertising close this store on the groping human mind?

THE MORAL EQUIVALENT OF WAR

By William James [1]

THE war against war is going to be no holiday excursion or camping party. The military feelings are too deeply grounded to abdicate their place among our ideals until better substitutes are offered than the glory and shame that come to nations as well as to individuals from the ups and downs of politics and the vicissitudes of trade. There is something highly paradoxical in the modern man's relation to war. Ask all our millions, north and south, whether they would vote now (were such a thing possible) to have our war for the Union expunged from history, and the record of a peaceful transition to the present time substituted for that of its marches and battles, and probably hardly a handful of eccentrics would say yes. Those ancestors, those efforts, those memories and legends, are the most ideal part of what we now own together, a sacred spiritual possession worth more than all the blood poured out. Yet ask those same people whether they would be willing in cold blood to start another civil war now to gain another similar possession, and not one man or women would vote for the proposition. In modern eyes, precious though wars may be, they must not be waged solely for the sake of the ideal har vest. Only when forced upon one, only when an enemy's injustice leaves us no alternative, is a war now thought permissible.

It was not thus in ancient times. The earlier men were hunting men, and to hunt a neighboring tribe, kill the males, loot the village and possess the females, was the most profitable, as well as the most exciting, way of living. Thus

[1] Reprinted by special permission of the American Association for International Conciliation.

were the more martial tribes selected, and in chiefs and peoples a pure pugnacity and love of glory came to mingle with the more fundamental appetite for plunder.

Modern war is so expensive that we feel trade to be a better avenue to plunder; but modern man inherits all the innate pugnacity and all the love of glory of his ancestors. Showing war's irrationality and horror is of no effect upon him. The horrors make the fascination. War is the *strong* life; it is life *in extremis;* war-taxes are the only ones men never hesitate to pay, as the budgets of all nations show us.

History is a bath of blood. The Iliad is one long recital of how Diomedes and Ajax, Sarpedon and Hector *killed.* No detail of the wounds they made is spared us, and the Greek mind fed upon the story. Greek history is a panorama of jingoism and imperialism — war for war's sake, all the citizens being warriors. It is horrible reading, because of the irrationality of it all — save for the purpose of making "history" — and the history is that of the utter ruin of a civilization in intellectual respects perhaps the highest the earth has ever seen.

Those wars were purely piratical. Pride, gold, women, slaves, excitement, were their only motives. In the Peloponnesian war, for example, the Athenians ask the inhabitants of Melos (the island where the "Venus of Milo" was found), hitherto neutral, to own their lordship. The envoys meet, and hold a debate which Thucydides gives in full, and which, for sweet reasonableness of form, would have satisfied Matthew Arnold. "The powerful exact what they can," said the Athenians, "and the weak grant what they must." When the Meleans say that sooner than be slaves they will appeal to the gods, the Athenians reply: "Of the gods we believe and of men we know that, by a law of their nature, wherever they can rule they will. This law was not made by us, and we are not the first to have acted upon it; we did but inherit it, and we know that you and all mankind, if you were as strong as we are, would do as we do. So much for the gods; we have told you why we expect to stand as high in their good opinion as you." Well, the Mcleans still refused, and their town was taken. "The Athenians," Thucydides quietly says, "thereupon put to death all who were of military age and made slaves of the women and children. They then colonized the island, sending thither five hundred settlers of their own."

Alexander's career was piracy pure and simple, nothing but an orgy of power and plunder, made romantic by the character of the hero. There was no rational principle in it, and the moment he died his generals and governors attacked one another. The cruelty of those times is incredible. When Rome finally conquered Greece, Paulus Æmilius was told by the Roman Senate to reward his soldiers for their toil by "giving" them the old kingdom of Epirus. They sacked seventy cities and carried off a hundred and fifty thousand inhabitants as slaves. How many they killed I know not; but in Etolia they killed all the senators, five hundred and fifty in number. Brutus was "the noblest Roman of them all," but to reanimate his soldiers on the eve of Philippi he similarly promises to give them the cities of Sparta and Thessalonica to ravage, if they win the fight.

Such was the gory nurse that trained societies to cohesiveness. We inherit the warlike type; and for most of the capacities of heroism that the human race is full of we have to thank this cruel history. Dead men tell no tales, and if there were any tribes of other type than this they have left no survivors. Our ancestors have bred pugnacity into our bone and marrow, and thousands of years of peace won't breed it out of us. The popular imagination fairly fattens on the thought of wars. Let public opinion once reach a certain fighting pitch, and no ruler can withstand it. In the

Boer war both governments began with bluff, but couldn't stay there, the military tension was too much for them. In 1898 our people had read the word WAR in letters three inches high for three months in every newspaper. The pliant politician McKinley was swept away by their eagerness, and our squalid war with Spain became a necessity.

At the present day, civilized opinion is a curious mental mixture. The military instincts and ideals are as strong as ever, but are confronted by reflective criticisms which sorely curb their ancient freedom. Innumerable writers are showing up the bestial side of military service. Pure loot and mastery seem no longer morally avowable motives, and pretexts must be found for attributing them solely to the enemy. England and we, our army and navy authorities repeat without ceasing, arm solely for "peace," Germany and Japan it is who are bent on loot and glory. "Peace" in military mouths to-day is a synonym for "war expected." The word has become a pure provocative, and no government wishing peace sincerely should allow it ever to be printed in a newspaper. Every up-to-date dictionary should say that "peace" and "war" mean the same thing, now *in posse*, now *in actu*. It may even reasonably be said that the intensely sharp competitive *preparation* for war by the nations *is the real war*, permanent, unceasing; and that the battles are only a sort of public verification of the mastery gained during the "peace"-interval.

It is plain that on this subject civilized man has developed a sort of double personality. If we take European nations, no legitimate interest of any one of them would seem to justify the tremendous destructions which a war to compass it would necessarily entail. It would seem as though common sense and reason ought to find a way to reach agreement in every conflict of honest interests. I myself think it our bounden duty to believe in such international rationality as possible. But, as things stand, I see how desperately hard it is to bring the peace-party and the war-party together, and I believe that the difficulty is due to certain deficiencies in the program of pacificism which set the militarist imagination strongly, and to a certain extent justifiably, against it. In the whole discussion both sides are on imaginative and sentimental ground. It is but one utopia against another, and everything one says must be abstract and hypothetical. Subject to this criticism and caution, I will try to characterize in abstract strokes the opposite imaginative forces, and point out what to my own very fallible mind seems the best utopian hypothesis, the most promising line of conciliation.

In my remarks, pacificist though I am, I will refuse to speak of the bestial side of the war-régime (already done justice to by many writers) and consider only the higher aspects of militaristic sentiment. Patriotism no one thinks discreditable; nor does any one deny that war is the romance of history. But inordinate ambitions are the soul of every patriotism, and the possibility of violent death the soul of all romance. The militarily patriotic and romantic-minded everywhere, and especially the professional military class, refuse to admit for a moment that war may be a transitory phenomenon in social evolution. The notion of a sheep's paradise like that revolts, they say, our higher imagination. Where then would be the steeps of life? If war had ever stopped, we should have to reinvent it, on this view, to redeem life from flat degeneration.

Reflective apologists for war at the present day all take it religiously. It is a sort of sacrament. Its profits are to the vanquished as well as to the victor; and quite apart from any question of profit, it is an absolute good, we are told, for it is human nature at its highest dynamic. Its "horrors" are a cheap price to pay for rescue from the only alternative supposed, of a world of clerks and teachers, of co-education and zoophily, of "consumer's leagues" and "associated charities," of industrialism unlimited, and feminism unabashed. No scorn, no hardness, no valor any more! Fie upon such a cattle yard of a planet!

So far as the central essence of this feeling goes, no healthy minded person, it seems to me, can help to some degree partaking of it. Militarism is the great preserver of our ideals of hardihood, and human life with no use for hardihood would be contemptible. Without risks or prizes for the darer, history would be insipid indeed; and there is a type of military character which every one feels that the race should never cease to breed, for every one is sensitive to its superiority. The duty is incumbent on mankind, of keeping military characters in stock — of keeping them, if not for use, then as ends in themselves and as pure pieces of perfection, — so that Roosevelt's weaklings and mollycoddles may not end by making everything else disappear from the face of nature.

This natural sort of feeling forms, I think, the innermost soul of army-writings. Without any exception known to me, militarist authors take a highly mystical view of their subject, and regard war as a biological or sociological necessity, uncontrolled by ordinary psychological checks and motives. When the time of development is ripe the war must come, reason or no reason, for the justifications pleaded are invariably fictitious. War is, in short, a permanent human *obligation*. General Homer Lea, in his recent book "The Valor of Ignorance," plants himself squarely on this ground. Readiness for war is for him the essence of nationality, and ability in it the supreme measure of the health of nations.

Nations, General Lea says, are never stationary — they must necessarily expand or shrink, according to their vitality or decrepitude. Japan now is culminating; and by the fatal law in question it is impossible that her statesmen should not long since have entered, with extraordinary foresight, upon a vast policy of conquest — the game in which the first moves were her wars with China and Russia and her treaty with England, and of which the final objective is the capture of the Philippines, the Hawaiian Islands,. Alaska, and the whole of our coast west of the Sierra Passes. This will give Japan what her ineluctable vocation as a state absolutely forces her to claim, the possession of the entire Pacific Ocean; and to oppose these deep designs we Americans have, according to our author, nothing but our conceit, our ignorance, our commercialism, our corruption, and our feminism. General Lea makes a minute technical comparison of the military strength which we at present could oppose to the strength of Japan, and concludes that the islands, Alaska, Oregon, and Southern California, would fall almost without resistance, that San Francisco must surrender in a fortnight to a Japanese investment, that in three or four months the war would be over, and our republic, unable to regain what it had heedlessly neglected to protect sufficiently, would then "disintegrate," until perhaps some Cæsar should arise to weld us again into a nation.

A dismal forecast indeed! Yet not unplausible, if the mentality of Japan's statesmen be of the Cæsarian type of which history shows so many examples, and which is all that General Lea seems able to imagine. But there is no reason to think that women can no longer be the mothers of Napoleonic or Alexandrian characters; and if these come in Japan and find their opportunity, just such surprises as "The Valor of Ignorance" paints may lurk in ambush for us. Ignorant as we still are of the innermost recesses of Japanese mentality, we may be foolhardy to disregard such possibilities.

Other militarists are more complex and more moral in their considerations. The "Philosophie des Krieges," by S. R. Steinmetz, is a good example. War, according to this author, is an ordeal instituted by God, who weighs the nations in its balance. It is the essential form of the state, and the only function in which peoples can employ all their powers at once and convergently. No victory is possible save as the resultant of a totality of virtues, no defeat for which some vice or weakness is not responsible. Fidelity, cohesiveness, tenacity, heroism, conscience, education, inventiveness, economy, wealth, physical health and vigor — there isn't a moral or intellectual point of superiority that doesn't tell, when God holds his assizes and hurls the peoples upon one another. *Die Weltgeschichte ist das Weltgericht,* and Dr. Steinmetz does not believe that in the long run chance and luck play any part in apportioning the issues.

The virtues that prevail, it must be noted, are virtues anyhow, superiorities that count in peaceful as well as in military competition; but the strain on them, being infinitely intenser in the latter case, makes war infinitely more searching as a trial. No ordeal is comparable to its winnowings. Its dread hammer is the welder of men into cohesive states, and nowhere but in such states can human nature adequately develop its capacity. The only alternative is "degeneration."

Dr. Steinmetz is a conscientious thinker, and his book, short as it is, takes much into account. Its upshot can, it seems to me, be summed up in Simon Patten's word, that mankind was nursed in pain and fear, and that the transition to a "pleasure-economy" may be fatal to a being wielding no powers of defense against its disintegrative influences. If we speak of the *fear of emancipation from the fear-régime,* we put the whole situation into a single phrase; fear regarding ourselves now taking the place of the ancient fear of the enemy.

Turn the fear over as I will in my mind, it all seems to lead back to two unwillingnesses of the imagination, one æsthetic, and the other moral: unwillingness, first to envisage a future in which army-life, with its many elements of charm, shall be forever impossible, and in which the destinies of peoples shall nevermore be decided quickly, thrillingly, and tragically, by force, but only gradually and insipidly by "evolution"; and, secondly, unwillingness to see the supreme theatre of human strenuousness closed, and the splendid military aptitudes of men doomed to keep always in a state of latency and never show themselves in action. These insistent unwillingnesses, no less than other æsthetic and ethical insistencies, have, it seems to me, to be listened to and respected. One cannot meet them effectively by mere counter-insistency on war's expensiveness and horror. The horror makes the thrill; and when the question is of getting the extremest and supremest out of human nature, talk of expense sounds ignominious. The weakness of so much merely negative criticism is evident — pacificism makes no converts from the military party. The military party denies neither the bestiality nor the horror, nor the expense; it only says that these things tell but half the story. It only says that war is *worth* them; that, taking human nature as a whole, its wars are its best protection against its weaker and more cowardly self, and that mankind cannot *afford* to adopt a peace-economy.

Pacificists ought to enter more deeply into the æsthetical and ethical point of view of their opponents. Do that first in any controversy, says J. J. Chapman, *then move the point*, and your opponent will follow. So long as anti-militarists propose no substitute for war's disciplinary function, no *moral equivalent* of war, analogous, as one might say, to the mechanical equivalent of heat, so long they fail to realize the full inwardness of the situation. And as a rule they do fail. The duties, penalties, and sanctions pictured in the utopias they paint are all too weak and tame to touch the military-minded. Tolstoy's pacificism is the only exception to this rule, for it is profoundly pessimistic as regards all this world's values, and makes the fear of the Lord furnish the moral spur provided elsewhere by the fear of the enemy. But our socialistic peace-advocates all believe absolutely in this world's values; and instead of the fear of the Lord and the fear of the enemy, the only fear they reckon with is the fear of poverty if one be lazy. This weakness pervades all the socialistic literature with which I am acquainted. Even in Lowes Dickinson's exquisite dialogue,[1] high wages and short hours are the only forces invoked for overcoming man's distaste for repulsive kinds of labor. Meanwhile men at large still live as they always have lived, under a pain-and-fear economy — for those of us who live in an ease-economy are but an island in the stormy ocean — and the whole atmosphere of present-day utopian literature tastes mawkish and dishwatery to people who still keep a sense for life's more bitter flavors. It suggests, in truth, ubiquitous inferiority.

Inferiority is always with us, and merciless scorn of it is the keynote of the military temper. "Dogs, would you live forever?" shouted Frederick the Great. "Yes," say our utopians, "let us live forever, and raise our level gradually." The best thing about our "inferiors" to-day is that they are as tough as nails, and physically and morally almost as insensitive. Utopianism would see them soft and squeamish, while militarism would keep their callousness, but transfigure it into a meritorious characteristic, needed by "the service," and redeemed by that from the suspicion of inferiority. All the qualities of a man acquire dignity when he knows that the service of the collectivity

[1] "Justice and Liberty," N. Y., 1909.

that owns him needs them. If proud of the collectivity, his own pride rises in proportion. No collectivity is like an army for nourishing such pride; but it has to be confessed that the only sentiment which the image of pacific cosmopolitan industrialism is capable of arousing in countless worthy breasts is shame at the idea of belonging to *such* a collectivity. It is obvious that the United States of America as they exist to-day impress a mind like General Lea's as so much human blubber. Where is the sharpness and precipitousness, the contempt for life, whether one's own, or another's? Where is the savage "yes" and "no," the unconditional duty? Where is the conscription? Where is the blood-tax? Where is anything that one feels honored by belonging to?

Having said thus much in preparation, I will now confess my own utopia. I devoutly believe in the reign of peace and in the gradual advent of some sort of a socialistic equilibrium. The fatalistic view of the war-function is to me nonsense, for I know that war-making is due to definite motives and subject to prudential checks and reasonable criticisms, just like any other form of enterprise. And when whole nations are the armies, and the science of destruction vies in intellectual refinement with the sciences of production, I see that war becomes absurd and impossible from its own monstrosity. Extravagant ambitions will have to be replaced by reasonable claims, and nations must make common cause against them. I see no reason why all this should not apply to yellow as well as to white countries, and I look forward to a future when acts of war shall be formally outlawed as between civilized peoples.

All these beliefs of mine put me squarely into the anti-militarist party. But I do not believe that peace either ought to be or will be permanent on this globe, unless the states pacifically organized preserve some of the old elements of army-discipline. A permanently successful peace-economy cannot be a simple pleasure-economy. In the more or less socialistic future towards which mankind seems drifting we must still subject ourselves collectively to those severities which answer to our real position upon this only partly hos pitable globe. We must make new energies and hardihoods continue the manliness to which the military mind so faith fully clings. Martial virtues must be the enduring cement; intrepidity, contempt of softness, surrender of private interest, obedience to command, must still remain the rock upon which states are built — unless, indeed, we wish for dangerous reactions against commonwealths fit only for contempt, and liable to invite attack whenever a centre of crystallization for military-minded enterprise gets formed anywhere in their neighborhood.

The war-party is assuredly right in affirming and reaffirming that the martial virtues, although originally gained by the race through war, are absolute and permanent human goods. Patriotic pride and ambition in their military form are, after all, only specifications of a more general competitive passion. They are its first form, but that is no reason for supposing them to be its last form. Men now are proud of belonging to a conquering nation, and without a murmur they lay down their persons and their wealth, if by so doing they may fend off subjection. But who can be sure that *other aspects of one's country* may not, with time and education and suggestion enough, come to be regarded with similarly effective feelings of pride and shame? Why should men not some day feel that it is worth a blood-tax to belong to a collectivity superior in *any* ideal respect? Why should they not blush with indignant shame if the community that owns them is vile in any way whatsoever? Individuals, daily more numerous, now feel this civic passion. It is only a question of blowing on the spark till the whole population gets incandescent, and on the ruins of the old morals of military honour, a stable system of morals of civic honour builds itself up. What the whole community comes to believe in grasps the individual as in a vise. The war-function has graspt us so far; but constructive interests may some day seem no less imperative, and impose on the individual a hardly lighter burden.

Let me illustrate my idea more concretely. There is nothing to make one indignant in the mere fact that life is hard, that men should toil and suffer pain. The planetary conditions once for all are such, and we can stand it. But that so many men, by mere accidents of birth and opportunity, should have a life of *nothing else* but toil and pain and hardness and inferiority imposed upon them, should have *no* vacation, while others natively no more deserving never get any taste of this campaigning life at all, — *this* is capable of arousing indignation in reflective minds. It may end by seeming shameful to all of us that some of us have nothing but campaigning, and others nothing but unmanly ease. If now — and this is my idea — there were, instead of military conscription, a conscription of the whole youthful population to form for a certain number of years a part of the army enlisted against *Nature*, the injustice would tend to be evened out, and numerous other goods to the commonwealth would follow. The military ideals of hardihood and discipline would be wrought into the growing fibre of the people; no one would remain blind as the luxurious classes now are blind, to man's real relations to the globe he lives on, and to the permanently sour and hard founda tions of his higher life. To coal and iron mines, to freight trains, to fishing fleets in December, to dish-washing, clothes washing, and window-washing, to road-building and tunnel making, to foundries and stoke-holes, and to the frames of skyscrapers, would our gilded youths be drafted off, according to their choice, to get the childishness knocked out of them, and to come back into society with healthier sympathies and soberer ideas. They would have paid their blood tax, done their own part in the immemorial human warfare against nature, they would tread the earth more proudly, the women would value them more highly, they would be better fathers and teachers of the following generation.

Such a conscription, with the state of public opinion that would have required it, and the many moral fruits it would bear, would preserve in the midst of a pacific civilization the manly virtues which the military party is so afraid of seeing disappear in peace. We should get toughness without callousness, authority with as little criminal cruelty as possible, and painful work done cheerily because the duty is temporary, and threatens not, as now, to degrade the whole remainder of one's life. I spoke of the "moral equivalent" of war. So far, war has been the only force that can discipline a whole community, and until an equivalent discipline is organized, I believe that war must have its way. But I have no serious doubt that the ordinary prides and shames of social man, once developed to a certain intensity, are capable of organizing such a moral equivalent as I have sketched, or some other just as effective for preserving manliness of type. It is but a question of time, of skillful propagandism, and of opinion-making men seizing historic opportunities.

The martial type of character can be bred without war. Strenuous honour and disinterestedness abound elsewhere. Priests and medical men are in a fashion educated to it, and we should all feel some degree of it imperative if we were conscious of our work as an obligatory service to the state. We should be *owned*, as soldiers are by the army, and our pride would rise accordingly. We could be poor, then, without humiliation, as army officers now are. The only thing needed henceforward is to inflame the civic temper as past history has inflamed the military temper. H. G. Wells, as usual, sees the centre of the situation. "In many ways," he says, "military organization is the most peaceful of activities. When the contemporary man steps from the street, of clamorous insincere advertisement, push, adulteration, underselling and intermittent employment, into the barrack-yard, he steps on to a higher social plane, into an atmosphere of service and co-operation and of infinitely more honourable emulations. Here at least men are not flung out of employment to degenerate because there is no immediate work for them to do. They are fed and drilled and trained for better services. Here at least a man is supposed to win promotion by self-forgetfulness and not by self-seeking. And beside the feeble and irregular endowment of research by commercialism, its little short-sighted snatches at profit by innovation and scientific economy, see how remarkable is the steady and rapid development of method and appliances in naval and military affairs! Nothing is more striking than to compare the progress of civil conveniences which has been left almost entirely to the trader, to the progress in military apparatus during the last few decades. The house-appliances of to-day, for example, are little better than they were fifty years ago. A house of to-day is still almost as ill-ventilated, badly heated by wasteful fires, clumsily arranged and furnished as the house of 1858. Houses a couple of hundred years old are still satisfactory places of residence, so little have our standards risen. But the rifle or battleship of fifty years ago was beyond all comparison inferior to those we possess; in power, in speed, in convenience alike. No one has a use now for such superannuated things."[1]

Wells adds[2] that he thinks that the conceptions of order

[1] "First and Last Things," 1908, p. 215.   [2] *Ibid.*, p. 226.

P

and discipline, the tradition of service and devotion, of physical fitness, unstinted exertion, and universal responsibility, which universal military duty is now teaching European nations, will remain a permanent acquisition, when the last ammunition has been used in the fireworks that celebrate the final peace. I believe as he does. It would be simply preposterous if the only force that could work ideals of honour and standards of efficiency into English or American natures should be the fear of being killed by the Germans or the Japanese. Great indeed is Fear; but it is not, as our military enthusiasts believe and try to make us believe, the only stimulus known for awakening the higher ranges of men's spiritual energy. The amount of alteration in public opinion which my utopia postulates is vastly less than the difference between the mentality of those black warriors who pursued Stanley's party on the Congo with their cannibal war-cry of "Meat! Meat" and that of the "general-staff" of any civilized nation. History has seen the latter interval bridged over: the former one can be bridged over much more easily.

THE PROLONGATION OF PEACE [1]

By Simeon Strunsky

ONE historic controversy which history has passed over in silence goes back only a matter of twenty-odd years to the time when Behring announced the discovery of his anti-toxin for diphtheria. Of course people immediately took sides. Against Behring and his serum it was argued that the Klebs-Loeffler bacillus had been active from the beginning of mankind, not to mention the rabbit and the guinea-pig. It was absurd to suppose that the human body would ever

[1] Reprinted from "The Yale Review" by special permission of the editors, and the author of the essay.

cease to be a host for some form of parasite or other. Children had always been dying of acute sore throat and would continue to die. Diphtheria, dispassionately regarded, had its rôle in natural selection. It eliminated the weaklings, and so worked directly against racial degeneracy. But even more important were its effects in the spiritual progress of mankind. Diphtheria was a moral tonic for parentage. It braced up the mothers of the race. It supplied them with an opportunity for displaying the valuable qualities of service and self-sacrifice while the child was sick, and of tight-lipped resignation when the child died.

The advocates of antitoxin usually replied with a mixture of practical and humanitarian considerations. They pointed out the enormous economic waste attributable to the Klebs-Loeffler bacillus. Assuming that every child, when he grew up, represented an addition of at least $5,000 to the national wealth, the ravages of diphtheria easily ran into hundreds of million dollars annually. There was the heavy cost of medical service. There was the large expenditure connected with the final disposition of the little victims who failed to recover. There was the loss of family income, arising either from the father's enforced idleness at the sick bed, as often happens, or in any case from a depressed vitality which for several months was bound to affect the father's earning powers. From the humanitarian point of view people deplored the wastage of human life, regarded not as an economic factor but as something desirable in itself. They drew heart-rending pictures of little faces aglow with fever, of little bodies contorted with pain, of little throats choking for breath. They spoke of the agony of mothers.

The force of this argument the anti-Behringites did not attempt to deny. They yielded to no one in their pity for suffering. But as men who faced life squarely they could only ask: How shall it be otherwise? Has Behring found the secret of immortality?

If this controversy, as I have said, has been neglected by the historians and is not to be traced even in the newspaper files of the period, the probable reason is that the controversy never took place; at least not in the exact form I have given to it. And yet that is precisely the form which the debate would have assumed if the quarrel over the Klebs-Loeffler bacillus had been carried on after the fashion in which the great quarrel over the Gobineau-Bernhardi war bacillus is conducted to-day. On the one hand, you have the same insistence on the fact that war always has been, and therefore, in all likelihood, always will be; the same emphasis on war as a biological factor in the survival of races; the same glorification of war as a moral factor, its enmity to sloth, cowardice, luxury, selfishness. On the other hand, you have the economic wastage of the battlefield, the prodigious cost of armaments, young life blasted in its promise, trenches, hospitals, widows, orphans. And the outcome of the debate is the same. "No one deplores more than I do the horrors of war," says Gobineau-Bernhardi, "but have you found a way to stop all war?"

Thus both sides keep hard at it, in utter disregard of the fact that since the discovery of an antitoxin in 1894 the mortality rate for diphtheria has been reduced from forty-five per cent to ten per cent.

It is amazing how easily men who believe that war is an evil thing will let themselves be manœuvred into the indefensible position of maintaining that the only alternative to war according to Bernhardi is the abolition of war. Either it must be twenty years of world history splashed with at least half a dozen heavy blood-lettings — Chino-Japanese war, Spanish-American war, Boer war, Russo-Japanese war, Balkan wars, the European war — or else it must be an endless future of unbroken peace. Only it is wrong to say manœuvred. The anti-militarist too often plunges of his own free will into this Sedan of perpetual peace. It is true that there are some who believe that war may be eliminated provided we make the effort and pay the price. But there are a great many of us who do not go so far as Tolstoi and non-resistance, yet for whom there is apparently no middle ground between Gobineau-Bernhardi on the one hand and the dream of perpetual peace on the other. We feel that six great wars and a dozen small wars in the course of twenty years are an evil and unnecessary thing. "Oh, then, you believe there is a time coming when men will forget how to fight, when Frenchmen and Germans and Hindus and Japanese will foregather like the Biblical lion and lamb?" No, that is not what we believe. But radical Bernhardi-ism and radical pacifism have so shaped the debate that apparently you must be with one or the other. Between the two lies No Man's Land. And the man who is nearer in heart to the pacifist ideal, lets it go at that, puts on the pacifist uniform, and shoulders a gun in defense of a cause that is not altogether his own.

He forgets, as I have already said, that it is not necessary to bring forward the elixir of life as an alternative to letting children die of diphtheria, that a reduction in mortality from forty-five per cent to ten per cent is a very good thing in itself. The scientists at the Rockefeller Institute are not tackling the problem of the elimination of death, but they are very much concerned with the problem of prolonging life. Ever so much has been written and said about the elimination of war, and very little about the prolongation of peace.

Coupled with this fundamental error of conception which speaks of the "end of war," of a "permanent peace," of a "warless world," is the error of judgment which would have the great ideal attained through some mechanical device. It is seemingly inevitable that it should be so. If peace is to be eternal and unshaken, you cannot turn for prevention to that erratic, untamed, ungauged, and utterly unscientific instrument, the human heart. The only perfect safety devices against rear-end collisions and faulty elevator cables are automatic devices. To the discussion of such automatic safeguards all sorts of minds and hearts have devoted themselves. Scientifically trained minds and prophetic spirits, men to whom the problem appeals only as a problem and men to whom the ideal is a flaming and a holy thing, all agree in searching for the machine that will clutch the slipping cable of peace and hold it firm.

It is now eighteen years since Jean de Bloch wrote a book in seven volumes to demonstrate that war had become impossible. His was the technical argument. It was not a question whether peace is better than war. It was the simple fact that the business of slaughter had become so complicated and so perfected that war meant only a furious tugging back and forth without definite advantage. De Bloch laid stress on trench warfare which rendered the defensive in battle impregnable. He foresaw the rôle of the machine gun, of blockade, of wholesale starvation. After eighteen years de Bloch is now spoken of by students of war as having come into his own. The two years' deadlock in the trenches of Europe has vindicated him. The only thing that remains to be explained is the fact, that in spite of two years' deadlock, there is still going on in the European trenches something that has every appearance of being war.

And there are some things which de Bloch did not foresee. He anticipated the trench, but he did not foresee the monster guns which reduce trenches to rubbish. He foresaw the machine gun, but he did not foresee the clouds of poison gas which drive the artillerist from his machine. But more than that. Assume that de Bloch had been right throughout and that war on land had indeed become impossible. There are other spheres for the aspiring soul of man. When men have lost the art of fighting on land, they will fight under the sea and in the air. When submarine and Zeppelin have found their antidote, men will fight at a distance of two thousand miles with incendiary vibrations and explosive air waves. De Bloch allowed a psychological error to creep into his technical argument. He thought that war had become too terrible for the spirit of man. It is the idea which Mr. H. G. Wells has exploited in his imaginative forecasts of the future social order. When you can drop just one atomic bomb and wipe out Paris or Berlin, war will have become monstrous and impossible. But de Bloch and Mr. Wells have underestimated the capacities of the human soul for inflicting and enduring terror. After the murder of women and babes from the air, it is no longer easy to believe that a mechanical device like the atomic bomb will keep men from fighting forevermore.

And just as Jean de Bloch, fifteen years before the Austrian ultimatum to Servia, had shown that war is technically bankrupt, Mr. Norman Angell proved, only two years before the greatest of wars, that war was an economic impossibility. He showed that war brought with it no profit to the conqueror, that it entailed a wastage of wealth which drained winner and vanquished alike, and that it needed only the general realization of this truth to convince men of the futility of war. I am not of those who think that the present war has made speedy havoc of Mr. Angell's theories. On the contrary I think that of all preventives for war his comes nearest to the heart of the question by laying stress on the human factor, by postulating that people must grow aware of the folly of war before they will stop fighting. To that extent his remedy is not mechanical. His error consists in assuming that men, having attained that knowledge, will forever after live up to it. Perhaps he did not even mean to stress his point so far. The fact remains that Mr. Angell to-day has let himself be classed with the ultra-pacifists. He has been manœuvred into the position of maintaining that there is such a thing as a perpetual and unfailing guarantee against war.

At first sight, the scheme outlined by William James in his little book, "A Moral Equivalent for War," seems to be anything but mechanical. He looks for the roots of war in the spirit of man. He recognizes that one of the great hindrances to the popularity of the pacifist ideal is the simple fact that peace is drab and that war is exciting. He knows that there enters into war the spirit of adventure, of service, and of sacrifice, and he sets himself to find an outlet for the militant impulses of mankind. William James found it in the scheme of a civic army organized and disciplined for the difficult and dangerous works of peace. A conscription of the young men of the nation for service in the coal mines, in the draining of swamps, in the building of public works, gives one a touch of Plato's republic, vivified by the spirit of modern humanitarianism. "Who will do the dirty work?" has been the stock argument flung against the Socialists. The mobilized young men of the nation will do it, says William James, in substance, the same young men who have always been doing the world's dirty work on the battlefields; provided you can train the young man to see that there is as much glory in digging a trench for an aqueduct as for a machine gun emplacement, that the smell of coal gas is as ennobling a thing, at least, as the stink of poison fumes.

A difficult proviso, of course, and James did not underestimate the difficulty; but that is not the fatal point. Again the error emerges of supposing that when you have organized your civic army you will have infallibly prevented the organization of a military army, that you will have eliminated war. A substitute is something which you put in place of something you have discarded. And when you offer a substitute for war you at once confront the ancient doubt whether war can ever be eliminated. William James's civic army is the ancient sword beaten into a ploughshare and the spear into a pruning hook. Translate James into these terms and he offers no brighter chances of success than the original proposal has attained these twenty-five hundred years. A permanent, unbroken ploughshare and pruning-hook existence for the human race? No. But if Isaiah had spoken only of putting aside the sword and taking up the ploughshare, only of hanging up the spear and taking down the pruning hook, it would have come nearer to human limitations. No; William James's substitution of civic service for war, like Percy MacKaye's substitution of the community pageant for war, is after all a business of externals, of mechanical devices. When the blood instinct surges up in man he will not go out into the stadium and dance it off with Mr. MacKaye. He may more probably pick up a shovel and sweat it off with William James; but not always.

One more of these mechanical devices against war and I have done. This time it is another variant of the economic argument. It is a fairly common position, but it has been best stated, perhaps, by Professor Edwin R. A. Seligman in a paper contributed to a composite volume of studies on the great war. Professor Seligman finds that economic rivalry is at the bottom of the present war. He shows how capital, piling up in the old, rich nations and eager for new fields of exploitation, has brought about friction and conflict. May we ever expect a condition of world peace, asks Professor Seligman at the end of his article. Well, perhaps, yes. When the wealth of the earth has been equalized, when capital ceases to be exported, when China, for instance, has become as thoroughly saturated with capital as England is to-day, and holds out no temptations to British and German investors, the reason for war will have disappeared and permanent peace will come.

Just when that will be, the reader is left to judge for himself. Perhaps two hundred years from now China will be saturated with money to the exuding point and we may have world peace, unless it should turn out that the Congo and Morocco are not quite saturated with capital; in which case we should probably have to wait another century. To tell the truth, it is plain that Professor Seligman does not believe in world peace. The subject does not interest him much till the very end of his article. Only then and in deference to the ancient dreams of the race, he permits himself a little idealistic speculation. Once he does take up the subject, he thinks millennially. He speaks only of permanent peace, and when it comes it will come through a mechanical device — capitalistic saturation. That there were wars in the world before capital began looking for foreign markets, that there might be things to quarrel about after international exploitation has ceased, does not enter into consideration.

"How about world peace?" says the pacifist. "Ah, yes, world peace, beautiful ideal, very. It will come some day, five hundred years from now, when China is saturated with money of her own. Kindly pass the cigars." But if one were to ask Professor Seligman not what he thinks of permanent peace, but whether he considers it inevitable for China to be at war with somebody in the next fifty years, he would ponder the question a little more seriously.

For the difference between permanent peace or the elimination of war, as usually understood, and the prolongation of peace as I understand it, is this: world peace means fighting as much as ever till about the year 2345 and then heaven forevermore. Whereas the prolongation of peace means that from now till the year 2345 and after there shall be six wars or a dozen wars only instead of the fifty wars indicated by our present ratio. I am ready to admit that war is as inevitable as death and taxes. Men will always pay taxes. The question is how high are taxes to be. Men will always die. The question is how soon. Men will always fight. The question is how often.

When the anti-militarist speaks of a United States of Europe that is to arise after the war, he is accused of indulging in millennial dreams, and the only rejoinder he can think of is to demonstrate the feasibility of the millennium. It seems to occur to neither party that the establishment of the United States of Europe does not guarantee the millennium. The United States of America had a civil war which lasted four years and this in spite of the fact that the States of the Union were not the European states of to-day. The Colonies had never engaged in war with each other. They had behind them almost none of the complex of forces and traditions that makes for international war. Eighty-five years after they had become a nation, they went to war with each other. And the United Counties of England have known civil war, and the United Provinces of France and the United Cantons of Switzerland. If it is the absolute prevention of war you are striving for, the Union of Europe is no guarantee.

Why this knockdown argument against the United States of Europe is never used by the anti-pacifist I am unable to understand. Unless it be that the anti-pacifist instinctively recognizes that this argument would in the long run be fatal to himself. It would be a knockdown blow that would ultimately help to clarify his opponent's ideas. For if your believer in things as they have been were to say ·
"Well, what of your United States of Europe? Has there

been no war within the United States of America?" the
average pacifist would be compelled to sift his own thoughts
and so discover what he really means. "Yes, one civil war
in one hundred and forty years," he would reply, "and how
many wars have there been in Europe during that time?"
"Oh, then, you don't mean the abolition of war, you mean
reducing the frequency of war?" "Yes: isn't that worth
while?" "Oh, in that case," and the militarist immediately
feels the disadvantage of combating a fairly reasonable citizen instead of a fanatic.

It is the same when we speak of the establishment of a
system of law and order among the nations such as obtains
within each separate nation and each community. For them
again your anti-pacifist is in a position to say, "Law as
between nations? Does law function so perfectly within the
nations? Is there no such thing as lynch law in the country
you offer as a model for the United States of Europe? Is
there no such thing as the *duello* in Europe? Is there no
such thing as the unwritten law in America and the *crime
passionel* in France, when public opinion virtually demands
that in certain cases a man shall not go to court but shall
shoot to kill?" To which the moderate pacifist: "True.
It is nevertheless a fact that men do go to court ever so
much more often than they used to and they use the dirk
and pistol ever so much less. People do not shoot and stab
on pretty nearly every occasion as they used to do." And
there, of course, is the nub of the whole problem.

How was it with the beginnings of the movement away
from the curse of private warfare in the Dark Ages of Europe? The church took the matter in hand. But though
the church subscribed to the ideal of everlasting and unbroken peace, the practical common sense of the ecclesias-
tics of the tenth century suggested a moderate programme.
The church councils did not impose peace everywhere and

every day in the week upon the militant barons. The peace of the church specified a number of classes against whom violence must not be practised at any time — against clerics, women, pilgrims, peasants, against ecclesiastical buildings, cattle, and agricultural implements. The "truce of God," which grew out of the peace of the church, forbade private warfare on certain days and in certain seasons. It began with a prohibition against fighting of all kinds from noon on Saturday to prime on Monday. The barons may have chafed at the loss of a good day and a half but to some extent they obeyed. Within a short time the truce of God had been stretched from Wednesday evening to Monday morning and during all of Lent, Advent, the feasts of the blessed Virgin, the twelve apostles, and a few other saints. One can almost imagine the shrewd churchmen cautiously feeling the pulse of their public and adding a saint or two as the opportunity offered. At the height of its development the truce of God left less than one-quarter of the year for the barons to fight in and even within that restricted space the provisions of the peace of the church held good with regard to those classes and objects which were perpetually immune against private assault.

I am bound to confess that the authority from whom I have drawn my information goes on to say that the truce of God produced on the whole "surprisingly mediocre results." It was apparently more than human nature could stand that a baron who had been insulted in his honor and his interests on Thursday morning should wait till noon of the following Monday before exacting satisfaction. But some results there were. The beginning had been made, and when monarchy arose in the later centuries to assert its authority against the feudalists it borrowed the provisions of the truce of God and peace of the church and embodied them into the king's peace. From that time, I imagine, the progress of law and order simply meant a steady reduction in the number of private quarrels; not because differences of opinion arose more frequently on a Sunday or within the bounds of a church building, or because of an increase in the number of classes immune against sudden assault, but primarily because of a reduction in the number of causes for which people felt it incumbent to fight.   How this happened it is not difficult to surmise.   If a baron did not like the color of his neighbor's mantle on Thursday morning and was prevented from fighting him on that cause till Monday noon, there was a chance that by Monday noon the offense would not seem so serious.   In that way does habit fix its clutches on man.   And in that way, I imagine, have we progressed from the time when men fought over the color of a coat or the theft of a sheep or because their sword hilts clashed in a crowd, to the present when men fight out private quarrels over the very few causes I have mentioned above.

But this much should be noted before we pass on.   In those bad times when men fought over the color of a coat or the possession of a herd of cattle, it was not the physical pain involved in looking at a scarlet coat with yellow trimmings that stirred the fighting blood, it was often not the money value of the disputed cattle.   The true cause was the injury to a man's honor inflicted by the unæsthetic coat or the ravished cattle.   That honor was at the bottom of private warfare is shown by the simple fact that there was no private warfare against merchants, peasants, pilgrims, and clerics, who had no honor to offend.

The progress from private feud to the law of the king or commonwealth may thus be described as a steady degeneration in the sensitiveness of private honor with which, in the higher circles of European society, the sense of honor is still sometimes confused.   The number of causes upon which a man will fight varies directly with his social status, though it is to be noted that the life-and-death combat of the mediæval barons has atrophied to a few ceremonial flourishes of the rapier or the discharge of a pistol into the air. It is obvious that about the honor which is appeased by a sword prick in the lower joint of the thumb there is more sensitiveness than sense.

There is no monarch or parliament in the civilized world to-day that will refuse to go into a treaty for the arbitration of differences with a foreign power provided the issue does not touch the honor or the vital interests of a nation. The two, of course, are in the last analysis the same thing. A nation's honor is of vital interest to the nation, and on the other hand no nation can surrender a vital interest without injury to its honor. Shall we ask nations and governments to sacrifice national honor or vital interests? No. But we may draw the attention of rulers and parliaments to the theory of emotions popularized by William James when he asserts that men are afraid because they run away and men hate because they clench their fists and scowl. If we were to give up the habit of saying that a nation will fight for a cause involving its honor, and said instead that when a nation fights its honor is presumably involved, we should get nearer to a solution of the problem. If we could only get a nation under a particular set of circumstances not to fight, it is likely that it will ultimately find that its honor has not been injured; not always, but as a rule. In the case of the mediæval baron, as the habit declined of fighting over the offensive color of a coat or the tilt of a hat, the sense of honor ceased to be mutilated by coats and hats. What the nations have inherited from an evil past is still that habit of finding a cause for war, and therefore an injury to one's honor, in the tilt of another nation's hat. Obviously the way to the prolongation of peace is through the elimination of many of the irritants that have hitherto stirred a nation's honor. This may seem a craven and ignoble policy. But the mediæval baron must have felt it a craven thing not to draw his sword when the color of his neighbor's coat of mail or the head feathers on his neighbor's charger offended him.

Civilized communities have already outgrown a mass of smiles, sneers, jostlings, hints, words, and phrases for which the Dark Ages went to war, but too many of those acts, signs, and ceremonials in which the national honor is supposed to be imbedded unfortunately survive. Civilized nations still recognize a large number of actions which, if performed by another nation, automatically lead to war. There is the national flag, insult to which means either reparation or war. There are the lives of nationals in a foreign country. There is the tradition which invests every army lieutenant and naval ensign on foreign soil with greater powers of peace and war than the President of the United States exercises. For you can criticise and oppose a President's policy even if it is foreign policy, but automatically the whole nation rallies behind the young subaltern who gets into trouble with the mob in a foreign city. There is the tradition which prescribes that when a nation has been committed to an act of folly or crime by its representative, it may explain or mitigate or countercharge or offer reparation but it cannot in honor disavow. The peace of the world is founded on the proud principle that the citizen of no par ticular consequence at home and the army or naval officer of no particular authority at home, become the depositaries of the nation's honor, the nation's fortunes, and the nation's policy when they set foot on foreign soil.

Into this mass of rights, privileges, proprieties, and tradi tions the awakened conscience of humanity has thrust the sterilized needle of common sense, and we are to-day witnessing a process which isolates the fundamental principles of true national honor and really vital interests from the dead sediment of etiquette which has hitherto been supposed to embody the national honor. The way to surer and larger peace is through the clearing away of this clutter of things "not arbitrable." . . .

I have tried to formulate something of a case for the man who is opposed to the Bernhardi ideal of war and yet does not wish to be driven into defending the kingdom of heaven on earth. It is the weakness of the ultra-pacifist from the historic point of view, that he would write *finis* to the book of international evolution. We have not done that even to the book of national evolution. The absolute rule of law does not obtain in any community. The pacifist writes at the end of the novel, "And they lived happy ever afterward." Opposed to him is the man who regards himself as an uncompromising realist and says, "Oh, no, the man and the woman will go on quarrelling to the end of time." Between the two there is room for the plain observer of life who merely predicts for his hero and heroine a steady progress through misunderstanding and strife to a tolerable condition of sympathy and forbearance.

GROUP THREE

(To Accompany Chapter III)

A MODERN SYMPOSIUM[1]

By G. Lowes Dickinson

(*The Speech of Ellis*)

[As Wilson] sat down a note was passed along to me from Ellis, asking permission to speak next. I assented willingly; for Ellis, though some of us thought him frivolous, was, at

[1] Pp. 90–108. Reprinted by special permission of the author and of the publishers, Doubleday, Page & Co.

Q

any rate, never dull. His sunburnt complexion, his fair curly hair, and the light in his blue eyes made a pleasant impression, as he rose and looked down upon us from his six feet.

"This," he began, "is really an extraordinary discovery Wilson has made, that fathers have children, and children fathers! One wonders how the world has got on all these centuries in ignorance of it. It seems so obvious, once it has been stated. But that, of course, is the nature of great truths; as soon as they are announced they seem to have been always familiar. It is possible, for that very reason, that many people may underestimate the importance of Wilson's pronouncement, forgetting that it is the privilege of genius to formulate for the first time what every one has been dimly feeling. We ought not to be ungrateful; but perhaps it is our duty to be cautious. For great ideas naturally suggest practical applications, and it is here that I foresee difficulties. What Wilson's proposition in fact amounts to, if I understand him rightly, is that we ought to open as wide as possible the gates of life, and make those who enter as comfortable as we can. Now, I think we ought to be very careful about doing anything of the kind. We know, of course, very little about the conditions of the unborn. But I think it highly probable that, like labour, as described by the political economists, they form throughout the universe a single mobile body, with a tendency to gravitate wherever the access is freest and the conditions most favourable. And I should be very much afraid of attracting what we may call, perhaps, the unemployed of the universe in undue proportions to this planet, by offering them artificially better terms than are to be obtained elsewhere. For that, as you know, would defeat our own object. We should merely cause an exodus, as it were, from the outlying and rural districts, Mars, or the moon, or whatever the place may be; and the amount of distress and difficulty on the earth would be greater than ever. At any rate, I should insist, and I daresay Wilson agrees with me there, on some adequate test. And I would not advertise too widely what we are doing. After all, other planets must be responsible for their own unborn; and I don't see why we should become a kind of dumping-ground of the universe for every one who may imagine he can better himself by migrating to the earth. For that reason, among others, I would not open the gate too wide. And, perhaps, in view of this consideration, we might still permit some people not to marry. At any rate, I wouldn't go further, I think, than a fine for recalcitrant bachelors. Wilson, I daresay, would prefer imprisonment for a second offence, and in case of contumacy, even capital punishment. On such a point I am not, I confess, an altogether impartial judge, as I should certainly incur the greater penalty. Still, as I have said, in the general interests of society, and in view of the conditions of the universal market, I would urge caution and deliberation. And that is all I have to say at present on this very interesting subject.

"The other point that interested me in Wilson's remarks was not, indeed, so novel as the discovery about fathers having children, but it was, in its way, equally important. I mean, the announcement made with authority that the human race really does, as has been so often conjectured, progress. We may take it now, I suppose, that that is established, or Wilson would not have proclaimed it. And we are, therefore, in a position roughly to determine in what progress consists. This is a task which, I believe, I am more competent to attempt perhaps even than Wilson himself, because I have had unusual opportunities of travel, and have endeavoured to utilize them to clear my mind of prejudices. I flatter myself that I can regard with perfect impartiality the ideals of different countries, and in particular those of the new world which, I presume, are to dominate the future. In attempting to estimate what progress means, one could not do better, I suppose, than describe the civilization of the United States. For in describing that, one will be describing the whole civilization of the future, seeing that what America is our colonies are, or will become, and what our colonies are we, too, may hope to attain, if we make the proper sacrifices to preserve the unity of the empire. Let us see, then, what, from an objective point of view, really is the future of this progressing world of ours.

"Perhaps, however, before proceeding to analyse the spiritual ideals of the American people, I had better give some account of their country. For environment, as we all know now, has an incalculable effect upon character. Consider, then, the American continent! How simple it is! How broad! How large! How grand in design! A strip of coast, a range of mountains, a plain, a second range, a second strip of coast! That is all! Contrast the complexity of Europe, its lack of symmetry, its variety, irregularity, disorder, and caprice! The geography of the two continents already foreshadows the differences in their civilizations. On the one hand simplicity and size; on the other a hole-and-corner variety: there immense rivers, endless forests, interminable plains, indefinite repetition of a few broad ideas; here distracting transitions, novelties, surprises, shocks, distinctions in a word, already suggesting Distinction. Even in its physical features America is the land of quantity, while Europe is that of quality. And as with the land, so with its products. How large are the American fruits! How tall the trees! How immense the oysters! What has Europe by comparison? Mere flavor and form, mere beauty, delicacy, and grace! America, one would say, is the latest work of the great artist — we are told, indeed, by geologists, that it is the youngest of the continents — conceived at an age when he had begun to repeat himself, broad, summary, impressionist, audacious in empty space; whereas Europe would seem to represent his pre-Raphaelite period, in its wealth of detail, its variety of figure, costume, architecture, landscape, its crudely contrasted colours and minute precision of individual form.

"And as with the countries, so with their civilizations. Europe is the home of class, America of democracy. By democracy I do not mean a mere form of government—in that respect, of course, America is less democratic than England; I mean the mental attitude that implies and engenders Indistinction. Indistinction, I say, rather than equality, for the word equality is misleading, and might seem to imply, for example, a social and economic parity of conditions, which no more exists in America than it does in Europe. Politically, as well as socially, America is a plutocracy; her democracy is spiritual and intellectual; and its essence is, the denial of all superiorities save that of wealth. Such superiorities, in fact, hardly exist across the Atlantic. All men there are intelligent, all efficient, all energetic; and as these are the only qualities they possess, so they are the only ones they feel called upon to admire. How different is the case with Europe! How innumerable and how confusing the gradations! For diversities of language and race, indeed, we may not be altogether responsible; but we have superadded to these, distinctions of manner, of feeling, of perception, of intellectual grasp and spiritual insight, unknown to the simpler and vaster consciousness of the West. In addition, in short, to the obvious and fundamentally natural standard of wealth, we have invented others impalpable and artificial in their character; and however rapidly these may be destined to disappear as the race progresses, and the influence of the West begins to dominate the East, they do, nevertheless, still persist, and give to our effete civilization the character of Aristocracy, that is of Caste. In all this we see, as I have suggested, the influence of environment. The old-world stock, transplanted across the ocean, imitates the characteristics of its new home. Sloughing off artificial distinctions, it manifests itself in bold simplicity, broad as the plains, turbulent as the rivers, formless as the mountains, crude as the fruits of its adopted country.

"Yet while thus forming themselves into the image of the new world, the Americans have not disdained to make use of such acquisitions of the Past as might be useful to them in the task that lay before them. They have rejected our ideals and our standards; but they have borrowed our capital and our inventions. They have thus been able — a thing unknown before in the history of the world — to start the battle against Nature with weapons ready forged. On the material results they have thus been able to achieve it is the less necessary for me to dilate, that they keep us so fully informed of them themselves. But it may be interesting to note an important consequence in their spiritual life, which has commonly escaped the notice of observers. Thanks to Europe, America has never been powerless in the face of Nature; therefore has never felt Fear; therefore never known Reverence; and therefore never experienced Religion. It may seem paradoxical to make such an assertion about the descendants of the Puritan Fathers; nor do I forget the notorious fact that America is the home of the sects, from the followers of Joseph Smith to those of Mrs. Eddy. But these are the phenomena that illustrate my point. A nation which knew what religion was, in the European sense; whose roots were struck in the soil of spiritual conflict, of temptations and visions in haunted forests or desert sands by the Nile, of midnight risings, scourgings of the flesh, dirges in vast cathedrals, and the miracle of the Host solemnly veiled in a glory of painted light — such a nation would never have accepted Christian Science as a religion. No! Religion in America is a parasite without roots. The questions that have occupied Europe from the dawn of her history, for which she has fought more fiercely than for empire or liberty, for which she has fasted in deserts, agonized in cells, suffered on the cross, and at the stake, for which she has sacrificed wealth, health, ease, intelligence, life, these questions of the meaning of the world, the origin and destiny of the soul, the life after death, the existence of God, and his relation to the universe, for the American people simply do not exist. They are as inaccessible, as impossible to them, as the Sphere to the dwellers in Flatland. That whole dimension is unknown to them. Their healthy and robust intelligence confines itself to the things of this world. Their religion, if they have one, is what I believe they call 'healthy-mindedness.' It consists in ignoring everything that might suggest a doubt as to the worth of existence, and so conceivably paralyse activity. 'Let us eat and drink,' they say, with a hearty and robust good faith; omitting as irrelevant and morbid the discouraging appendix, 'for to-morrow we die.' Indeed! What has death to do with buildings twenty-four stories high, with the fastest trains, the noisiest cities, the busiest crowds in the world, and generally the largest, the finest, the most accelerated of everything that exists? America has sloughed off religion; and as, in the history of Europe, religion has underlain every other activity, she has sloughed off, along with it, the whole European system of spiritual life. Literature, for instance, and Art, do not exist across the Atlantic. I am aware, of course, that Americans write books and paint pictures. But their books are not Literature, nor their pictures Art, except in so far as they represent a faint adum bration of the European tradition. The true spirit of America has no use for such activities. And even if, as must occasionally happen in a population of eighty millions, there is born among them a man of artistic instincts, he is immediately and inevitably repelled to Europe, whence he derives his training and his inspiration, and where alone he can live, observe and create. That this must be so from the nature of the case is obvious when we reflect that the spirit of Art is disinterested contemplation, while that of America is cupidous acquisition. Americans, I am aware, believe that they will produce Literature and Art, as they produce coal and steel and oil, by the judicious application of intelligence and capital; but here they do themselves injustice. The qualities that are making them masters of the world, unfit them for slighter and less serious pursuits. The Future is for them, the kingdom of elevators, of telephones, of motor-cars, of flying-machines. Let them not idly hark back, misled by effete traditions, to the old European dream of the kingdom of heaven. *'Excudent alii'* let them say, 'for Europe, Letters and Art; *tu regere argento populos, Morgane, memento*, let America rule the world by Syndicates and Trusts!' For such is her true destiny; and that she conceives it to be such, is evidenced by the determination with which she has suppressed all irrelevant activities. Every kind of disinterested intellectual operation she has severely repudiated. In Europe we take delight in the operations of the mind as such, we let it play about a subject, merely for the fun of the thing; we approve knowledge for its own sake; we appreciate irony and wit. But all this is unknown in America. The most intelligent people in the world, they severely limit their intelligence to the adaptation of means to ends. About the ends themselves they never permit themselves to speculate; and for this reason, though they calculate, they never think, though they invent, they never discover, and though they talk, they never converse. For thought implies speculation; reflection, discovery; conversation, leisure; and all alike imply a disinterestedness which has no place in the American system. For the same reason they do not play; they have converted games into battles; and battles in which every weapon is legitimate so long as it is victorious. An American foot-ball match exhibits in a type the American spirit, short, sharp, scientific, intense, no loitering by the road, no enjoyment of the process, no favour, no quarter, but a fight to the death with victory as the end, and anything and everything as the means.

"A nation so severely practical could hardly be expected to attach the same importance to the emotions as has been attributed to them by Europeans. Feeling, like Intellect, is not regarded, in the West, as an end in itself. And it is not uninteresting to note that the Americans are the only great nation that have not produced a single lyric of love worth recording. Physically, as well as spiritually, they are a people of cold temperament. Their women, so much and, I do not doubt, so legitimately admired, are as hard as they are brilliant; their glitter is the glitter of ice. Thus happily constituted, Americans are able to avoid the im mense waste of time and energy involved in the formation and maintenance of subtle personal relations. They marry, of course, they produce children, they propagate the race; but I would venture to say, they do not love, as Europeans have loved; they do not exploit the emotion, analyse and enjoy it, still less express it in manners, in gesture, in epigram, in verse. And hence the kind of shudder produced in a cultivated European by the treatment of emotion in American fiction. The authors are trying to express something they have never experienced, and to graft the European tradition on to a civilization which has none of the elements necessary to nourish and support it.

"From this brief analysis of the attitude of Americans towards life, the point with which I started will, I hope, have become clear, that it is idle to apply to them any of the tests which we apply to a European civilization. For they have rejected, whether they know it or not, our whole scheme of values. What, then, is their own? What do they recognize as an end? This is an interesting point on which I have reflected much in the course of my travels. Sometimes I have thought it was wealth, sometimes power, sometimes activity. But a poem, or at least a production in metre, which I came across in the States, gave me a new idea upon the subject. On such a point I speak with great diffidence; but I am inclined to think that my author was right; that the real end which Americans set before themselves is Acceleration. To be always moving, and always moving faster, that they think is the beatific life; and with their happy detachment from philosophy and specula tion, they are not troubled by the question, Whither? If they are asked by Europeans, as they sometimes are, what is the point of going so fast? their only feeling is one of gen- uine astonishment. Why, they reply, you go fast! And what more can be said? Hence, their contempt for the leisure so much valued by Europeans. Leisure they feel to be a kind of standing still, the unpardonable sin. Hence, also, their aversion to play, to conversation, to everything that is not work. I once asked an American who had been describ ing to me the scheme of his laborious life, where it was that the fun came in? He replied, without hesitation and without regret, that it came in nowhere. How should it? It could only act as a brake; and a brake upon Acceleration is the last thing tolerable to the American genius.

"The American genius, I say: but after all, and this is the real point of my remarks, what America is Europe is becoming. We, who sit here, with the exception, of course, of Wilson, represent the Past, not the Future. Politicians, professors, lawyers, doctors, no matter what our calling, our judgments are determined by the old scale of values. Intellect, Beauty, Emotion, these are the things we count precious; to wealth and to progress we are indifferent, save as conducing to these. And thus, like the speakers who preceded me, we venture to criticise and doubt, where the modern man, American or European, simply and whole-heartedly, accepts. For this it would be idle for us to blame ourselves, idle even to regret; we should simply and objectively note that we are out of court. All that we say may be true, but it is irrelevant. 'True,' says the man of the Future, 'we have no religion, literature, or art; we don't know whence we come, nor whither we go; but, what is more important, we don't care. What we do know is, that we are moving faster than any one ever moved before; and that there is every chance of our moving faster and faster. To inquire "whither" is the one thing that we recognize as blasphemous. The principle of the Universe is Acceleration, and we are its exponents; what is not accelerated will be extinguished; and if we cannot answer ultimate questions, that is the less to be regretted in that, a few centuries hence, there will be nobody left to ask them.'

"Such is the attitude which I believe to be that of the Future, both in the West and in the East. I do not pretend to sympathize with it; but my perception of it gives a peculiar piquancy to my own position. I rejoice that I was born at the end of an epoch; that I stand as it were at the summit, just before the plunge into the valley below; and looking back, survey and summarize in a glance the ages that are past. I rejoice that my friends are Socrates and Plato, Dante, Michelangelo, Goethe instead of Mr. Carnegie and Mr. Pierpont Morgan. I rejoice that I belong to an effete country; and that I sit at table with almost the last representatives of the culture, the learning and the ideals of centuries of civilization. I prefer the tradition of the Past to that of the Future; I value it the more for its contrast with that which is to come; and I am the more at ease inasmuch as I feel myself divested of all responsibility towards generations whose ideals and standards I am unable to appreciate.

"All this shows, of course, merely that I am not one of the people so aptly described by Wilson as the 'new generation.' But I flatter myself that my intellectual apprehension is not coloured by the circumstances of my own case, and that I have given you a clear and objective picture of what it is that really constitutes progress. And with that proud consciousness in my mind, I resume my seat."

PASSING OF THE THIRD FLOOR BACK [1]

By Jerome K. Jerome

THE neighborhood of Bloomsbury Square towards four o'clock of a November afternoon is not so crowded as to secure to the stranger, of appearance anything out of the common, immunity from observation. Tibb's boy, screaming at the top of his voice that *she* was his honey, stopped suddenly, stepped backwards on to the toes of a voluble young lady wheeling a perambulator, and remained deaf, apparently, to the somewhat personal remarks of the voluble young lady. Not until he had reached the next corner — and then more as a soliloquy than as information to the street — did Tibb's boy recover sufficient interest in his own affairs to remark that *he* was her bee. The voluble young lady herself, following some half-a-dozen yards behind, forgot her wrongs in contemplation of the stranger's back.

[1] Reprinted by special permission of the author and of the publishers, Dodd, Mead, & Co.

There was this that was peculiar about the stranger's back: that instead of being flat it presented a decided curve. "It ain't a 'ump, and it don't look like kervitcher of the spine," observed the voluble young lady to herself. "Blimy if I don't believe 'e's taking 'ome 'is washing up his back."

The constable at the corner, trying to seem busy doing nothing, noticed the stranger's approach with gathering interest. "That's an odd sort of a walk of yours, young man," thought the constable. "You take care you don't fall down and tumble over yourself."

"Thought he was a young man," murmured the constable, the stranger having passed him. "He had a young face right enough."

The daylight was fading. The stranger, finding it impossible to read the name of the street upon the corner house, turned back.

"Why, 'tis a young man," the constable told himself; "a mere boy."

"I beg your pardon," said the stranger; "but would you mind telling me my way to Bloomsbury Square."

"This is Bloomsbury Square," explained the constable; "leastways round the corner is. What number might you be wanting?"

The stranger took from the ticket pocket of his tightly buttoned overcoat a piece of paper, unfolded it and read it out: "Mrs. Pennycherry. Number Forty-eight."

"Round to the left," instructed him the constable; "fourth house. Been recommended there?"

"By — by a friend," replied the stranger. "Thank you very much."

"Ah," muttered the constable to himself; "guess you won't be calling him that by the end of the week, young ——

"Funny," added the constable, gazing after the retreating figure of the stranger. "Seen plenty of the other sex as looked young behind and old in front. This cove looks young in front and old behind. Guess he'll look old all round if he stops long at mother Pennycherry's: stingy old cat."

Constables whose beat included Bloomsbury Square had their reasons for not liking Mrs. Pennycherry. Indeed it might have been difficult to discover any human being with reasons for liking that sharp-featured lady. Maybe the keeping of second-rate boarding houses in the neighbourhood of Bloomsbury does not tend to develop the virtues of generosity and amiability.

Meanwhile the stranger, proceeding upon his way, had rung the bell of Number Forty-eight. Mrs. Pennycherry, peeping from the area and catching a glimpse, above the railings, of a handsome if somewhat effeminate masculine face, hastened to readjust her widow's cap before the looking glass while directing Mary Jane to show the stranger, should he prove a problematical boarder, into the dining-room, and to light the gas.

"And don't stop gossiping, and don't you take it upon yourself to answer questions. Say I'll be up in a minute," were Mrs. Pennycherry's further instructions, "and mind you hide your hands as much as you can."

"What are you grinning at?" demanded Mrs. Pennycherry, a couple of minutes later, of the dingy Mary Jane.

"Wasn't grinning," explained the meek Mary Jane, "was only smiling to myself."

"What at?"

"Dunno," admitted Mary Jane. But still she went on smiling.

"What's he like then?" demanded Mrs. Pennycherry.

"'E ain't the usual sort," was Mary Jane's opinion.

"Thank God for that," ejaculated Mrs. Pennycherry piously.

"Says 'e's been recommended, by a friend."

"By whom?"

"By a friend. 'E didn't say no name."

Mrs. Pennycherry pondered. "He's not the funny sort, is he?"

Not that sort at all. Mary Jane was sure of it.

Mrs. Pennycherry ascended the stairs still pondering. As she entered the room the stranger rose and bowed. Nothing could have been simpler than the stranger's bow, yet there came with it to Mrs. Pennycherry a rush of old sensations long forgotten. For one brief moment Mrs. Pennycherry saw herself an amiable well-bred lady, widow of a solicitor: a visitor had called to see her. It was but a momentary fancy. The next instant Reality reasserted itself. Mrs. Pennycherry, a lodging-house keeper, existing precariously upon a daily round of petty meannesses, was prepared for contest with a possible new boarder, who fortunately looked an inexperienced young gentleman.

"Someone has recommended me to you," began Mrs. Pennycherry; "may I ask who?"

But the stranger waved the question aside as immaterial.

"You might not remember — him," he smiled. "He thought that I should do well to pass the few months I am given — that I have to be in London, here. You can take me in?"

Mrs. Pennycherry thought that she would be able to take the stranger in.

"A room to sleep in," explained the stranger, "— any room will do — with food and drink sufficient for a man, is all that I require."

"For breakfast," began Mrs. Pennycherry, "I always give ——"

"What is right and proper, I am convinced," interrupted the stranger. "Pray do not trouble to go into detail, Mrs. Pennycherry. With whatever it is I shall be content."

Mrs. Pennycherry, puzzled, shot a quick glance at the stranger, but his face, though the gentle eyes were smiling, was frank and serious.

"At all events you will see the room," suggested Mrs. Pennycherry, "before we discuss terms."

"Certainly," agreed the stranger. "I am a little tired and shall be glad to rest there."

Mrs. Pennycherry led the way upward; on the landing of the third floor, paused a moment undecided, then opened the door of the back bedroom.

"It is very comfortable," commented the stranger.

"For this room," stated Mrs. Pennycherry, "together with full board, consisting of ——"

"Of everything needful. It goes without saying," again interrupted the stranger with his quiet grave smile.

"I have generally asked," continued Mrs. Pennycherry, "four pounds a week. To you —" Mrs. Pennycherry's voice, unknown to her, took to itself the note of aggressive generosity — "seeing you have been recommended here, say three pounds ten."

"Dear lady," said the stranger, "that is kind of you. As you have divined, I am not a rich man. If it be not imposing upon you I accept your reduction with gratitude."

Again Mrs. Pennycherry, familiar with the satirical method, shot a suspicious glance upon the stranger, but not a line was there, upon that smooth fair face, to which a sneer could for a moment have clung. Clearly he was as simple as he looked.

"Gas, of course, extra."

"Of course," agreed the stranger.

"Coals ——"

"We shall not quarrel," for a third time the stranger interrupted. "You have been very considerate to me as it is. I feel, Mrs. Pennycherry, I can leave myself entirely in your hands."

The stranger appeared anxious to be alone. Mrs. Pennycherry, having put a match to the stranger's fire, turned to depart. And at this point it was that Mrs. Pennycherry, the holder hitherto of an unbroken record for sanity, behaved in a manner she herself, five minutes earlier in her career, would have deemed impossible — that no living soul who had ever known her would have believed, even had Mrs. Pennycherry gone down upon her knees and sworn it to them.

"Did I say three pound ten?" demanded Mrs. Pennycherry of the stranger, her hand upon the door. She spoke crossly. She was feeling cross, with the stranger, with herself — particularly with herself.

"You were kind enough to reduce it to that amount," replied the stranger; "but if upon reflection you find yourself unable ——"

"I was making a mistake," said Mrs. Pennycherry, "it should have been two pound ten."

"I cannot — I will not accept such sacrifice," exclaimed the stranger; "the three pound ten I can well afford."

"Two pound ten are my terms," snapped Mrs. Pennycherry. "If you are bent on paying more, you can go elsewhere. You'll find plenty to oblige you."

Her vehemence must have impressed the stranger. "We will not contend further," he smiled. "I was merely afraid that in the goodness of your heart ——"

"Oh, it isn't as good as all that," growled Mrs. Pennycherry.

"I am not so sure," returned the stranger. "I am somewhat suspicious of you. But wilful woman must, I suppose, have her way."

R

The stranger held out his hand, and to Mrs. Pennycherry, at that moment, it seemed the most natural thing in the world to take it as if it had been the hand of an old friend and to end the interview with a pleasant laugh — though laughing was an exercise not often indulged in by Mrs. Pennycherry.

Mary Jane was standing by the window, her hands folded in front of her, when Mrs. Pennycherry reëntered the kitchen. By standing close to the window one caught a glimpse of the trees in Bloomsbury Square and through their bare branches of the sky beyond.

"There's nothing much to do for the next half hour, till Cook comes back. I'll see to the door if you'd like a run out?" suggested Mrs. Pennycherry.

"It would be nice," agreed the girl so soon as she had recovered power of speech; "it's just the time of day I like."

"Don't be longer than the half hour," added Mrs. Pennycherry.

Forty-eight Bloomsbury Square, assembled after dinner in the drawing-room, discussed the stranger with that freedom and frankness characteristic of Forty-eight Bloomsbury Square, towards the absent.

"Not what I call a smart young man," was the opinion of Augustus Longcord, who was something in the City

"Thpeaking for mythelf," commented his partner Isidore, "hav'n'th any uthe for the thmart young man. Too many of him, ath it ith."

"Must be pretty smart if he's one too many for you," laughed his partner. There was this to be said for the repartee of Forty-eight Bloomsbury Square: it was simple of construction and easy of comprehension.

"Well it made me feel good just looking at him," declared Miss Kite, the highly coloured. "It was his clothes, I suppose — made me think of Noah and the ark — all that sort of thing."

"It would be clothes that would make you think — if anything," drawled the languid Miss Devine. She was a tall, handsome girl, engaged at the moment in futile efforts to recline with elegance and comfort combined upon a horsehair sofa. Miss Kite, by reason of having secured the only easy-chair, was unpopular that evening; so that Miss Devine's remark received from the rest of the company more approbation than perhaps it merited.

"Is that intended to be clever, dear, or only rude?" Miss Kite requested to be informed.

"Both," claimed Miss Devine.

"Myself, I must confess," shouted the tall young lady's father, commonly called the Colonel, "I found him a fool."

"I noticed you seemed to be getting on very well together," purred his wife, a plump, smiling little lady.

"Possibly we were," retorted the Colonel. "Fate has accustomed me to the society of fools."

"Isn't it a pity to start quarrelling immediately after dinner, you two," suggested their thoughtful daughter from the sofa, "you'll have nothing left to amuse you for the rest of the evening."

"He didn't strike me as a conversationalist," said the lady who was cousin to a baronet; "but he did pass the vegetables before he helped himself. A little thing like that shows breeding."

"Or that he didn't know you and thought maybe you'd leave him half a spoonful," laughed Augustus the wit.

"What I can't make out about him ——" shouted the Colonel.

The stranger entered the room.

The Colonel, securing the evening paper, retired into a

corner. The highly coloured Kite, reaching down from the mantelpiece a paper fan, held it coyly before her face. Miss Devine sat upright on the horsehair sofa, and rearranged her skirts.

"Know anything?" demanded Augustus of the stranger, breaking the somewhat remarkable silence.

The stranger evidently did not understand. It was necessary for Augustus, the witty, to advance further into that odd silence.

"What's going to pull off the Lincoln handicap? Tell me, and I'll go out straight and put my shirt upon it."

"I think you would act unwisely," smiled the stranger; "I am not an authority upon the subject."

"Not! Why they told me you were Captain Spy of the *Sporting Life* — in disguise."

It would have been difficult for a joke to fall more flat. Nobody laughed, though why Mr. Augustus Longcord could not understand, and maybe none of his audience could have told him, for at Forty-eight Bloomsbury Square Mr. Augustus Longcord passed as a humorist. The stranger himself appeared unaware that he was being made fun of.

"You have been misinformed," assured him the stranger.

"I beg your pardon," said Mr. Augustus Longcord.

"It is nothing," replied the stranger in his sweet low voice, and passed on.

"Well what about this theatre," demanded Mr. Longcord of his friend and partner; "do you want to go or don't you?" Mr. Longcord was feeling irritable.

"Goth the ticketh — may ath well," thought Isidore.

"Damn stupid piece, I'm told."

"Motht of them thupid, more or leth. Pity to wathte the ticketh," argued Isidore, and the pair went out.

"Are you staying long in London?" asked Miss Kite, raising her practised eyes towards the stranger.

"Not long," answered the stranger. "At least, I do not know. It depends."

An unusual quiet had invaded the drawing-room of Forty-eight Bloomsbury Square, generally noisy with strident voices about this hour. The Colonel remained engrossed in his paper. Mrs. Devine sat with her plump white hands folded on her lap, whether asleep or not it was impossible to say.

The lady who was cousin to a baronet had shifted her chair beneath the gasolier, her eyes bent on her everlasting crochet work. The languid Miss Devine had crossed to the piano, where she sat fingering softly the tuneless keys, her back to the cold barely-furnished room.

"Sit down," commanded saucily Miss Kite, indicating with her fan the vacant seat beside her. "Tell me about yourself. You interest me." Miss Kite adopted a pretty authoritative air towards all youthful-looking members of the opposite sex. It harmonised with the peach complexion and the golden hair, and fitted her about as well.

"I am glad of that," answered the stranger, taking the chair suggested. "I so wish to interest you."

"You're a very bold boy." Miss Kite lowered her fan, for the purpose of glancing archly over the edge of it, and for the first time encountered the eyes of the stranger looking into hers. And then it was that Miss Kite experienced precisely the same curious sensation that an hour or so ago had troubled Mrs. Pennycherry when the stranger had first bowed to her. It seemed to Miss Kite that she was no longer the Miss Kite that, had she risen and looked into it, the fly-blown mirror over the marble mantelpiece would, she knew, have presented to her view; but quite another Miss Kite — a cheerful, bright-eyed lady verging on middle age, yet still good-looking in spite of her faded complexion and somewhat thin brown locks. Miss Kite felt a pang of jealousy shoot through her; this middle-aged

Miss Kite seemed, on the whole, a more attractive lady. There was a wholesomeness, a broadmindedness about her that instinctively drew one towards her. Not hampered, as Miss Kite herself was, by the necessity of appearing to be somewhere between eighteen and twenty-two, this other Miss Kite could talk sensibly, even brilliantly: one felt it. A thoroughly "nice" woman this other Miss Kite; the real Miss Kite, though envious, was bound to admit it. Miss Kite wished to goodness she had never seen the woman. The glimpse of her had rendered Miss Kite dissatisfied with herself.

"I am not a boy," explained the stranger; "and I had no intention of being bold."

"I know," replied Miss Kite. "It was a silly remark. Whatever induced me to make it, I can't think. Getting foolish in my old age, I suppose."

The stranger laughed. "Surely you are not old."

"I'm thirty-nine," snapped out Miss Kite. "You don't call it young?"

"I think it a beautiful age," insisted the stranger; "young enough not to have lost the joy of youth, old enough to have learnt sympathy."

"Oh, I daresay," returned Miss Kite, "any age you'd think beautiful. I'm going to bed." Miss Kite rose. The paper fan had somehow got itself broken. She threw the fragments into the fire.

"It is early yet," pleaded the stranger, "I was looking forward to a talk with you."

"Well, you'll be able to look forward to it," retorted Miss Kite. "Good-night."

The truth was, Miss Kite was impatient to have a look at herself in the glass, in her own room with the door shut. The vision of that other Miss Kite — the clean-looking lady of the pale face and the brown hair had been so vivid,

Miss Kite wondered whether temporary forgetfulness might not have fallen upon her while dressing for dinner that evening.

The stranger, left to his own devices, strolled towards the loo table, seeking something to read.

"You seem to have frightened away Miss Kite," remarked the lady who was cousin to a baronet.

"It seems so," admitted the stranger.

"My cousin, Sir William Bosster," observed the crocheting lady, "who married old Lord Egham's niece — you never met the Eghams?"

"Hitherto," replied the stranger, "I have not had that pleasure."

"A charming family. Cannot understand — my cousin Sir William, I mean, cannot understand my remaining here. 'My dear Emily' — he says the same thing every time he sees me: 'My dear Emily, how can you exist among the sort of people one meets with in a boarding-house.' But they amuse me."

A sense of humour, agreed the stranger, was always of advantage.

"Our family on my mother's side," continued Sir William's cousin in her placid monotone, "was connected with the Tatton-Joneses, who when King George the Fourth ——" Sir William's cousin, needing another reel of cotton, glanced up, and met the stranger's gaze.

"I'm sure I don't know why I'm telling you all this," said Sir William's cousin in an irritable tone. "It can't possibly interest you."

"Everything connected with you interests me," gravely the stranger assured her.

"It is very kind of you to say so," sighed Sir William's cousin, but without conviction; "I am afraid sometimes I bore people."

The polite stranger refrained from contradiction.

"You see," continued the poor lady, "I really am of good family."

"Dear lady," said the stranger, "your gentle face, your gentle voice, your gentle bearing, all proclaim it."

She looked without flinching into the stranger's eyes, and gradually a smile banished the reigning dulness of her features.

"How foolish of me." She spoke rather to herself than to the stranger. "Why, of course, people — people whose opinion is worth troubling about — judge of you by what you are, not by what you go about saying you are."

The stranger remained silent.

"I am the widow of a provincial doctor, with an income of just two hundred and thirty pounds per annum," she argued. "The sensible thing for me to do is to make the best of it, and to worry myself about these high and mighty relations of mine as little as they have ever worried themselves about me."

The stranger appeared unable to think of anything worth saying.

"I have other connections," remembered Sir William's cousin; "those of my poor husband, to whom instead of being the 'poor relation' I could be the fairy god-mama. They are my people — or would be," added Sir William's cousin tartly, "if I wasn't a vulgar snob."

She flushed the instant she had said the words and, rising, commenced preparations for a hurried departure.

"Now it seems I am driving you away," sighed the stranger.

"Having been called a 'vulgar snob,'" retorted the lady with some heat, "I think it about time I went."

"The words were your own," the stranger reminded her.

"Whatever I may have thought," remarked the indignant dame, "no lady — least of all in the presence of a total stranger — would have called herself ——" The poor dame paused, bewildered. "There is something very curious the matter with me this evening, that I cannot understand," she explained, "I seem quite unable to avoid insulting myself."

Still surrounded by bewilderment, she wished the stranger good night, hoping that when' next they met she would be more herself. The stranger, hoping so also, opened the door and closed it again behind her.

"Tell me," laughed Miss Devine, who by sheer force of talent was contriving to wring harmony from the reluctant piano, "how did you manage to do it? I should like to know."

"How did I do what?" inquired the stranger.

"Contrive to get rid so quickly of those two old frumps?"

"How well you play!" observed the stranger. "I knew you had genius for music the moment I saw you."

"How could you tell?"

"It is written so clearly in your face."

The girl laughed, well pleased. "You seem to have lost no time in studying my face."

"It is a beautiful and interesting face," observed the stranger.

She swung round sharply on the stool and their eyes met. "You can read faces?"

"Yes."

"Tell me, what else do you read in mine?"

"Frankness, courage ——"

"Ah, yes, all the virtues. Perhaps. We will take them for granted." It was odd how serious the girl had suddenly become. "Tell me the reverse side."

"I see no reverse side," replied the stranger. "I see but a fair girl, bursting into noble womanhood."

"And nothing else? You read no trace of greed, of vanity,

of sordidness, of ——" An angry laugh escaped her lips. "And you are a reader of faces!"

"A reader of faces." The stranger smiled. "Do you know what is written upon yours at this very moment? A love of truth that is almost fierce, scorn of lies, scorn of hypocrisy, the desire for all things pure, contempt of all things that are contemptible — especially of such things as are contemptible in woman. Tell me, do I not read aright?"

I wonder, thought the girl, is that why those two others both hurried from the room? Does everyone feel ashamed of the littleness that is in them when looked at by those clear, believing eyes of yours?

The idea occurred to her: "Papa seemed to have a good deal to say to you during dinner. Tell me, what were you talking about?"

"The military looking gentleman upon my left? We talked about your mother principally."

"I am sorry," returned the girl, wishful now she had not asked the question. "I was hoping he might have chosen another topic for the first evening!"

"He did try one or two," admitted the stranger; "but I have been about the world so little, I was glad when he talked to me about himself. I feel we shall be friends. He spoke so nicely, too, about Mrs. Devine."

"Indeed," commented the girl.

"He told me he had been married for twenty years and had never regretted it but once!"

Her black eyes flashed upon him, but meeting his, the suspicion died from them. She turned aside to hide her smile.

"So he regretted it — once."

"Only once," explained the stranger, "a passing irritable mood. It was so frank of him to admit it. He told me —

I think he has taken a liking to me. Indeed he hinted as much. He said he did not often get an opportunity of talking to a man like myself — he told me that he and your mother, when they travel together, are always mistaken for a honeymoon couple. Some of the experiences he related to me were really quite amusing." The stranger laughed at recollection of them — "that even here, in this place, they are generally referred to as 'Darby and Joan.'"

"Yes," said the girl, "that is true. Mr. Longcord gave them that name, the second evening after our arrival. It was considered clever — but rather obvious I thought myself."

"Nothing — so it seems to me," said the stranger, "is more beautiful than the love that has weathered the storms of life. The sweet, tender blossom that flowers in the heart of the young — in hearts such as yours — that, too, is beautiful. The love of the young for the young, that is the beginning of life. But the love of the old for the old, that is the beginning of — of things longer."

"You seem to find all things beautiful," the girl grumbled.

"But are not all things beautiful?" demanded the stranger.

The Colonel had finished his paper. "You two are engaged in a very absorbing conversation," observed the Colonel, approaching them.

"We were discussing Darbies and Joans," explained his daughter. "How beautiful is the love that has weathered the storms of life!"

"Ah!" smiled the Colonel, "that is hardly fair. My friend has been repeating to cynical youth the confessions of an amorous husband's affection for his middle-aged and somewhat ——" The Colonel in playful mood laid his hand upon the stranger's shoulder, an action that necessitated his looking straight into the stranger's eyes. The Colonel drew himself up stiffly and turned scarlet.

Somebody was calling the Colonel a cad. Not only that, but was explaining quite clearly, so that the Colonel could see it for himself, why he was a cad.

"That you and your wife lead a cat and dog existence is a disgrace to both of you. At least you might have the decency to try and hide it from the world — not make a jest of your shame to every passing stranger. You are a cad, sir, a cad!"

Who was daring to say these things? Not the stranger, his lips had not moved. Besides, it was not his voice. Indeed it sounded much more like the voice of the Colonel himself. The Colonel looked from the stranger to his daughter, from his daughter back to the stranger. Clearly they had not heard the voice — a mere hallucination. The Colonel breathed again.

Yet the impression remaining was not to be shaken off. Undoubtedly it was bad taste to have joked to the stranger upon such a subject. No gentleman would have done so.

But then no gentleman would have permitted such a jest to be possible. No gentleman would be forever wrangling with his wife — certainly never in public. However irritating the woman, a gentleman would have exercised self-control.

Mrs. Devine had risen, was coming slowly across the room. Fear laid hold of the Colonel. She was going to address some aggravating remark to him — he could see it in her eye — which would irritate him into savage retort. Even this prize idiot of a stranger would understand why boarding-house wits had dubbed them "Darby and Joan," would grasp the fact that the gallant Colonel had thought it amusing, in conversation with a table acquaintance, to hold his own wife up to ridicule.

"My dear," cried the Colonel, hurrying to speak first,

"does not this room strike you as cold? Let me fetch you a shawl."

It was useless: the Colonel felt it. It had been too long the custom of both of them to preface with politeness their deadliest insults to each other. She came on, thinking of a suitable reply: suitable from her point of view, that is. In another moment the truth would be out. A wild, fantastic possibility flashed through the Colonel's brain: If to him, why not to her?

"Letitia," cried the Colonel, and the tone of his voice surprised her into silence, "I want you to look closely at our friend. Does he not remind you of someone?"

Mrs. Devine, so urged, looked at the stranger long and hard. "Yes," she murmured, turning to her husband, "he does, who is it?"

"I cannot fix it," replied the Colonel; "I thought that maybe you would remember."

"It will come to me," mused Mrs. Devine. "It is some one — years ago, when I was a girl — in Devonshire. Thank you, if it isn't troubling you, Harry. I left it in the dining-room."

It was, as Mr. Augustus Longcord explained to his partner Isidore, the colossal foolishness of the stranger that was the cause of all the trouble. "Give me a man, who can take care of himself — or thinks he can," declared Augustus Longcord, "and I am prepared to give a good account of myself. But when a helpless baby refuses even to look at what you call your figures, tells you that your mere word is sufficient for him, and hands you over his cheque-book to fill up for yourself — well, it isn't playing the game."

"Auguthuth," was the curt comment of his partner, "you're a fool."

"All right, my boy, you try," suggested Augustus.

"Jutht what I mean to do," asserted his partner.

"Well," demanded Augustus one evening later, meeting Isidore ascending the stairs after a long talk with the stranger in the dining-room with the door shut.

"Oh, don't arth me," retorted Isidore, "thilly ath, thath what he ith."

"What did he say?"

"What did he ·thay! talked about the Jewth: what a grand rathe they were — how people mithjudged them· all that thort of rot.

"Thaid thome of the motht honorable men he had ever met had been Jewth. Thought I wath one of 'em!"

"Well, did you get anything out of him?"

"Get anything out of him. Of courthe not. Couldn't very well thell the whole rathe, ath it were, for a couple of hundred poundth, after that. Didn't theem worth it."

There were many things Forty-eight Bloomsbury Square came gradually to the conclusion were not worth the doing· — Snatching at the gravy; pouncing out of one's turn upon the vegetables and helping oneself to more than one's fair share; manœuvring for the easy-chair; sitting on the evening paper while pretending not to have seen it — all such-like tiresome bits of business. For the little one made out of it, really it was not worth the bother. Grumbling everlastingly at one's food; grumbling everlastingly at most things; abusing Pennycherry behind her back; abusing, for a change, one's fellow-boarders; squabbling with one's fellow-boarders about nothing in particular; sneering at one's fellow-boarders; talking scandal of one's fellow-boarders; making senseless jokes about one's fellow-boarders; talking big about oneself, nobody believing one — all such-like vulgarities. Other boarding-houses might indulge in them: Forty-eight Bloomsbury Square had its dignity to consider.

The truth is, Forty-eight Bloomsbury Square was coming

to a very good opinion of itself: for the which not Bloomsbury Square so much as the stranger must be blamed. The stranger had arrived at Forty-eight Bloomsbury Square with the preconceived idea — where obtained from Heaven knows — that its seemingly commonplace, mean-minded, coarse-fibred occupants were in reality ladies and gentlemen of the first water; and time and observation had apparently only strengthened this absurd idea. The natural result was, Forty-eight Bloomsbury Square was coming round to the stranger's opinion of itself.

Mrs. Pennycherry, the stranger would persist in regarding as a lady born and bred, compelled by circumstances over which she had no control to fill an arduous but honorable position of middle-class society — a sort of foster-mother, to whom were due the thanks and gratitude of her promiscuous family; and this view of herself Mrs. Pennycherry now clung to with obstinate conviction. There were disadvantages attaching, but these Mrs. Pennycherry appeared prepared to suffer cheerfully. A lady born and bred cannot charge other ladies and gentlemen for coals and candles they have never burnt; a foster-mother cannot palm off upon her children New Zealand mutton for Southdown. A mere lodging-house-keeper can play these tricks, and pocket the profits. But a lady feels she cannot: Mrs. Pennycherry felt she no longer could.

To the stranger Miss Kite was a witty and delightful conversationalist of most attractive personality. Miss Kite had one failing: it was lack of vanity. She was unaware of her own delicate and refined beauty. If Miss Kite could only see herself with his, the stranger's eyes, the modesty that rendered her distrustful of her natural charms would fall from her. The stranger was so sure of it Miss Kite determined to put it to the test. One evening, an hour before dinner, there entered the drawing-room, when the

stranger only was there and before the gas was lighted, a
pleasant, good-looking lady, somewhat pale, with neatly-
arranged brown hair, who demanded of the stranger if he
knew her. All her body was trembling, and her voice
seemed inclined to run away from her and become a sob.
But when the stranger, looking straight into her eyes, told
her that from the likeness he thought she must be Miss
Kite's younger sister, but much prettier, it became a laugh
instead: and that evening the golden-haired Miss Kite disappeared never to show her high-coloured face again; and
what perhaps, more than all else, might have impressed some
former habitué of Forty-eight Bloomsbury Square with awe,
it was that no one in the house made even a passing inquiry
concerning her.

Sir William's cousin the stranger thought an acquisition
to any boarding-house. A lady of high-class family! There
was nothing outward or visible perhaps to tell you that she
was of high-class family. She herself, naturally, would
not mention the fact, yet somehow you felt it. Unconsciously she set a high-class tone, diffused an atmosphere of
gentle manners. Not that the stranger had said this in so
many words; Sir William's cousin gathered that he thought
it, and felt herself in agreement with him.

For Mr. Longcord and his partner, as representatives
of the best type of business men, the stranger had a great
respect. With what unfortunate results to themselves has
been noted. The curious thing is that the Firm appeared
content with the price they had paid for the stranger's
good opinion — had even, it was rumoured, acquired a
taste for honest men's respect — that in the long run
was likely to cost them dear. But we all have our pet
extravagance.

The Colonel and Mrs. Devine both suffered a good deal
at first from the necessity imposed upon them of learning,

somewhat late in life, new tricks. In the privacy of their own apartment they condoled with one another.

"Tomfool nonsense," grumbled the Colonel, "you and I starting billing and cooing at our age!"

"What I object to," said Mrs. Devine, "is the feeling that somehow I am being made to do it."

"The idea that a man and his wife cannot have their little joke together for fear of what some impertinent jacka napes may think of them! it's damn ridiculous," the Colonel exploded.

"Even when he isn't there," said Mrs. Devine, "I seem to see him looking at me with those vexing eyes of his. Really the man quite haunts me."

"I have met him somewhere," mused the Colonel, "I'll swear I've met him somewhere. I wish to goodness he would go."

A hundred things a day the Colonel wanted to say to Mrs. Devine, a hundred things a day Mrs. Devine would have liked to observe to the Colonel. But by the time the opportunity occurred — when nobody else was by to hear — all interest in saying them was gone.

"Women will be women," was the sentiment with which the Colonel consoled himself. "A man must bear with them — must never forget that he is a gentleman."

"Oh, well, I suppose they're all alike," laughed Mrs. Devine to herself, having arrived at that stage of despair when one seeks refuge in cheerfulness. "What's the use of putting oneself out — it does no good, and only upsets one."

There is a certain satisfaction in feeling you are bearing with heroic resignation the irritating follies of others. Colonel and Mrs. Devine came to enjoy the luxury of much self-approbation.

But the person seriously annoyed by the stranger's bigoted

s

belief in the innate goodness of everyone he came across was the languid, handsome Miss Devine. The stranger would have it that Miss Devine was a noble-souled, high-minded young woman, something midway between a Flora Macdonald and a Joan of Arc. Miss Devine, on the contrary, knew herself to be a sleek, luxury-loving animal, quite willing to sell herself to the bidder who could offer her the finest clothes, the richest foods, the most sumptuous surroundings. Such a bidder was to hand in the person of a retired bookmaker, a somewhat greasy old gentleman, but exceedingly rich and undoubtedly fond of her.

Miss Devine, having made up her mind that the thing had got to be done, was anxious that it should be done quickly. And here it was that the stranger's ridiculous opinion of her not only irritated but inconvenienced her. Under the very eyes of a person — however foolish — convinced that you are possessed of all the highest attributes of your sex, it is difficult to behave as though actuated by only the basest motives. A dozen times had Miss Devine determined to end the matter by formal acceptance of her elderly admirer's large and flabby hand, and a dozen times — the vision intervening of the stranger's grave, believing eyes — had Miss Devine refused decided answer. The stranger would one day depart. Indeed, he had told her himself, he was but a passing traveller. When he was gone it would be easier. So she thought at the time.

One afternoon the stranger entered the room where she was standing by the window, looking out upon the bare branches of the trees in Bloomsbury Square. She remembered afterwards, it was just such another foggy afternoon as the afternoon of the stranger's arrival three months before. No one else was in the room. The stranger closed the door, and came towards her with that curious, quick-leaping step of his. His long coat was tightly buttoned, and in his hands he carried his old felt hat and the massive knotted stick that was almost a staff.

"I have come to say good-bye," explained the stranger. "I am going."

"I shall not see you again?" asked the girl.

"I cannot say," replied the stranger. "But you will think of me?"

"Yes," she answered with a smile, "I can promise that."

"And I shall always remember you," promised the stranger, "and I wish you every joy — the joy of love, the joy of a happy marriage."

The girl winced. "Love and marriage are not always the same thing," she said.

"Not always," agreed the stranger, "but in your case they will be one."

She looked at him.

"Do you think I have not noticed?" smiled the stranger, "a gallant, handsome lad, and clever. You love him and he loves you. I could not have gone away without knowing it was well with you."

Her gaze wandered towards the fading light.

"Ah, yes, I love him," she answered petulantly. "Your eyes can see clearly enough, when they want to. But one does not live on love, in our world. I will tell you the man I am going to marry if you care to know." She would not meet his eyes. She kept her gaze still fixed upon the dingy trees, the mist beyond, and spoke rapidly and vehemently: "The man who can give me all my soul's desire — money and the things that money can buy. You think me a woman, I'm only a pig. He is moist, and breathes like a porpoise; with cunning in place of a brain, and the rest of him mere stomach. But he is good enough for me."

She hoped this would shock the stranger and that now, perhaps, he would go. It irritated her to hear him only laugh.

"No," he said, "you will not marry him."

"Who will stop me?" she cried angrily.

"Your Better Self."

His voice had a strange ring of authority, compelling her to turn and look upon his face. Yes, it was true, the fancy that from the very first had haunted her. She had met him, talked to him — in silent country roads, in crowded city streets, where was it? And always in talking with him her spirit had been lifted up: she had been — what he had always thought her.

"There are those," continued the stranger (and for the first time she saw that he was of a noble presence, that his gentle, childlike eyes could also command), "whose Better Self lies slain by their own hand and troubles them no more. But yours, my child, you have let grow too strong; it will ever be your master. You must obey. Flee from it and it will follow you; you cannot escape it. Insult it and it will chastise you with burning shame, with stinging self-reproach from day to day." The sternness faded from the beautiful face, the tenderness crept back. He laid his hand upon the young girl's shoulder. "You will marry your lover," he smiled. "With him you will walk the way of sunlight and of shadow."

And the girl, looking up into the strong, calm face, knew that it would be so, that the power of resisting her Better Self had passed away from her for ever.

"Now," said the stranger, "come to the door with me. Leave-takings are but wasted sadness. Let me pass out quietly. Close the door softly behind me."

She thought that perhaps he would turn his face again, but she saw no more of him than the odd roundness of his back under the tightly buttoned coat, before he faded into the gathering fog.

Then softly she closed the door.

THE STORY OF THE LAST TRUMP [1]

By H. G. WELLS

"AFTER this war," said Wilkins, "after its revelation of horrors and waste and destruction, it is impossible that people will tolerate any longer that system of diplomacy and armaments and national aggression that has brought this catastrophe upon mankind. This is the war that will end war."

"Osborn," said Boon, "Osborn."

"But after all the world has seen ——!"

"The world doesn't see," said Boon.

Boon's story of the Last Trump may well come after this to terminate my book. It has been by no means an easy task to assemble the various portions of this manuscript. It is written almost entirely in pencil, and sometimes the writing is so bad as to be almost illegible. But here at last it is, as complete, I think, as Boon meant it to be. It is his epitaph upon his dream of the Mind of the Race.

2

The story of the Last Trump begins in heaven, and it ends in all sorts of places round about the world.

Heaven, you must know, is a kindly place, and the blessed ones do not go on forever singing Alleluia, whatever you may have been told. For they, too, are finite creatures, and must be fed with their eternity in little bits, as one feeds a chick or a child. So there are mornings and changes and freshness, there is time to condition their lives. And the children are still children, gravely eager about their

[1] From "Boon," pp. 301–308. Reprinted by special permission of the author and the publishers, the George H. Doran Company.

playing and ready always for new things; just children they are, but blessèd as you see them in the pictures beneath the careless feet of the Lord God. And one of these blessèd children routing about in an attic — for heaven is, of course, full of the most heavenly attics, seeing that it has children — came upon a number of instruments stored away, and laid its little chubby hands upon them. . . .

Now, indeed, I cannot tell what these instruments were, for to do so would be to invade mysteries. . . . But one I may tell of, and that was a great brazen trumpet which the Lord God had made when He made the world — for the Lord God finishes all His jobs — to blow when the time for our Judgement came round. And He had made it and left it; there it was, and everything was settled exactly as the Doctrine of Predestination declares. And this blessèd child conceived one of those unaccountable passions of childhood for its smoothness and brassiness, and he played with it and tried to blow it, and trailed it about with him out of the attic into the gay and golden streets, and, after many fitful wanderings, to those celestial battlements of crystal of which you have doubtless read. And there the blessèd child fell to counting the stars, and forgot all about the trumpet beside him until a flourish of his elbow sent it over.

Down fell the trump, spinning as it fell, and for a day or so, which seemed but moments in heaven, the blessèd child watched its fall until it was a glittering little speck of brightness. . . .

When it looked a second time the trump was gone. . . . I do not know what happened to that child when at last it was time for Judgement Day and that shining trumpet was missed. I know that Judgement Day is long overpassed, because of the wickedness of the world; I think perhaps it was in 1000 A.D. when the expected Day should have dawned that never came, but no other heavenly particulars do I know at all, because now my scene changes to the narrow ways of this Earth. . . . And the Prologue in heaven ends.

3

And now the scene is a dingy little shop in Caledonian Market, where things of an incredible worthlessness lie in wait for such as seek after an impossible cheapness. In the window, as though it had always been there and never anywhere else, lies a long, battered, discoloured trumpet of brass that no prospective purchaser has ever been able to sound. In it mice shelter, and dust and fluff have gathered after the fashion of this world. The keeper of the shop is a very old man, and he bought the shop long ago, but already this trumpet was there; he has no idea whence it came, nor its country or origin, nor anything about it. But once in a moment of enterprise that led to nothing he decided to call it an Ancient Ceremonial Shawm, though he ought to have known that whatever a shawm may be the last thing it was likely to be is a trumpet, seeing that they are always mentioned together. And above it hung concertinas and melodeons and cornets and tin whistles and mouth-organs and all that rubbish of musical instruments which delight the hearts of the poor. Until one day two blackened young men from the big motor works in the Pansophist Road stood outside the window and argued.

They argued about these instruments in stock and how you made these instruments sound, because they were fond of argument, and one asserted and the other denied that he could make every instrument in the place sound a note. And the argument rose high, and led to a bet.

"Supposing, of course, that the instrument is in order," said Hoskin, who was betting he could.

"That's understood," said Briggs.

And then they called as witnesses certain other young and black and greasy men in the same employment, and after much argument and discussion that lasted through the afternoon, they went in to the little old dealer about tea-time, just as he was putting a blear-eyed, stinking paraffin-lamp to throw an unfavorable light upon his always very unattractive window. And after great difficulty they arranged that for the sum of one shilling, paid in advance, Hoskin should have a try at every instrument in the shop that Briggs chose to indicate.

And the trial began.

The third instrument that was pitched upon by Briggs for the trial was the strange trumpet that lay at the bottom of the window, the trumpet that you, who have read the Introduction, know was the trumpet for the Last Trump. And Hoskin tried and tried again, and then, blowing desperately, hurt his ears. But he could get no sound from the trumpet. Then he examined the trumpet more carefully and discovered the mice and fluff and other things in it, and demanded that it should be cleaned; and the old dealer, nothing loath, knowing they were used to automobile-horns and such-like instruments, agreed to let them clean it on condition that they left it shiny. So the young men, after making a suitable deposit, — which, as you shall hear, was presently confiscated, — went off with the trumpet, proposing to clean it next day at the works and polish it with the peculiarly excellent brass polish employed upon the honk-honk horns of the firm. And this they did, and Hoskin tried again.

But he tried in vain. Whereupon there arose a great argument about the trumpet, whether it was in order or not, whether it was possible for any one to sound it. For if not, then clearly it was outside the condition of the bet.

Others among the young men tried it, including two who

played wind instruments in a band and were musically knowing men. After their own failure they were strongly on the side of Hoskin and strongly against Briggs, and most of the other young men were of the same opinion.

"Not a bit of it," said Briggs, who was a man of resource. "*I'll* show you that it can be sounded."

And taking the instrument in his hand, he went toward a peculiarly powerful foot blow-pipe that stood at the far end of the tool-shed. "Good old Briggs!" said one of the other young men, and opinion veered about.

Briggs removed the blow-pipe from its bellows and tube, and then adjusted the tube very carefully to the mouthpiece of the trumpet. Then with great deliberation he produced a piece of beeswaxed string from a number of other strange and filthy contents in his pocket, and tied the tube to the mouthpiece. And then he began to work the treadle of the bellows.

"Good old Briggs!" said the one who had previously admired him.

And then something incomprehensible happened.

It was a flash. Whatever else it was it was a flash. And a sound that seemed to coincide exactly with the flash.

Afterward the young men agreed to it that the trumpet blew to bits. It blew to bits and vanished, and they were all flung upon their faces — not backward, be it noted, but on their faces — and Briggs was stunned and scared. The tool-shed windows were broken and the various apparatus and cars around were much displaced, and *no traces of the trumpet were ever discovered.*

That last particular puzzled and perplexed poor Briggs very much. It puzzled and perplexed him the more because he had had an impression so extraordinary, so incredible, that he was never able to describe it to any other living person. But his impression was this: that the flash that came with the sound came not from the trumpet, but to it, that it smote down to it and took it, and that its shape was in the exact likeness of a hand and arm of fire.

4

And that was not all; that was not the only strange thing about the disappearance of that battered trumpet. There was something else even more difficult to describe, an effect as though for one instant something opened.

The young men who worked with Hoskin and Briggs had that clearness of mind which comes of dealing with machinery, and all felt this indescribable something else, as if for an instant the world was not the world, but something lit and wonderful, larger.

This is what one of them said of it.

"I felt," he said, "just for a minute as though I was blown to kingdom come."

"It is just how it took me," said another. "'Lord,' I says, 'here's Judgement Day!' and there I was sprawling among the files.   "

But none of the others felt that he could say anything more definite than that.

5

Moreover, there was a storm. All over the world there was a storm that puzzled meteorology, a moment's gale that left the atmosphere in a state of wild commotion, rains, tornadoes, depressions, irregularities for weeks. News came of it from all the quarters of the earth.

All over China, for example, that land of cherished graves, there was a dust-storm; dust leaped into the air. A kind of earthquake shook Europe — an earthquake that seemed to have at heart the peculiar interests of Mr. Algernon

Ashton: everywhere it cracked mausoleums and shivered the pavements of cathedrals, swished the flower-beds of cemeteries, and tossed tombstones aside. A crematorium in Texas blew up. The sea was greatly agitated, and the beautiful harbour of Sydney, in Australia, was seen to be littered with sharks floating upside down in manifest distress.

And all about the world a sound was heard like the sound of a trumpet instantly cut short.

6

But this much is only the superficial dressing of the story. The reality is something different. It is this: that in an instant, and for an instant, the dead lived, and all that are alive in the world did for a moment see the Lord God and all His powers, His hosts of angels, and all His array looking down upon them. They saw Him as one sees by a flash of lightning in the darkness, and then instantly the world was opaque again, limited, petty, habitual. That is the tremendous reality of this story. Such glimpses have happened in individual cases before. The lives of the saints abound in them. Such a glimpse it was that came to Rabindranath Tagore upon the burning ghat at Benares. But this was not an individual but a world experience; the flash came to every one. Not always was it quite the same, and thereby the doubter found his denials when presently a sort of discussion broke out in the obscurer Press. For this one testified that it seemed that "One stood very near to me," and another saw "all the hosts of heaven flame up toward the Throne."

And there were others who had a vision of brooding watchers, and others who imagined great sentinels before a veiled figure, and some one who felt nothing more divine than a sensation of happiness and freedom such as one gets from a sudden burst of sunshine in the spring. . . . So that one is forced to believe that something more than wonderfully wonderful, something altogether strange, was seen, and that all these various things that people thought they saw were only interpretations drawn from their experiences and their imaginations. It was a light, it was beauty, it was high and solemn, it made this world seem a flimsy transparency. . . .

Then it had vanished. . . .

And people were left with the question of what they had seen, and just how much it mattered.

7

A little old lady sat by the fire in a small sitting-room in West Kensington. Her cat was in her lap, her spectacles were on her nose; she was reading the morning's paper, and beside her, on a little occasional table, was her tea and a buttered muffin. She had finished the crimes and she was reading about the Royal Family. When she had read all there was to read about the Royal Family, she put down the paper, deposited the cat on the hearth-rug, and turned to her tea. She had poured out her first cup and she had just taken up a quadrant of muffin when the trump and the flash came. Through its instant duration she remained motionless with the quadrant of muffin poised halfway to her mouth. Then very slowly she put the morsel down.

"Now, what was that?" she said.

She surveyed the cat, but the cat was quite calm. Then she looked very, very hard at her lamp. It was a patent safety-lamp, and had always behaved very well. Then she stared at the window, but the curtains were drawn, and everything was in order.

"One might think I was going to be ill," she said, and resumed her toast.

8

Not far away from this old lady, not more than three-quarters of a mile at most, sat Mr. Parchester in his luxurious study, writing a perfectly beautiful, sustaining sermon about the Need of Faith in God. He was a handsome, earnest, modern preacher, he was rector of one of our big West End churches, and he had amassed a large, fashionable congregation. Every Sunday, and at convenient intervals during the week, he fought against Modern Materialism, Scientific Education, Excessive Puritanism, Pragmatism, Doubt, Levity, Selfish Individualism, Further Relaxation of the Divorce Laws, all the Evils of our Time — and anything else that was unpopular. He believed quite simply, he said, in all the old, simple, kindly things. He had the face of a saint, but he had rendered this generally acceptable by growing side-whiskers. And nothing could tame the beauty of his voice.

He was an enormous asset in the spiritual life of the metropolis — to give it no harsher name — and his fluent periods had restored faith and courage to many a poor soul hovering on the brink of the dark river of thought. . . .

And just as beautiful Christian maidens played a wonderful part in the last days of Pompeii, in winning proud Roman hearts to a hated and despised faith, so Mr. Parchester's naturally graceful gestures, and his simple, melodious, trumpet voice won back scores of our half-pagan rich women to church attendance and the social work of which his church was the centre. . . .

And now by the light of an exquisitely shaded electric lamp he was writing this sermon of quiet, confident belief (with occasional hard smacks, perfect stingers in fact, at current

unbelief and rival leaders of opinion), in the simple, divine
faith of our fathers. . . .

When there came this truncated trump and this vision. . . .

9

Of all the innumerable multitudes who for the infinitesimal
fraction of a second had this glimpse of the Divinity, none
were so blankly and profoundly astonished as Mr. Parchester. For — it may be because of his subtly spiritual
nature — he *saw*, and seeing believed. He dropped his
pen and let it roll across his manuscript, he sat stunned,
every drop of blood fled from his face and his lips and his
eyes dilated.

While he had just been writing and arguing about God,
there *was* God!

The curtain had been snatched back for an instant. It
had fallen again; but his mind had taken a photographic
impression of everything that he had seen — the grave
presences, the hierarchy, the effulgence, the vast concourse,
the terrible, gentle eyes. He felt it, as though the vision
still continued, behind the bookcases, behind the pictured
wall and the curtained window : *even now there was judgement!*

For quite a long time he sat, incapable of more than ap-
prehending this supreme realization. His hands were held
out limply upon the desk before him. And then very slowly
his staring eyes came back to immediate things, and fell
upon the scattered manuscript on which he had been
engaged. He read an unfinished sentence and slowly recovered its intention. As he did so, a picture of his congregation came to him as he saw it from the pulpit during his
evening sermon, as he had intended to see it on the Sunday
evening that was at hand, with Lady Rupert in her sitting
and Lady Blex in hers and Mrs. Munbridge, the rich and
in her Jewish way very attractive Mrs. Munbridge, running

them close in her adoration, and each with one or two friends they had brought to adore him, and behind them the Hexhams and the Wassinghams and behind them others and others and others, ranks and ranks of people, and the galleries on either side packed with worshippers of a less dominant class, and the great organ and his magnificent choir waiting to support him and supplement him, and the great altar to the left of him, and the beautiful new Lady Chapel, done by Roger Fry and Wyndham Lewis and all the latest people in art, to the right. He thought of the listening multitude, seen through the haze of the thousand electric candles, and how he had planned the paragraphs of his discourse so that the notes of his beautiful voice should float slowly down, like golden leaves in autumn, into the smooth tarn of their silence, word by word, phrase by phrase, until he came to —

"Now to God the Father, God the Son ——"

And all the time he knew that Lady Blex would watch his face and Mrs. Munbridge, leaning those graceful shoulders of hers a little forward, would watch his face. . . .

Many people would watch his face.

All sorts of people would come to Mr. Parchester's services at times. Once it was said Mr. Balfour had come. Just to hear him. After his sermons, the strangest people would come and make confessions in the beautifully furnished reception-room beyond the vestry. All sorts of people. Once or twice he had asked people to come and listen to him; and one of them had been a very beautiful woman. And often he had dreamt of the people who might come: prominent people, influential people, remarkable people. But never before had it occurred to Mr. Parchester that, a little hidden from the rest of the congregation, behind the thin veil of this material world, there was another auditorium. And that God also, God also, watched his face.

And watched him through and through.

Terror seized upon Mr. Parchester.

He stood up, as though Divinity had come into the room before him. He was trembling. He felt smitten and about to be smitten.

He perceived that it was hopeless to **try** to hide what he had written, what he had thought, the unclean egotism **he** had become.

"I did not know," he said at last.

The click of the door behind him warned him that he was not alone. He turned, and saw Miss Skelton, his typist, for it was her time to come for his manuscript and copy it out in the specially legible type he used. For a moment he stared at her strangely.

She looked at him with those deep, adoring eyes of hers: "Am I too soon, sir?" she asked in her slow, unhappy voice, and seemed prepared for a noiseless departure.

He did not answer immediately. Then he said: "Miss Skelton, the Judgement of God is close at hand!"

And seeing she stood perplexed, he said —

"Miss Skelton, how can you expect me to go on acting and mouthing this Tosh when the Sword of Truth hangs over us?"

Something in her face made him ask a question.

"Did *you* see anything?" he asked.

"I thought it was because I was rubbing my eyes."

"Then indeed there is a God! And He is watching us now. And all this about us, this sinful room, this foolish costume, this preposterous life of blasphemous pretension ——!"

He stopped short, with a kind of horror on his face.

With a hopeless gesture he rushed by her. He appeared wild-eyed upon the landing before his man-servant, who was carrying a scuttle of coal upstairs.

"Brompton," he said, "what are you doing?"

"Coal, sir."

"Put it down, man!" he said. "Are you not an immortal soul? God is here! As close as my hand! Repent! Turn to Him! The Kingdom of Heaven is at hand!"

10

Now if you are a policeman perplexed by a sudden and unaccountable collision between a taxicab and an electric standard, complicated by a blinding flash and a sound like an abbreviated trump from an automobile horn, you do not want to be bothered by a hatless clerical gentleman suddenly rushing out of a handsome private house and telling you that "the Kingdom of Heaven is at hand!" You are respectful to him because it is the duty of a policeman to be respectful to gentlemen, but you say to him, "Sorry I can't attend to that now, sir. One thing at a time. I've got this little accident to see to." And if he persists in dancing round the gathering crowd and coming at you again, you say: "I'm afraid I must ask you just to get away from here, sir. You aren't being an 'elp, sir." And if, on the other hand, you are a well-trained clerical gentleman, who knows his way about in the world, you do not go on pestering a policeman on duty after he has said that, even although you think God is looking at you and Judgement is close at hand. You turn away and go on, a little damped, looking for some one else more likely to pay attention to your tremendous tidings.

And so it happened to the Reverend Mr. Parchester.

He experienced a curious little recession of confidence. He went on past quite a number of people without saying anything further, and the next person he accosted was a flower-woman sitting by her basket at the corner of Chexington Square. She was unable to stop him at once when he began to talk to her because she was tying up a big bundle of white chrysanthemums and had an end of string behind her teeth. And her daughter who stood beside her was the sort of girl who wouldn't say "Bo!" to a goose.

"Do you know, my good woman," said Mr. Parchester, "that while we poor creatures of earth go about our poor business here, while we sin and blunder and follow every sort of base end, close to us, above us, around us, watching us, judging us, are God and His holy angels? I have had a vision, and I am not the only one. I have *seen*. We are *in* the Kingdom of Heaven now and here, and Judgement is all about us now! Have you seen nothing? No light? No sound? No warning?"

By this time the old flower-seller had finished her bunch of flowers and could speak. "I saw it," she said. "And Mary — she saw it."

"Well?" said Mr. Parchester.

"But, Lord! It don't *mean* nothing!" said the old flower-seller.

II

At that a kind of chill fell upon Mr. Parchester. He went on across Chexington Square by his own inertia.

He was still about as sure that he had seen God as he had been in his study, but now he was no longer sure that the world would believe that he had. He felt perhaps that this idea of rushing out to tell people was precipitate and inadvisable. After all, a priest in the Church of England is only one unit in a great machine; and in a world-wide spiritual crisis it should be the task of that great machine to act as one resolute body. This isolated crying aloud in the street was unworthy of a consecrated priest. It was a dissenting kind of thing to do. A vulgar individualistic screaming.

He thought suddenly that he would go and tell his bishop — the great Bishop Wampach. He called a taxicab, and within half an hour he was in the presence of his commanding officer. It was an extraordinarily difficult and painful interview. . . .

You see, Mr. Parchester believed. The Bishop impressed him as being quite angrily resolved not to believe. And for the first time in his career Mr. Parchester realized just how much jealous hostility a beautiful, fluent, and popular preacher may arouse in the minds of the hierarchy. It wasn't, he felt, a conversation. It was like flinging oneself into the paddock of a bull that has long been anxious to gore one.

"Inevitably," said the bishop, "this theatricalism, this star-turn business, with its extreme spiritual excitements, its exaggerated soul crises and all the rest of it, leads to such a breakdown as afflicts you. Inevitably! You were at least wise to come to me. I can see you are only in the beginning of your trouble, that already in your mind fresh hallucinations are gathering to overwhelm you, voices, special charges and missions, strange revelations. . . . I wish I had the power to suspend you right away, to send you into retreat. "

Mr. Parchester made a violent effort to control himself. "But I tell you," he said, "that I saw God!" He added, as if to reassure himself: "More plainly, more certainly, than I see you."

"Of course," said the Bishop, "this is how strange new sects come into existence; this is how false prophets spring out of the bosom of the Church. Loose-minded, excitable men of your stamp ——"

Mr. Parchester, to his own astonishment, burst into tears. "But I tell you," he wept, "He is here. I have seen. I know."

"Don't talk such nonsense!" said the Bishop. "There is no one here but you and I."

Mr. Parchester expostulated. "But," he protested, "He is omnipresent."

The Bishop controlled an expression of impatience. "It is characteristic of your condition," he said, "that you are unable to distinguish between a matter of fact and a spiritual truth. . . . Now listen to me. If you value your sanity and public decency and the discipline of the Church, go right home from here and go to bed. Send for Broadhays, who will prescribe a safe sedative. And read something calming and graceful and purifying. For my own part, I should be dis posed to recommend the 'Life of Saint Francis of Assisi.'" . . .

12

Unhappily Mr. Parchester did not go home. He went out from the Bishop's residence stunned and amazed, and suddenly upon his desolation came the thought of Mrs. Munbridge. . . .

She would understand. . . .

He was shown up to her own little sitting-room. She had already gone up to her room to dress, but when she heard that he had called, and wanted very greatly to see her, she slipped on a loose, beautiful tea-gown, négligé thing, and hurried to him. He tried to tell her everything, but she only kept saying "There! there!" She was sure he wanted a cup of tea, he looked so pale and exhausted. She rang to have the tea equipage brought back; she put the dear saint in an arm-chair by the fire; she put cushions about him, and ministered to him. And when she began partially to comprehend what he had experienced, she suddenly realized that she too had experienced it. That vision had been a brain-wave between their two linked and sympathetic brains. And that thought glowed in her as she brewed his tea with her own hands. He had been weeping! How tenderly he felt all these things! He was more sensitive than a woman. What madness to have expected understanding from the Bishop! But that was just like his unworldliness. He was not fit to take care of himself. A wave of tenderness carried her away. "Here is your tea!" she said, bending over him, and fully conscious of her fragrant warmth and sweetness, and suddenly, she could never afterwards explain why she was so, she was moved to kiss him on his brow. . . .

How indescribable is the comfort of a true-hearted womanly friend! The safety of it! The consolation! . . .

About half-past seven that evening Mr. Parchester returned to his own home, and Brompton admitted him. Brompton was relieved to find his employer looking quite restored and ordinary again.

"Brompton," said Mr. Parchester, "I will not have the usual dinner to-night. Just a single mutton cutlet and one of those quarter-bottles of Perrier Jouet on a tray in my study. I shall have to finish my sermon to-night."

And he had promised Mrs. Munbridge he would preach that sermon specially for her.

13

And as it was with Mr. Parchester and Brompton and Mrs. Munbridge, and the taxi-driver and the policeman and the little old lady and the automobile mechanics and Mr. Parchester's secretary and the Bishop, so it was with all the rest of the world. If a thing is sufficiently strange and great no one will perceive it. Men will go on in their own ways though one rose from the dead to tell them that the King dom of Heaven was at hand, though the Kingdom itself and all its glory became visible, blinding their eyes. They and their ways are one.   Men will go on in their ways as rabbits will go on feeding in their hutches within a hundred yards of a battery of artillery.   For rabbits are rabbits, and made to eat and breed, and men are human beings and creatures of habit and custom and prejudice ; and what has made them, what will judge them, what will destroy them — they may turn their eyes to it at times as the rabbits will glance at the concussion of the guns, but it will never draw them away from eating their lettuce and sniffing after their does. . . .

TWO PLAYS[1]

BY ALFRED SUTRO

THE MAN ON THE KERB

A Duologue

The Persons of the Play

JOSEPH MATTHEWS
MARY (HIS WIFE)

TIME — *The present*

SCENE — *Their home in the West End*

SCENE: *An underground room, bare of any furniture except two or three broken chairs, a tattered mattress on the stone floor and an old trunk. On a packing-chest are a few pots and pans and a kettle. A few sacks are spread over the floor, close to the empty grate; the walls are discoloured, with plentiful signs of damp oozing through. Close to the door, at back, is a window, looking on to the area; two of the panes are broken and stuffed with paper.*

On the mattress a child is sleeping, covered with a tattered old mantle; MARY *is bending over her, crooning a song. The woman is still quite young, and must have been very pretty; but her cheeks are hollow and there are great circles round her eyes; her face is very pale and bloodless. Her dress is painfully worn and shabby, but displays pathetic attempts at neatness. The only light in the room comes from the street lamp on the pavement above.*

---

[1] *These plays have been copyrighted in America by the author's agents, Messrs. Samuel French Ltd., 26 Southampton Street, Strand, to whom all applications for production, both in England and America, should be addressed. Reprinted here by the special permission of the American publishers from the volume entitled* "Five Little Plays," *Brentano's, New York, 1916.*

JOE *comes down the area steps, and enters. His clothes are of the familiar colourless, shapeless kind one sees at street corners; he would be a pleasant-looking young fellow enough were it not that his face is abnormally lined, and pinched, and weather-beaten. He shambles in, with the intense weariness of a man who has for hours been forcing benumbed limbs to move; he shakes himself, on the threshold, dog-fashion, to get rid of the rain.* MARY *first makes sure that the child is asleep, then rises eagerly and goes to him. Her face falls as she notes his air of dejection.*

MARY. [*Wistfully.*] Nothing, Joe?

JOE. Nothing. Not a farthing. Nothing.

[MARY *turns away and checks a moan.*

JOE. Nothing at all. Same as yesterday — worse than yesterday — I *did* bring home a few coppers — And **you**?

MARY. A lady gave Minnie some food ——

JOE. [*Heartily.*] Bless her for that!

MARY. Took her into the pastrycook's, Joe ——

JOE. And the kiddie had a tuck-out? Thank **God**! And you?

MARY. Minnie managed to hide a great big bun for **me**.

JOE. The lady didn't give you anything?

MARY. Only a lecture, Joe, for bringing the child **out** on so bittter a day.

JOE. [*With a sour laugh, as he sits on a chair.*] Ho, ho! Always so ready with their lectures, aren't they? "Shouldn't beg, my man! Never give to beggars in the street!" — Look at me, I said to one of them. Feel my arm. **Tap** my chest. I tell you I'm starving, and they're starving at home. — "Never give to beggars in the street."

MARY. [*Laying a hand on his arm.*] Oh, Joe, you're wet!

JOE. It's been raining hard the last three hours — pouring. My stars, it's cold. Couldn't we raise a bit of fire, Mary?

MARY. With what, Joe?

JOE. [*After a look round, suddenly getting up, seizing a ricketty chair by the wall, breaking off the legs.*] With this! Wonderful fine furniture they give you on the Hire System — so solid and substantial — as advertised. [*He breaks the flimsy thing up, as he speaks.*] And to think we paid for this muck, in the days we were human beings — paid about three times its value! And to think of the poor devils, poor devils like us, who sweated their life-blood out to make it — and of the blood-sucking devils who sold it and got fat on it — and now back it goes to the devil it came from, and we can at least get warm for a minute. [*He crams the wood into the grate.*] Got any paper, Mary?

MARY. [*Taking an old newspaper from the trunk.*] Here, Joe.

JOE. That will help to build up a fire. [*He glances at it, then lays it carefully underneath the wood.* MARY *gets lamp from table.*] The Daily Something or other — that tells the world what a happy people we are — how proud of belonging to an Empire on which the sun never sets. And I'd sell Gibraltar to-night for a sausage with mashed potatoes, and let Russia take India if some one would give me a clerkship at a pound a week. — There, in you go! A match, Mary?

MARY. [*Standing above* JOE, *handing him one.*] Oh, Joe, be careful — we've only two left!

JOE. I'll be careful. Wait, though — I'll see whether there's a bit of tobacco still in my pipe. [*He fishes the pipe out of his pocket.*] A policeman who warned me away from the kerb gave me some tobacco. "Mustn't beg," he said. "Got a pipe? Well, here's some tobacco." I believe he'd have given me money. But it was the first kind word I had heard all day, and it choked me. — There's just a bit left at the bottom. [*He bustles.*] Now, first the fire. [*He puts the match to the paper — it kindles.*] And then my pipe. [*The fire burns up; he throws himself in front of it.*] Boo-o-oh, I'm sizzling. . . . I got so wet that I felt the water running into my lungs — my feet didn't seem to belong to me — and as for my head and nose! [*Yawns.*] Well, smoke's good — by the powers, I'm getting warm — come closer to it, Mary. It's a little after midnight now — and I left home, this fine, luxurious British home, just as soon as it was light. And I've tramped the streets all day. Net result, a policeman gave me a pipeful of tobacco, I lunched off a bit of bread that I saw floating down the gutter — and I dined off the kitchen smell of the Café Royal. That's my day.

MARY. [*Stroking his hand.*] Poor boy, poor boy!

JOE. I stood for an hour in Leicester Square when the theatres emptied, thinking I might earn a copper, calling a cab, or something. There they were, all streaming out, happy and clean and warm — broughams and motor-cars — supper at the Savoy and the Carlton — and a hundred or two of us others in the gutter, hungry — looking at them. They went off to their supper — it was pouring, and I got soaked — and there I stood, dodging the policemen, dodging the horses' heads and the motors — and it was always — get away, you loafer, get away — get away — get away ——

MARY. We've done nothing to deserve it, Joe ——

JOE. [*With sudden fury.*] Deserve it! What have I ever done wrong! Wasn't *my* fault the firm went bankrupt and I couldn't get another job. I've a first-rate character — I'm respectable — what's the use? I want to work — they won't let me!

MARY. That illness of mine ate up all our savings. O Joe, I wish I had died!

JOE. And left me alone? That's not kind of you,

Mary. How about Mrs. Willis? Is she worrying about the rent?

MARY. Well, she'd like to have it, of course — they're so dreadfully poor themselves — but she says she won't turn us out. And I'm going to-morrow to her daughter's upstairs — she makes matchboxes, you know — and I don't see why I shouldn't try — I could earn nearly a shilling a day.

JOE. A shilling a day! Princely! [*His pipe goes out. He takes a last puff at it, squints into it to make sure all the tobacco is gone, then lays it down with a sigh.*] I reckon *I*'ll try making 'em too. I went to the Vestry again, this morning, to see whether they'd take me as sweeper — but they've thirty names down, ahead of me. I've tried chopping wood, but I can't — I begin to cough the third stroke — there's something wrong with me inside, somewhere. I've tried every Institution on God's earth — and there are others before me, and there is no vacancy, and I mustn't beg, and I mustn't worry the gentlemen. A shilling a day — can one earn as much as that! Why, Mary, that will be fourteen shillings a week — an income! We'll do it!

MARY. It's not quite a shilling, Joe — you have to find your own paste and odds and ends. And of course it takes a few weeks to learn, before you begin to make any money.

JOE. [*Crestfallen.*] Does it though? And what are we going to do, those few weeks? I thought there was a catch in it, somewhere. [*He gets up and stretches himself.*] Well, here's a free-born Englishman, able to conduct correspondence in three languages, bookkeeping by double entry, twelve years' experience — and all he's allowed to do is to starve. [*He stretches himself, again.*]

> But in spite of all temptations
> To belong to other nations ——

[*With sudden passion.*] God! I wish I were a Zulu!

MARY. [*Edging to him.*] Joe ——

JOE. [*Turning*]. Well?

MARY. Joe, Joe, we've tried very hard, haven't we?

JOE. Tried! Is there a job in this world we'd refuse?
Is there anything we'd turn up our nose at? Is there any
chance we've neglected?

MARY. [*Stealing nervously to him and laying a hand on
his arm.*] Joe ——

JOE. [*Raising his head and looking at her.*] Yes — what
is it? [*She stands timidly with downcast eyes.*] Well? Out
with it, Mary!

MARY. [*Suddenly.*] It's this, Joe.

> [*She goes feverishly to the mattress, and from underneath
> it she pulls out a big, fat purse which she hands
> him.*]

JOE. [*Staring.*] A purse!

MARY. [*Nodding.*] Yes.

JOE. You ——

MARY. Found it.

JOE. [*Looking at her.*] Found?

MARY [*Awkwardly.*] In a way I did — yes.

JOE. How?

MARY. It came on to rain, Joe — and I went into a
Tube Station — and was standing by a bookstall, showing
Minnie the illustrated papers — and an old lady bought
one — and she took out her purse — this purse — and paid
for it — and laid the purse on the board while she fumbled
to pick up her skirts — and then some one spoke to her —
a friend, I suppose — and — there were lots of people standing about — I don't know how it was — I was out in the
street, with Minnie ——

JOE. You had the purse?

MARY. Yes ——

JOE. No one followed you?

MARY. No one. I couldn't run, as I had to carry Minnie.

JOE. What made you do it?

MARY. I don't know — something in me did it — She put the purse down just by the side of my hand — my fingers clutched it before I knew — and I was out in the street.

JOE. How much is there in it?

MARY. I haven't looked, Joe.

JOE. [*Wondering.*] You haven't looked?

MARY. No; I didn't dare.

JOE. [*Sorrowfully.*] I didn't think we'd come to this, Mary.

MARY. [*Desperately.*] We've got to do something. Before we can earn any money at making matchboxes we'll have to spend some weeks learning. And you've not had a decent meal for a month — nor have I. If there's money inside this purse you can get some clothes — and for me too — I need them! It's not as though the old lady would miss it — she's rich enough — her cloak was real sable — and no one can find us out — they can't tell one piece of money from the other. It's heavy, Joe — I think there's a lot inside.

JOE. [*Weighing it mechanically.*] Yes — it's heavy ——

MARY. [*Eagerly.*] Open it, Joe.

JOE. [*Turning to her again.*] Why didn't you?

MARY. I just thought I'd wait — I'd an idea something might have happened; that some one might have stopped you in the street, some one with a heart — and that he'd have come in with you to-night — and seen us — seen Minnie — and said — "Well, here's money — I'll put you on your legs again" — And then we'd have given the purse back, Joe.

JOE. [*As he still mechanically balances it in his hand.*] Yes.

MARY. Can't go on like this, can we? You'll cough all night again, as you did yesterday — and the stuff they gave you at the Dispensary's no good. If you had clothes, you might get some sort of a job perhaps — you know you had to give up trying because you were so shabby

JOE. They laugh at me.

MARY. [*With a glance at herself.*] And I'm really ashamed to walk through the streets ——

JOE. I know — though I'm getting used to it. Besides, there's the kiddie. Let's have a look at her.

MARY. Be careful you don't wake her, Joe!

JOE. There's a fire.

MARY. She'll be hungry.

JOE. You said that she had some food?

MARY. That was at three o'clock. And little things aren't like us — they want their regular meals. Night after night she has been hungry, and I've had nothing to give her. That's why I took the purse.

JOE. [*Still holding it mechanically and staring at it.*] Yes. And, after all, why not?

MARY. We can get the poor little thing some warm clothes, some good food ——

JOE. [*Under his breath.*] A thief's daughter.

[*Covers his face with his hands.*

MARY. Joe!

JOE. Not nice, is it? Can't be helped, of course. And who cares? For three months this game has gone on — we getting shabbier, wretcheder, hungrier — no one bothers — all *they* say is "keep off the pavement." Let's see what's in the purse.

MARY. [*Eagerly.*] Yes, yes!

JOE. [*Lifting his head as he is on the point of opening the purse.*] That's the policeman passing.

MARY. [*Impatiently.*] Never mind that ——

JOE. [*Turning to the purse again.*] First time in my life I've been afraid when I heard the policeman.

> [*He has his finger on the catch of the purse when he pauses for a moment — then acting on a sudden impulse, makes a dart for the door, opens it, and is out, and up the area steps.*

MARY. [*With a despairing cry.*] Joe!

> [*She flings herself on the mattress, and sobs silently, so as not to awaken the child. JOE returns, hanging his head, dragging one foot before the other.*

MARY. [*Still sobbing, but trying to control herself.*] Why did you do that?

JOE. [*Humbly.*] I don't know ——

MARY. You gave it to the policeman?

JOE. Yes.

MARY. What did you tell him?

JOE. That you had found it.

MARY. Where?

JOE. In a Tube Station. Picked it up because we were starving. That we hadn't opened it. And that we lived here, in this cellar.

MARY. [*With a little shake.*] I expect he'll keep it himself!

JOE. [*Miserably.*] Perhaps.

> [*There is silence for a moment; she has ceased to cry; suddenly she raises herself violently on her elbow.*

MARY. You fool! You fool!

JOE. [*Pleading.*] Mary!

MARY. With your stupid ideas of honesty! What have they done for you, or me?

JOE. [*Dropping his head again.*] It's the kiddie, you know — her being a thief's daughter ——

MARY. Is that worse than being the daughter of a pair of miserable beggars?

JOE. [*Under his breath.*] I suppose it is, somehow ——

MARY.   You'd rather she went hungry?

JOE.   [*Despairingly.*]   I don't know how it was — hearing his tramp up there ——

MARY.   You were afraid?

JOE.   I don't want you taken to prison.

MARY.   [*With a wail.*]   I'll be taken to the graveyard soon, in a pauper's coffin!

JOE.   [*Starts suddenly.*]   Suppose we did that?

MARY.   [*Staring.*]   The workhouse?

JOE.   Why not, after all?   That's what it will come to, sooner or later.

MARY.   They'd separate us.

JOE.   At least you and the kiddie'd have food.

MARY.   They'd separate us.   And I love you, Joe. My poor, poor Joe!   I love you.

[*She nestles up to him and takes his hand.*]

JOE.   [*Holding her hand in his, and bending over her.*] You forgive me for returning the purse?

MARY.   [*Dropping her head on his shoulder.*]   Forgive you!   You were right.   It was the cold and the hunger maddened me.   You were right!

JOE.   [*Springing to his feet, with sudden passion.* MARY *staggers back.*]   I *wasn't* right — I was a coward, a criminal — a vile and wicked fool.

MARY.   [*Startled.*]   Joe!

JOE.   I had money there — money in my hand — money that you need so badly, you, the woman I love with all my ragged soul — money that would have put food into the body of my little girl — money that was mine, that belonged to me — and I've given it back, because of my rotten honesty!   What right have I to be honest?   They've made a dog of me — what business had I to remember I was a man?

MARY.   [*Following him and laying a hand on his arm.*] Hush, Joe — you'll wake Minnie.

Joe. [*Turning and staring haggardly at her.*] I could have got clothes — a job, perhaps — we might have left this cellar. We could have gone out to-morrow and bought things — gone into shops — we might have had food, coal ——

Mary. Don't, Joe — what's the use? And who knows — it may prove a blessing to us. You told the policeman where we lived?

Joe. A blessing! I'll get up to-morrow, after having coughed out my lungs all night — and I'll go into the streets and walk there from left to right and from right to left, standing at this corner and at that, peering into men's faces, watching people go to their shops and their offices, people who are warm and comfortable — and so it will go on, till the end comes.

Mary. [*Standing very close to him, almost in a whisper.*] Why not now, Joe?

Joe. [*With a startled glance at her.*] The end?

Mary. There's no room for us in this world ——

Joe. If I'd taken that money ——

Mary. It's too late for that now. And I'm glad you didn't — yes, I am — I'm glad. We'll go before God clean-handed. And we'll say to Him we didn't steal, or do anything He didn't want us to. And we'll tell Him we've died because people wouldn't allow us to live.

Joe. [*With a shudder.*] No. Not that — we'll wait, Mary. Don't speak of that.

Mary. [*Wistfully.*] You've thought of it too?

Joe. Thought of it! Don't, Mary, don't! It's bad enough, in the night, when I lie there and think of to-morrow! Something will happen — it must.

Mary. What? We haven't a friend in the world.

Joe. I may meet some one I used to know.

Mary. You've met them before — they always refuse——

Joe. [*Passionately.*] I've done nothing wrong — I

U

haven't drunk or gambled — I can't help being only a clerk, and unable to do heavy work! I can't help my lungs being weak! I've a wife and a child, like other people — and all we ask is to be allowed to live!

MARY. [*Pleading.*] Let's give it up, Joe. Go away together, you'd sleep without coughing. Sleep, that's all. And God will be kinder than men.

JOE. [*Groaning.*] Don't, Mary — don't!

MARY. Joe, I can't stand it any longer — I can't. Not only myself — but Minnie — Joe, it's too much for me! I can't stand Minnie crying, and asking me for her breakfast, as she will in the morning. Joe, dear Joe, let there be no morning!

JOE. [*Completely overcome.*] Oh, Mary, Mary!

MARY. It's not *your* fault, dear — you've done what you could. Not *your* fault they won't let you work — you've tried hard enough. And no woman ever had a better husband than you've been to me. I love you, dear Joe. And let's do it — let's make an end. And take Minnie with us.

JOE. [*Springing up.*] Mary, I'll steal something tomorrow.

MARY. And they'd send you to prison. Besides, then God would be angry. Now we can go to Him and need not be ashamed. Let us, dear Joe — oh, do let us! I'm so tired!

JOE. No.

MARY. [*Sorrowfully.*] You won't?

JOE. [*Doggedly.*] No. We'll go to the workhouse.

MARY. You've seen them in there, haven't you?

JOE. Yes.

MARY. You've seen them standing at the window, staring at the world? And they'd take you away from me.

JOE. That's better than ——

MARY. [*Firmly.*] I won't do it, Joe. I've been a good

wife to you — I've been a good mother: and I love you, though I'm ragged and have pawned all my clothes; and I'll strangle myself rather than go to the workhouse and be shut away from you.

JOE. [*With a loud cry.*] No! I'll *make* them give me something; and if I *have* to kill, it shan't be my wife and child! To-morrow I'll come home with food and money — to-morrow ——

> [*There is a sudden wail from the child;* JOE *stops and stares at her;* MARY *goes quickly to the mattress and soothes the little girl.*

MARY. Hush, dear, hush — no, it's not morning yet, not time for breakfast. Go to sleep again, dear. Yes, daddy's come back, and things are going to be all right now — No, dear, you can't be hungry, really — remember those beautiful cakes. Go to sleep, Minnie, dear. You're cold? [*She takes off her ragged shawl and wraps it round the child.*] There, dear, you won't be cold now. Go to sleep, Minnie ——

> [*The child's wail dies away, as* MARY *soothes her back to sleep.*

JOE. [*Staggering forward with a sudden cry.*] God, O God, give us bread!

THE CURTAIN SLOWLY FALLS

THE BRACELET

A Play in One Act

The Persons of the Play

HARVEY WESTERN
HIS HONOUR JUDGE BANKET
MARTIN
WILLIAM
MRS. WESTERN
MRS. BANKET
MISS FARREN
SMITHERS

TIME — *The present*

*The dining-room in an upper middle-class house near the
Park. It is furnished in the conventional modern style,
soberly and without imagination. The room is on the ground
floor, facing the street; the door is to the right, and leads
into the hall. To the left of this door is a sideboard, glittering with silver. Three tall windows, at the back, heavily
curtained; between them hang two or three family por-
traits. The table, on which there is the usual débris of a
meal that is over — coffee-cups, liqueur-glasses, etc. —
has been laid for four persons, and their four chairs are
still around it. The fireplace, with its rather crude and
ambitious mantelpiece, is in the centre of the left wall;
and uncomfortable-looking heavy armchairs are on each
side of it. On the mantelpiece are a marble clock and a
few bits of china. In the angle formed at the left side is a*

small Queen Anne writing-table, open. To th'
the room is a large sofa. The floor is heavily carpe.
and there are many rugs scattered about.

When the curtain rises, the room is in darkness.
WILLIAM, *the footman, enters hurriedly and switches on the*
electric light. He rushes to the table, looks eagerly around,
shifting cups and glasses, napkins, etc., then goes on his
hands and knees and searches on the carpet. After a mo-
ment, SMITHERS, *the lady's-maid, follows him.*

SMITHERS. [*Eagerly.*] Can't you find it?
WILLIAM. [*Sulkily.*] No. Not yet. Give me time.
SMITHERS. [*Feeling along the table-cloth.*] Under one of those rugs, perhaps.
WILLIAM. Well, I'm looking. [*Motor-horn sounds sharply, off.*] All right, all right!
SMITHERS. [*With a jerk of the head.*] Missis is telling him to do it.
WILLIAM. [*On all fours, crawling about.*] Very like her voice, too, when she's angry. Drat the thing! Where can it be?
[*He peers into the coal-scuttle.*
SMITHERS. No good looking in there, stupid.
WILLIAM. They always say it's the unlikeliest places——
[MARTIN, *the butler, comes in.*
MARTIN. Come, come, haven't you found it?
WILLIAM. No, Mr. Martin. It ain't here.
MARTIN. [*Bustling about.*] Must be, must be. She says ——
WILLIAM. I can't help what she says. It ain't.
MARTIN. [*Looking under the sofa.*] Just you hustle, young man, and don't give me any back-answers.
[*Having completed his examination of the sofa, he*
moves to the sideboard, and fusses round that.

SMITHERS. [*Methodically shaking out each napkin.*] I tell you she's cross.

MARTIN. [*Hard at work, searching.*] Doesn't mind disturbing *us*, in the midst of our supper!

WILLIAM. [*Who, all the time, has been on all fours searching.*] We're dirt, that's what we are — dirt.

MARTIN. [*Reprovingly.*] William, I've told you before——

WILLIAM. Very sorry, Mr. Martin, but this is the first time I've accepted an engagement at a stockbroker's. [*He has been crawling round the curtains at the back, shaking them; pulling hard at one of them he dislodges the lower part.*] Lor! *Now* I've done it!

SMITHERS. Clumsy!

MARTIN. [*Severely.*] That comes of too much talk. Never mind the curtain — go on looking.

> [WILLIAM *drops on to his hands and knees again;* HARVEY WESTERN *comes into the room, perturbed and restless. He is a well-preserved man of fifty.*

HARVEY. I say — not found it?

MARTIN. Not yet, sir.

HARVEY. Nuisance. *Must* be here, you know.

MARTIN. Is it a very valuable one, sir?

HARVEY. [*Who has gone to the table, and is turning things over.*] No, no, not particularly — but that's not the point.
> [*He looks under the table.*

MARTIN. [*Still seeking.*] When did madam find that she'd lost it, sir?

HARVEY. Oh, about five minutes after we'd started. And we've turned over everything in the car. It's certainly not there. [*He fusses around the table.*

MARTIN. Is madam quite sure she was wearing it, sir?

SMITHERS. [*Fretfully.*] Yes, yes, of course she was wearing it. I put it on her myself.

MARTIN. Where did madam put her cloak on, sir?

SMITHERS. In here. I brought it in.

MARTIN. You didn't notice whether ——

SMITHERS. No. Don't you think if we moved *all* the rugs ——

> [*She moves across the room and joins* WILLIAM, *who is still grovelling on the floor, and goes on her knees by his side.*

HARVEY. It must be here *somewhere*.

> [*They are all searching furiously —* WILLIAM *by the windows, peering into the spaces between the wall and the carpets,* MARTIN *at the sideboard,* SMITHERS *gathering the rugs together, all on their hands and knees, while* HARVEY, *bent double, is looking under the table.* MRS. WESTERN *comes in stonily, followed by the* JUDGE *and* MRS. BANKET. MRS. WESTERN *is a handsome woman of forty-five, with a rather stern, cold face; the* JUDGE, *a somewhat corpulent, genial man of fifty-five; and his wife, an amiable nullity, seven or eight years younger. They are all in evening-dress, the ladies in opera-cloaks.*

MRS. WESTERN. [*Pausing on the threshold.*] Well!

HARVEY. [*Rising and dusting himself.*] No trace of it.

MRS. WESTERN. [*Looking around.*] A nice mess you've made of the room!

MARTIN. You told us to look, Madam.

JUDGE. [*Going to the fire and standing with his back to it.*] I'm afraid we'll be shockingly late, Alice.

MRS. WESTERN. [*Firmly.*] I don't go without my bracelet.

> [*She goes to the table, and proceeds to shift the cups and glasses.*

MRS. BANKET. [*Moving to the other side of the table, and doing the same.*] Quite right, dear — I wouldn't.

> [*They all search, except the* JUDGE, *who shrugs his shoulders placidly, then takes a cigarette from his case, and lights it. The three servants still are grovelling on the floor.*

MRS. WESTERN. I *know* I had it while I was drinking my coffee ——

JUDGE. My experience is, one should never look for things. They find themselves.

MRS. WESTERN. [*Shortly.*] Nonsense.

JUDGE. A fact. Or at least one should *pretend* to be looking for something else. My glasses now. When I lose them I declare loudly I can't find my cigar-case. That disheartens the glasses — they return at once.

MRS. BANKET. [*Reproachfully.*] Don't be so irritating, Tom!

JUDGE. That's all very well, but how about me? I was asked here to dine. I've dined — I'm not complaining about the dinner. But now the curtain's up—and here am I watching half-a-dozen people looking very hard for a thing that isn't there.

MRS. BANKET. Tom, Tom, it's those laughs you get in Court that make you so fond of talking. Don't you see how you're vexing your sister?

MRS. WESTERN. Oh, I'm used to Tom. Harvey, I think you might be looking.

HARVEY. My dear, I've been turning round and round in this corner like a bird in a cage.

MARTIN. [*Who all this time, like the other servants, has been crawling around the different articles of furniture in the room, suddenly rises to his feet and addresses his mistress firmly but respectfully.*] It's not here, madam.

> [*The other servants also rise; and stand, each in their*

JUDGE. That, I imagine, is perfectly clear; and I congratulate the witness on the manner in which he has given his evidence. [*He throws his cigarette into the fire and steps forward.*] Now, my dear Alice ——

MRS. WESTERN. [*Sitting doggedly in the chair in front of the table and proceeding to pull off her gloves.*] I don't go without my bracelet.

JUDGE. Heaven forbid that I should speak slightingly of a gift of Harvey's — but really it isn't of such priceless value.

MRS. WESTERN. That has nothing to do with it.

MRS. BANKET. Of course not. Oh, these men!

HARVEY. [*Stepping forward.*] Tom's right. Let's go. Look here, I'll get you another.

MRS. WESTERN. [*Drily.*] Thanks — I want *that* one. — Smithers, and you, William, just look again in the hall.

SMITHERS. Yes, m'm.

MRS. WESTERN. And then help the chauffeur — turn out *everything* in the car.

SMITHERS. Yes, m'm.

MRS. WESTERN. Bring the rugs into the house, and shake them.

SMITHERS. Yes, m'm. [*She and* WILLIAM *go.*

JUDGE. [*Going back to the fire.*] Sumptuary laws — that's what we want. If women didn't wear bracelets, they couldn't lose them.

MRS. WESTERN. Martin, William is honest, isn't he?

HARVEY. [*Protesting.*] Oh, hang it, Alice!

MARTIN. Quite, madam — excellent character — a little flighty, but a most respectable young man.

MRS. WESTERN. I've seen him reading a sporting paper.

JUDGE. A weakness, my dear Alice, common to the best of us. I do it myself sometimes, but I'm willing to be searched.

MRS. BANKET. O Tom, *do* be quiet!

MRS. WESTERN. [*To the* JUDGE.] You're very un-sympathetic. [*Turning to* MARTIN *again.*] None of the other servants came in after we left?

MARTIN. No, madam.

MRS. WESTERN. You're sure?

MARTIN. Quite sure, madam. They were all downstairs, having their supper.

MRS. WESTERN. Most mysterious! Incomprehensible!

JUDGE. [*Looking at his watch.*] Past nine! We shall plunge into the play — like body-snatchers, looking for the corpse of the plot — and we shall never know what it was that the heroine did.

MRS. WESTERN. [*Ignoring him, to* MARTIN.] Smithers I'll answer for.

MARTIN. Oh yes, madam. If I *might* make a sugges-tion ——

MRS. WESTERN. Well?

MARTIN. It couldn't have fallen anywhere into your dress, madam?

MRS. WESTERN. Nonsense, how could it? [*She gets up and shakes herself.*] Absurd.   [*She sits again.*

MARTIN. Into your cloak?

MRS. WESTERN. Silk! No. That'll do, Martin. You might help the others outside.   [MARTIN *goes.*

JUDGE. [*With a step forward.*] Now, admirable sister ——

MRS. WESTERN. Didn't it strike you that Martin's manner was rather strange?

HARVEY. [*Fretfully.*] Really you *must* not suspect the servants!

MRS. WESTERN. [*Turning to him.*] *Must* not — must! That's scarcely the way to speak to me, Harvey.

HARVEY. [*Deprecatingly.*] My dear ——

MRS. WESTERN. And I wasn't suspecting — I was merely asking a question of my brother.

JUDGE. Come, Alice, let's go.

MRS. WESTERN. [*Shaking her head.*] You three go. You'll excuse me.

JUDGE. [*Cheerfully.*] If you insist ——

MRS. BANKET. [*Coming forward.*] No, no. *Do* come, Alice!

MRS. WESTERN. I can't — I'm so puzzled. [*With a sudden idea.*] Oh!

HARVEY. [*Who is behind her to the left, between her and the* JUDGE.] What? Have you found it?

MRS. WESTERN. No, no — of course not. But ring, please, will you?

HARVEY. Why?

MRS. WESTERN. I want you to ring. [*He presses the bell by the fireplace.*] I just remember Miss Farren came in while we were having coffee.

HARVEY. [*Indignantly.*] Alice!

MRS. WESTERN. I asked her to write a card to Harrod's — she'll have written it in here.

HARVEY. [*Angrily.*] I say — really!

MRS. WESTERN. [*Coldly.*] No need to snub me again — before our guests! I need scarcely say I am not *suspecting* Miss Farren — but in justice to her ——

MRS. BANKET. But, Alice, she'll have gone out — you told her she might ——

MRS. WESTERN. Only to her sister's close by — and she may not have gone yet. Why don't they answer the bell? Ring again, Harvey.

JUDGE. The poor things are still searching.

HARVEY. [*Firmly.*] Alice, I protest, I do indeed ——

MRS. WESTERN. Don't be so foolishly sentimental — it's ridiculous at your age. The young woman is in my employ, as governess to my children. [MARTIN *comes in.*] Has Miss Farren gone out yet?

MARTIN.   No, madam.   I believe she's in her room, dressing.

MRS. WESTERN.   Ask her to come.

MARTIN.   Yes, madam.   `   [*He goes.*

JUDGE.   [*Shaking his head.*]   No sense of proportion, that's the truth — they've no sense of proportion.

MRS. BANKET.   Tom!

JUDGE.   A fact, my dear — but you can't help it.   You've every quality in the world but just that — you *will* always look through the wrong end of the telescope.

MRS. BANKET.   Really, Tom, this isn't the moment for your nonsense — and if you only knew how stupid you are when you try to be funny!

HARVEY.   [*Going nervously to* MRS. WESTERN.]   I say, I really do think ——

MRS. WESTERN.   [*Roughly.*]   I don't care *what* you think. Leave me alone!

> [*There is silence.   The* JUDGE, *sitting by the fire, whistles loudly "Waltz me around again, Willie!"* HARVEY *has gone moodily across the room and stands by the sideboard.* MRS. BANKET *is sitting behind the table.   After a moment the door opens, and* MISS FARREN *comes in, with hat and cloak on, and goes straight to* MRS. WESTERN.   *She is an extremely pretty girl of twenty.*

MISS FARREN.   You want me, Mrs. Western?

MRS. WESTERN.   Oh, Miss Farren, I've lost my bracelet.

MISS FARREN.   Really!   I'm so sorry!   Where?

MRS. WESTERN.   I don't know.   You didn't see it, of course, after we'd gone?

MISS FARREN.   [*Shaking her head.*]   No — and no one came in.   I was writing the letter to Harrod's.

MRS. WESTERN.   No one at all?

MISS FARREN. No — I'm sure of that. And I'd hardly got to my room when I heard the car come back.

MRS. WESTERN. Well, thank you, Miss Farren.

MISS FARREN. It's very annoying. You're sure it's not in the car?

JUDGE. My dear Miss Farren, it's not in the car, it's not anywhere, and I'm beginning to believe it never was at all. Come, Alice, let's go. We shan't see much of the play, but we can at least help the British drama by buying two programmes.

MISS FARREN. [*With a light laugh — then turning to* MRS. WESTERN *again.*] Do you want me any more, Mrs. Western?

MRS. WESTERN. No, thanks. [MISS FARREN *turns to go —* MRS. WESTERN, *who has suddenly cast an eager glance at her, as though attracted by something, calls her back.*] Oh Miss Farren!

MISS FARREN. [*Turning.*] Yes?

MRS. WESTERN. I wonder whether you'd be so good as to shift this aigrette of mine — it's hurting me.

MISS FARREN. Certainly.

> [*She comes back to* MRS. WESTERN, *and stands by her side; as she raises her arm* MRS. WESTERN *jumps up and seizes it by the wrist.*

MRS. WESTERN. My bracelet!

> [*Keeping a tight hold of* MISS FARREN'S *wrist, she holds it at arm's length. There is a general cry of amazement — the* JUDGE *and his wife start to their feet —* HARVEY *rushes eagerly towards her.*

JUDGE. Alice!

MRS. BANKET. Oh!

HARVEY. No, no ——

> [*These three exclamations are simultaneous.*

MRS. WESTERN. There it is! She took it!

JUDGE. Are you sure?

HARVEY. [*Breathless and urgent.*] Alice ——

MISS FARREN. [*Recovering from her shock and bewilderment.*] Mrs. Western, it isn't ——

MRS. WESTERN. [*Sternly, still holding the girl by the wrist.*] You dare to pretend ——

HARVEY. [*Who is now at the back of his wife's chair, looking closely at the bracelet.*] Let me look, let me look. . . . I say, Alice, you're wrong. It's not yours at all. The setting's different.

MRS. WESTERN. [*Angrily.*] What do you mean, different? You think I don't know my own bracelet? Are you mad? I say it's mine — and it is!

JUDGE. [*Stepping forward.*] Alice, be careful ——

MRS. WESTERN. Careful! You're as bad as he! Of course the thing's mine — I've been wearing it for weeks — and you think I can make a mistake? She found it, and took it.

MISS FARREN. [*Very distressed.*] No, no, Mrs. Western, really! It isn't yours! I assure you!

HARVEY. Alice, I declare to you ——

MRS. WESTERN. [*Roughly.*] Be quiet and go away. This is no business of yours.

HARVEY. [*Eagerly.*] But it is! It was I who bought the wretched thing — well, I am prepared to swear that this isn't the one!

MRS. WESTERN. [*A little shaken, looking at it again.*] You're prepared to. . . . [*She lifts her head.*] How can you talk such utter nonsense? There is not the least doubt — not the least!

JUDGE. [*Stopping HARVEY, who is about to protest violently.*] Alice, mind what you're saying. You'll get yourself into trouble. If Harvey says ——

MRS. BANKET. [*Contemptuously.*] He's saying it to shield her, that's all.

HARVEY. [*Indignantly.*] I'm not. It's not true. But you mustn't bring such an accusation. It's monstrous. And I won't allow ——

MRS. WESTERN. [*Drawing herself up.*] You — won't — allow! The girl takes my bracelet — and you won't allow!

MISS FARREN. [*Trying to free herself.*] Mrs. Western, I haven't, I haven't!

JUDGE. [*Impressively.*] Alice, will you listen to me?

MRS. WESTERN. No, I won't! This doesn't concern you, or any one, but me and this girl! Look at her — she knows!

MISS FARREN. Mrs. Western, you're hurting my arm. . . .

MRS. WESTERN. Come now — confess! I won't be hard on you if you confess ——

> [*She wrenches off the bracelet, and releases the girl, who staggers back, nursing her wrist.*]

HARVEY. [*Almost beside himself, stamping his foot.*] Alice, Alice, will you hear ——

MISS FARREN. Oh, you *have* hurt me! And you've no right — to say such things.

HARVEY. No, you haven't, you haven't!

MRS. WESTERN. Besides, a bracelet like that! [*She holds it up. To* MISS FARREN.] You won't confess? Very well, then. I'll send for a policeman.

HARVEY. [*Doggedly.*] The bracelet is hers.

MRS. WESTERN. [*Jeeringly.*] Turquoise and emeralds! Hers! A coincidence, perhaps. Very likely. I'll give her in charge at once.

HARVEY. The bracelet is hers, I tell you.

MRS. WESTERN. [*Turning furiously on him.*] You dare to say that?

HARVEY. [*Steadily.*] Yes. Because I myself — gave it to her.

[*There is a moment's almost stupefied silence;* HAR-
VEY *and* ALICE *are face to face.* MISS FARREN
to the left of her, MRS. BANKET *is still at the back,
the* JUDGE *by the fire.* MRS. WESTERN *breaks
the silence.*

MRS. WESTERN. [*Sternly.*] You — gave — it — her?

HARVEY. [*Steadily.*] Yes.

MRS. WESTERN. You ask me to believe that you gave
a bracelet to — this person — my children's governess?

HARVEY. I did.

MRS. WESTERN. An exact copy of the one you gave me?

HARVEY. I've told you — it's not an exact copy — there's
a difference in the setting.

MRS. BANKET. Nonsense, nonsense, it can't be — he's
just saying this ——

JUDGE. Fanny, don't interfere.

HARVEY. I'm saying what's true.

MRS. WESTERN. I refuse to believe it. It's incredible.
You've not sunk so low as that. It's a lie.

HARVEY. [*Indignantly.*] Alice!

MRS. WESTERN. Yes, a lie. A trumped-up story. The
girl has taken it ——

MISS FARREN. I have not!

MRS. WESTERN. You can tell that to the magistrate —
[*She turns to* HARVEY] and you too, if you like.

[*She moves to the bell.*

JUDGE. [*Putting out a hand to stop her.*] Alice ——

MRS. WESTERN. Leave me alone, Tom. I know what
I'm doing. I'll send for a policeman.

HARVEY. [*Imploringly.*] Alice, Alice ——

MRS. WESTERN. [*Pausing, with her hand on the bell.*]
I'll let the girl off, if you'll tell me the truth.

HARVEY. I *have* told you the truth.

MRS. WESTERN. You persist in this silly falsehood?

HARVEY. It isn't — I tell you it isn't!

MRS. WESTERN. Very well, then.

[*She presses the bell. At that moment the door bursts open, and* MARTIN *comes in triumphantly, with the bracelet on a salver.* SMITHERS *and* WILLIAM *are behind him, but do not pass beyond the threshold.*

MARTIN. [*Eagerly.*] Ma'am, ma'am, we've found the——

[MRS. WESTERN *has turned towards him, still holding the other bracelet in her hand.* MARTIN *catches sight of it, and stops dead short, staring bewilderedly at it.*

MRS. WESTERN. [*Calmly.*] Where did you find it?

[*She takes the bracelet off the salver and lays it on the table.*

MARTIN. [*With a great effort.*] It had fallen into the pocket of the car — there was a hole in the pocket — it had worked its way right down into the body.

MRS. WESTERN. Very well. Thank you.

[MARTIN *goes; the other servants have already slunk off. There is a moment's silence.* MRS. WESTERN *suddenly flings the bracelet she has in her hand in* MISS FARREN's *direction.*

MRS. WESTERN. [*Contemptuously.*] Here. I return you your property. And now pack up your things and leave the house.

HARVEY. [*Who has stepped forward and picked up the bracelet, standing between* MRS. WESTERN *and* MISS FARREN.] No.

MRS. WESTERN. [*Staring at him.*] What?

HARVEY. [*Violently.*] I say, No!

MRS. WESTERN. I have told the girl to leave my house.

HARVEY. *My* house — mine! And she shall stay in it! Or, at least, when she goes, it shall be without the slightest stain or suspicion ——

x

MRS. WESTERN. [*Scornfully.*] I am not accusing her of theft.

HARVEY. But you are insinuating — I declare solemnly before you all ——

JUDGE. [*Interposing.*] Harvey, one moment. . . . I am sure that Miss Farren would rather go to her room. . . .

MISS FARREN. Yes.

HARVEY. By all means. Here, take your bracelet. [*He gives it to her.*] But you don't leave this house — you understand that? *I* am master here.

[MISS FARREN *goes quietly.*

JUDGE. Now just listen to me, both of you. Be calm — all this excitement won't help. Harvey, you too. You and Alice will have your explanation ——

MRS. WESTERN. If the girl doesn't go to-night ——

HARVEY. I tell you again she shall not! And there's no need. I was a fool to give her that bracelet — she didn't want to take it ——

MRS. BANKET. Why *did* you?

HARVEY. I had given Alice one on her birthday.

MRS. WESTERN. Well?

HARVEY. And so I got *her* one.

MRS. WESTERN. Why?

HARVEY. Because —— [*He stops, very embarrassed.*]

MRS. WESTERN. Well?

HARVEY. Because — oh, because — well, she admired it — and *she* liked pretty things too. . . .

MRS. WESTERN. I don't think you need say anything more.

MRS. BANKET. No. He needn't. It's clear enough!

HARVEY. [*Eagerly.*] Look here, on my honour — I *am* fond of her, of course, in a way — but I'm old enough to be her father — and I swear to you all — I've seen her about, of course, a good deal — and I gave her that thing — but beyond that, nothing, nothing!

MRS. WESTERN. [*Sitting, and with a shrug of the shoulder.*] A ridiculous fairy tale!

JUDGE. My dear Alice, take my advice, and believe your husband.

MRS. WESTERN. You too!

MRS. BANKET. All alike, when there's a pretty face!

JUDGE. Let her find another situation, by all means. . . . But to turn a girl out, at a moment's notice! You couldn't.

MRS. WESTERN. [*Turning to the* JUDGE.] You are really suggesting that I should sleep under the same roof with ——

JUDGE. [*Almost sternly.*] You are condemning, without the slightest evidence. And condemning, remember, an utterly defenceless creature. This girl has a claim on you : were your suspicions justified, she would *still* have a claim.

MRS. WESTERN. Indeed!

MRS. BANKET. The nonsense he talks! It's really too silly!

JUDGE. You are extraordinary, you women! You exact such rigid morality from the governess and the housemaid! You're full of excuses when it's one of yourselves!

MRS. BANKET. [*Indignantly.*] Tom!

JUDGE. Well, that's true — we all know it! And here — I believe every word Harvey has said.

MRS. WESTERN. [*Scarcely believing her ears.*] You do!

JUDGE. Because he is a man of honour, and men of honour have their code. Their children's governess is safe. You will do well to believe it, too. Now, Fanny, we'll go. Be sensible, Alice — I tell you again, Harvey's right; the girl must not be — summarily dismissed : it would be an act of cruel injustice. Good-bye. [*He offers to kiss her — she turns away.*] As you like. Good-bye, Harvey, old man.

HARVEY. Good-bye, Tom. [*They shake hands.*] And thank you.

MRS. BANKET. [*Kissing* MRS. WESTERN.] My poor, dear Alice!

MRS. WESTERN. Good-bye, Fanny. I'm sorry that our party to-night ——

MRS. BANKET. Oh, that doesn't matter! Poor thing! I promise you that Tom shall have a good talking to!

[*She is too angry with* HARVEY *to say good-bye to him: she and the* JUDGE *go. The moment the door closes,* HARVEY *begins, feverishly and passionately.*

HARVEY. Now just listen. I'm going to speak to you — I'm going to say things — things that have been in my heart, in my life, for years. I'm not going to spare you. I'm going to tell you the truth, and the truth, and the truth!

MRS. WESTERN. [*Calmly, looking ironically at him.*] If it's the same kind of truth you've been giving us to-night ——

HARVEY. We've been married ten years. Oh, I know, we were neither of us very young. But anyhow the last five have been nothing but misery for me. Misery — do you hear that? You sitting there, calm and collected — not caring one damn for me ——

MRS. WESTERN. [*Quietly.*] That's not true.

HARVEY. It is, and you know it. The mother of my children! Satisfied with that. Never a word of kindness, or sympathy. And as for — affection!

MRS. WESTERN. We're not sweethearts — we're middle-aged people.

HARVEY. Well, I need something more. And, look here, I'll tell you. This girl has made life worth living. That's all. I'd come home at night dog-tired, all day in the City — sick of it, Stock Exchange, office, and the mud and the grime and the worry — there were you, with a nod, ah, Harvey, good evening — and you'd scarcely look up from your Committee Report or your Blue-book, or damned pamphlet or other ——

MRS. WESTERN. [*Contemptuously.*] You are one of the men who want their wife to be a mere sort of doll.

HARVEY. [*More and more vehemently.*] I want my wife to care for me! I want her to smile when I come in, and be glad — I want her to love me! You don't! By the Lord, I've sneaked upstairs, gone in and had a peep at the children — well, they'd be asleep. I tell you I've been hungry, hungry, for a word, for a look! And there, in the school-room, was this girl. I've played it low down, I know — she's fond of me. But I couldn't help it — I was lonely — that's what it was. I've gone up there night after night. *You* didn't know where I was — and you didn't care. In my study, you thought — the cold, chilly box that you call my study — glad to have me out of the way. Well, there I was, with this girl. It was something to look forward to, in the cab, coming home. It was something to catch hold of, when things went wrong, in that dreary grind of money-making. Her eyes lit up when they saw me. She'd ask me about things — if I coughed, she'd fuss me — she had pretty ways, and was pleased, oh, pleased beyond words, if I brought her home something ——

MRS. WESTERN. So this isn't the first time!

HARVEY. [*With a snarl.*] No, of course not! She admired that bracelet of yours — by Jove, I said to myself, I'll get her one like it! Whatever I brought home to *you* you'd scarcely say thank you — and usually it went into the drawer — I'd such shocking bad taste! *She'd* beam! Well, as ill-luck would have it, you took a fancy to this one. I told her she mustn't wear hers ——

MRS. WESTERN. [*Calmly and cuttingly.*] Conspiring behind my back.

HARVEY. [*Raging.*] Oh, if you knew what has gone on

behind your back! Not when I was with her — when I was alone! The things I've said about you — to myself! When I thought of this miserable life that had to be dragged on here, thought of your superior smile, your damnable cruelty ——

MRS. WESTERN. [*Genuinely surprised.*] Cruelty! Why?

HARVEY. What else? I'd go up to you timidly — bah, why talk of it? To you I've been the machine that made money — money to pay for the house, and the car, and the dressmakers' bills — a machine that had to be fed — and when you'd done that, you'd done all. Well, there was this girl ——

MRS. WESTERN. You had your children.

HARVEY. A boy of seven and a girl of five — in bed when I came home — and *your* children much more than mine — I'm a stranger to them! And anyhow, I wanted something more — something human, alive — that only a woman can give. And she gave it. Nothing between us, I swear — but just that. As Tom says, I've not been such a cur — and *you* ought to know me well enough, after all these years! . . . But there is the truth — she's fond of me · she is, it's a fact. And I *needed* that fondness — it has kept me going. And now — do you think I'll let her be thrust out into the street?

[*As he says these last words he drops into a chair, facing her, and looks fiercely and doggedly at her.*

MRS. WESTERN. [*Calmly.*] Stop now, and listen to me. I've let you rattle on. Will you hear me for one moment?

HARVEY. Go on.

MRS. WESTERN. All those things you've said about me — [*With a shrug.*] Well, what's the use? I suppose we're like most married people when they come to our age. I've interests of my own, that don't appeal to you ——

HARVEY. Blue-books and Committees!

MRS. WESTERN. I do useful work — oh yes, you may sneer — you always have sneered! If a woman tries to do something sensible with her life, instead of cuddling and kissing you all day, she's cold and cruel. We've drifted apart — well, your fault as much as mine. More, perhaps — but it's no good going into that — no good making reproaches. That's how things are — we must make the best of them. Wait, let me finish. About this girl. Granted that what you say is true — and I'm inclined to believe it ——

HARVEY. [*Genuinely grateful.*] At least thank you for that!

MRS. WESTERN. Or at any rate it's better policy to believe it, for every one's sake ——

HARVEY. [*Bitterly.*] That's right — that's more like you!

MRS. WESTERN. We gain nothing by abusing each other. And I didn't interrupt *you*. Let's look facts in the face. Here we are, we two — tied.

HARVEY. [*With a groan.*] Yes.

MRS. WESTERN. With our two children. If it weren't for them. . . . Well, we've *got* to remain together. Now there's this girl. It's quite evident, after what you've said, that she can't stop here ——

HARVEY. [*Jumping to his feet.*] She shall!

MRS. WESTERN. [*Fretfully.*] Oh, do be a man, and drop this mawkish sentiment! You say she's fond of you — you've *made* her fond of you. Was this a very pretty thing — for a man of your age to do?

HARVEY. [*Sullenly, as he drops back into his chair.*] Never mind my age.

MRS. WESTERN. Very well then — for a married man?

HARVEY. An unhappy man.

MRS. WESTERN.   Even granting that — though if you're unhappy it's your own fault — I've always been urging you to go on the County Council — What's to become of the girl, if she stops here?

HARVEY.   [*Desperately*]   I don't know — but I can't let her go — I tell you I can't!

MRS. WESTERN.   [*Scarcely able to conceal her disgust.*]   Oh, if you knew how painful it is to hear you whining like this! It's pitiable, really!   In the girl's own interest — how can she stop?

HARVEY.   She must.   I can't let her be turned out. It would break her heart.

MRS. WESTERN.   [*Turning right round, and staring at him.*] What?

HARVEY.   [*Doggedly.*]   Yes, it would.   She's very fond of me, that's the truth.   I know that I've been to blame — but it's too late for that now.   She's romantic, of course — what you'd call sentimental.   I dare say I've played on her feelings — she saw I was lonely.   She has a side that you've never suspected — a tender, sensitive side — she has ideals.

Well, do you realise what it would mean, with a girl like that?   No one knows her as I do.   I'm quite startled, sometimes, to find how fond she is of me.   Oh, have some sympathy!   It's difficult, I know — it's terribly difficult. But she loves me — that's the truth — and a young girl's love — why, she might throw herself into the river!   Oh yes, you smile — but she might!   What do *you* know of life, with your Blue-books?   Anyhow, I daren't risk it. By-and-by — there's no hurry, is there?   And I put it to you — be merciful!   You're not the ordinary woman — you have a brain — you're not conventional.   Don't act like the others.   Don't drive this girl out of the house.   It would end in tragedy.   Believe it!

MRS. WESTERN.   You can't really expect me to keep a

girl here, as governess to my children, who, as you say, is in love with you.

HARVEY. [*Pleading.*] I expect you — I'm asking you — to help her — and me.

MRS. WESTERN. [*Shaking her head.*] That's too much. We won't turn her out to-night — I'll give her a reference, and all that ——

HARVEY. [*Springing to his feet again.*] Alice, I can't let her go!

MRS. WESTERN. [*Conciliatorily.*] Ask Tom, ask any one ——

HARVEY. [*More and more passionately*] I tell you, I can't let her go!

MRS. WESTERN. Be sensible, Harvey — you must realise yourself there's no alternative ——

HARVEY. [*With a violent and uncontrollable outburst.*] I vow and declare to you — if she goes, I go too! And the consequences will be on your head!

[MRS. WESTERN *has also risen — they stand face to face, looking at each other — and for a moment there is silence. The door opens, and* MISS FARREN *comes in, dressed as before. She walks straight to* MRS. WESTERN.

MISS FARREN. Mrs. Western, my things are packed, and on the cab ——

HARVEY. [*Wildly.*] My poor child, you're *not* to go — I told you!

MISS FARREN. [*With a demure glance at him, stopping him as he is moving towards her.*] Of course I must — I can't stay here — that's not possible. My sister will take me in for to-night.

MRS. WESTERN. Miss Farren, my husband has explained to me — I withdraw all ——

MISS FARREN. [*Carelessly.*] Oh, that's all right —

though thank you all the same. And it really doesn't matter much. I was going to give notice to-morrow any-way ——

HARVEY. [*Starting violently.*] What!

MISS FARREN. Well, I put it off as long as I could, Mr. Western, because . . . But the fact is I'm going on the stage — musical comedy ——

HARVEY. [*Breathless, staggering back.*] You — are — going ——

MISS FARREN. I've accepted an engagement — oh, I'm only to be a show-girl at first — but they believe I'll do well. They've been wanting me some time. And my *fiancé* has persuaded me.

HARVEY. [*Collapsing utterly, dropping into the chair by the fire.*] Your ——

MISS FARREN. [*Gravely.*] My *fiancé* — yes. He's one of the comic men there.

MRS. WESTERN. [*Who has been watching them both with an unmoved face.*] I'll write a cheque for your salary, Miss Farren.   [*She goes to the desk at back.*

MISS FARREN. [*Coquettishly, to* HARVEY.] I ought to have told you, I know, Mr. Western. But it *was* so dull here — and you've been most awfully good to me. I can never be sufficiently grateful.

HARVEY. [*With difficulty, his face turned away.*] Don't mention it. And I hope you'll be happy.

MISS FARREN. [*Lightly.*] Thank you. I mean to try!

[MRS. WESTERN *returns with a cheque which she hands to* MISS FARREN.

MRS. WESTERN. Here, Miss Farren.

MISS FARREN. [*Putting it into her bag.*] Thank you so much. Good-bye.

MRS. WESTERN. If you should ever need a reference, don't be afraid to ——

Miss Farren. Oh, thanks, no more governessing for me. Good-bye!

[*She trips out, without another glance at* Harvey, *who sits huddled by the fire.* Mrs. Western *moves slowly to the door. At the threshold she pauses, turns, and looks at* Harvey.

Mrs. Western. I'll take care that the next governess — shall be quite as pretty as this one, Harvey.

[*She opens the door and goes.* Harvey *doesn't stir.*

THE CURTAIN FALLS

APPENDIX

DIRECTIONS FOR MAKING A PRÉCIS

I. What a *précis* is.

A. A *précis* is a condensed essay, giving in logical sequence the main thoughts or facts of the original author,[1] freed from all nonessential matter.

II. What a *précis* is not.

A. The *précis* is not a paragraph outline of the original article. Each main heading of the printed essay will usually cover several paragraphs; a paragraph outline ignores the distinction between the main headings and their minor subdivisions, ignores the very distinction which gives the *précis* value. Also whole paragraphs may be introduced in the original article merely to win over a hostile reader or interest an apathetic one, and consequently should be omitted from the *précis*.

B. Although the construction of an outline is a preparatory step, the final version of the *précis* is not to be written in any kind of outline form.

C. The *précis* should contain no comment, criticism, or thought not found in the original.

III. Steps in making a *précis*.

A. The central thought of the whole essay should be summarized in a sentence. It is well to write that sentence at the head of the *précis*.

---

[1] Or authors. A *précis* may represent the condensed information gathered from a body of correspondence, the letters of various writers.

B. The main divisions of the essay, that is, the main headings under which the author thought out the subject, should be distinguished from each other; and the basic thought of each division summarized in a sentence.

C. These sentences should be arranged as an outline, in the most coherent order, which will often, but not necessarily or always, be that of the printed essay.

D. From the outline thus formed, a condensed essay should be written, in which each sentence of the outline is developed into a paragraph. The thought development underlying the paragraph should follow the thought development of the original essay. Examples and other illustrative material should be used only when indispensable, and, when used, should be reproduced from the original with the most rigid accuracy.

E. All matter brought in for purposes of proof or illustration must be placed under the topic which its author intended it to prove or illustrate. Its presence under any other heading condemns the *précis* as inaccurate and unintelligent.

F. Space should be apportioned according to the importance apparently attached to the different points by the original writer. This will usually, but not necessarily or always, mean that space will be apportioned as in the printed article.

IV. The *précis* and the magazine article.

A. If the order of topics and proportionate space allotted to topics are not the same in a magazine article and a *précis* based on it, that fact does not necessarily mean that either is bad. The *précis* is written for readers concerned only with the logical development of thought or the bare statement of facts. Magazine articles are written to interest and to amuse, as well as to instruct; they may require an informal order or indirect presentation to. hold the reader's attention or lull his prejudice.

Printed in the United States of America.

THE following pages contain advertisements of books by the same author or on kindred subjects.

English Composition

By CHESTER NOYES GREENOUGH

Professor of English in Harvard University, and

FRANK W. C. HERSEY

Instructor in English in Harvard University

Cloth, 12mo, 379 pages, $1.40

1. The book makes a point of treating that part of the process of writing which takes place before any words are put on paper; namely, the perception of good descriptive and narrative material, and the use of books and periodicals for expository and argumentative material; weighing and estimating of one authority against another; the use of libraries, catalogues, and indexes, and the making of notes on books and lectures.

2. Throughout it treats English composition, not as a separate subject, but as a matter which runs through all subjects and which includes all the spoken and written business of the day.

3. In description and argument, which are sometimes thought to succeed by mere vividness, it emphasizes structural principles.

4. Instead of merely treating the principles of composition — unity, emphasis, and coherence — in the abstract, after briefly explaining them, it shows what modifications they undergo in the different kinds of composition.

5. The exercises and original problems are an important feature of the book.

CONTENTS

Introduction.

Part I. Gathering and weighing materials.

Part II. Exposition, including Biography and Criticism; Argument; Description; Narrative.

Part III. Structure, including sentences, paragraphs, and whole compositions considered with respect to unity, emphasis, and coherence.

Part IV. Diction, including grammar, spelling, pronunciation, abbreviations, representation of numbers, choice of words, number of words.

THE MACMILLAN COMPANY

Publishers   64-66 Fifth Avenue   New York

College Readings in English Prose

By FRANKLIN W. SCOTT

Assistant Professor of English, and

JACOB ZEITLIN

Associate in English in the University of Illinois

12mo, 653 pages, $1.40

"Six hundred pages crammed full of illustrative material in all forms of composition. Valuable as a reference book for models, most of which are new, selected from modern writers or speakers." — *School Review*, Chicago.

"The specimens selected for this volume of prose by Professors Scott and Zeitlin, of the University of Illinois, represent a greater range in subject matter, in typical forms and in variations of style than other texts of this sort. The book is all meat, more than 650 pages of it. The editors have taken account of the special interest of the engineering and agricultural student, and have provided material which will appeal particularly to his taste, without being so technical in treatment as to baffle the lay intelligence. Many of the selections are from contemporary writings. The book is divided in a large way into examples of exposition, argument, description, narrative, and letters. The appendix contains more than twenty-five students' themes which are classified under the same general heads." — *Journal of Education*, Boston.

"Wider in range than most similar volumes." — *English Journal*.

"The result is a volume which the general reader will find as entertaining and as instructive as the college student. The articles are arranged under the various heads of exposition, argument, description, narrative, and letters." — *San Francisco Chronicle*.

THE MACMILLAN COMPANY

Publishers   64-66 Fifth Avenue   New York

Modern Essays

SELECTED AND EDITED BY

JOHN MILTON BERDAN, Ph.D.
Assistant Professor of English in Yale College

JOHN RICHIE SCHULTZ, M.A.
AND
HEWETTE ELWELL JOYCE, B.A.
Instructors in English in Yale College

12mo, 448 pages, $1.25

A volume of thirty-three essays selected from contemporary authors, the great majority of whom are still alive and among the most able writers of the age. The essays were chosen because, in the opinion of the editors, each author succeeded in saying forcibly what he wished to say; the emphasis is on the form, not on the facts; on the method, not the content. A wide range, both in treatment and in subject matter, is to be found, and the various forms of exposition are thoroughly illustrated without being offensively labelled. Each essay offers a suggestive treatment for its particular subject and its particular audience. In order to enable the student to perceive clearly just what is gained and what is lost in each case, brief notes are prefixed to each essay, suggesting the scope and limitations of its particular type. A general theoretical introduction has been included in order to explain the point of view of the entire book. Among the authors may be mentioned Whistler, Lubbock, Bryce, Wu Tingfang, Lodge, Taft, Phelps, Rhodes, Chesterton, Bennett, Lang, Leacock, Sumner, Woodrow Wilson, Galsworthy. The book will be found adapted for use in courses on Exposition or Essay-Writing, following the general Freshman course, although it may also be used in a Freshman course when it is desired to devote considerable attention to Exposition.

THE MACMILLAN COMPANY
Publishers   64-66 Fifth Avenue   New York

CPSIA information can be obtained at www.ICGtesting.com
Printed in the USA
BVOW11s0326270116

434384BV00021B/183/P